The Naked State of Human Being

The Naked State of Human Being

The Meaning of Gymnos *in 2 Corinthians 5:3
and its Theological Implications*

Luis Iván Martínez Toledo

FOREWORD BY
Kim Papaioannou

WIPF & STOCK · Eugene, Oregon

THE NAKED STATE OF HUMAN BEING
The Meaning of Gymnos in 2 Corinthians 5:3 and its Theological Implications

Copyright © 2016 Luis Iván Martínez Toledo. All rights reserved. Except for brief quotations in critical publications or reviews, no part of this book may be reproduced in any manner without prior written permission from the publisher. Write: Permissions, Wipf and Stock Publishers, 199 W. 8th Ave., Suite 3, Eugene, OR 97401.

Wipf & Stock
An Imprint of Wipf and Stock Publishers
199 W. 8th Ave., Suite 3
Eugene, OR 97401

www.wipfandstock.com

PAPERBACK ISBN: 978-1-62564-998-0
HARDCOVER ISBN: 978-1-4982-8829-3

Manufactured in the U.S.A.

To my dear Mary,
and all who enjoy Bible studies

Contents

List of Figures · ix
List of Abbreviations · x
Foreword by Kim Papaioannou · xi
Preface · xiii
Acknowledgments · xv

1. Introduction · 1
    Dualism · 5
    Monism · 13
    The Problem · 22
    Presuppositions · 23
    Some Delimitations · 24

2. Literary Background · 26
    Gar, the Immediate Background · 27
    Oidamen, the Broad Background · 35
        Greek Background · 38
        Old Testament Background · 40
        Corinthian Correspondence Background · 44
    The Background on First Corinthians 15:35–55 · 46

The Significance of Anthropological Terms · 47
The Change of Nature · 68
Summary and Conclusion of chapter · 83

3. Gymnos in 2 Corinthians 5:3 · 85
   Literary Analysis · 86
      The Earthly Tent and the Building from God · 86
      The Process of Change · 102
   Naked State · 107
      Uses of the Term · 108
      Gymnos in Its Literary Context · 112
   Continuity of Identity · 118
      Gymnos and Koimaō · 119
      In the Twinkling of an Eye · 123

4. Theological Implications · 125
   The Concept of Death · 126
   Identity · 129
      Memory · 130
      Biblical Continuity of Identity · 135
   On Judgment · 144

5. Conclusion · 148
   Further Considerations · 153
   Applications · 154

Bibliography · 157

Figures

Figure 1. Anthropological characteristics in 1 Corinthians 15: 35–55. · 63

Figure 2. Kinds of bodies in 1 Corinthians 15:35–55. · 72

Figure 3. Psychikon and *pneumatikon* contrasted. · 74

Figure 4. Comparison between Adam and Christ. · 76

Figure 5. Two processes of change in 1 Corinthians 15. · 82

Figure 6. Textual evidences for *endysamenoi*. · 88

Figure 7. Biblical translations of *endysamenoi*. · 88

Figure 8. Earthly and heavenly existences in 2 Corinthians 4:7–5:10. · 92

Figure 9. Comparison of existences in 1 Corinthians 15 and 2 Corinthians 4–5. · 97

Figure 10. Syntactical diagram of 2 Corinthians 5:1–4. · 100

Figure 11. The place of gymnos in the process of change. · 114

Figure 12. Plant germination image. · 114

Abbreviations

ABD	*Anchor Bible Dictionary*
ANLEX	*Analytical Lexicon of the Greek New Testament*
AUSS	*Andrews University Seminary Studies Journal*
BDAG	*A Greek-English Lexicon of the New Testament and Other Early Christian Literature*
BEB	*Baker Encyclopedia of the Bible*
BECA	*Baker Encyclopedia of Christian Apologetics*
BKC	*Bible Knowledge Commentary*
CT	Critical Text
EDNT	*Exegetical Dictionary of the New Testament*
HSDAT	*Handbook of Seventh-day Adventist Theology*
JBL	*Journal of Biblical Literature*
LSJ	*A Greek-English Lexicon (Liddell, Scott and Jones)*
LXX	Septuagint
MT	Masoretic Text
NAS	*New American Standard Bible*
NTC	New Testament Commentary
OHPR	*Oxford Handbook of Philosophy of Religion*
TDNT	*Theological Dictionary of the New Testament*
WBC	Word Biblical Commentary

Foreword

IT IS A PLEASURE to recommend the work of Luis Ivan Martinez to all readers who take an interest in questions of the afterlife from a Biblical perspective. I have known Luis for the past seven years. As a PhD student he took several of my classes, and I also had the opportunity to help shape his dissertation. Currently he is building a distinguished career as a university professor in Mexico. Over time I have come to respect his ability to think outside the box and approach topics and themes with fresh insights, flair, and candor. Beyond academics, Luis is a pastor with a true pastor's heart, a care for other human beings that is reflected in his active involvement in different community projects.

The present volume is an adaptation of Luis' PhD dissertation. It combines a sharp academic outlook with pastoral tenderness as it tackles one of the great questions of human existence, namely, what happens when a person dies. Luis is unapologetically a monist. He believes that at death human consciousness ceases to function and the person remains in the tomb awaiting the resurrection. It is his desire to further explore, substantiate, and develop this outlook that led him to choose this topic for his PhD dissertation.

His study deals primarily with 2 Corinthians 5:1–10, one of the most difficult passages relating to the afterlife from a monist perspective, and one which has not received its due attention. In this passage Paul declares his desire not do die and be found "naked." Proponents of the continued existence after death see in this expression one of the surest proofs that Paul expected to continue to live after death. Those who reject continued existence

Foreword

at death, endeavor to brush away this passage by arguing the Paul's focus is primarily soteriological rather than anthropological.

Luis avoids evasion and tackles the topic head on. By detailed exegesis and comparison of the use of the relevant vocabulary in other ancient sources he demonstrates quite convincingly that the term "naked," the state which Paul wanted to avoid, was not a continued immaterial existence at death, but the cessation of life. Paul was hoping to see the coming of Jesus without facing death. The force and conviction of Luis' argument is such, that no subsequent commentary on 2 Corinthians 5:1–10 should be written without reference to his outlook as outlined in this volume.

Luis' contribution is not limited only to an exegesis on 2 Corinthians 5:1-10. His introduction contains a detailed discussion of terminology used by those who do not believe in continued existence at death, terms such as soul-sleep, or annihilationism, among others. It emerges that such terminology lacks unity, and is often inaccurate. He then proposes alternative terminology. The candor with which he critiques the use of such language, and the alternatives he suggests to replace such language, make his introduction extremely informative and worth reading in its own right.

Lastly, Luis' pastoral outlook comes in his concluding section where he discusses the hope of the believer. The cessation of existence of a person at death may sound like a painful reality, and indeed it is. But thankfully, it does not mark the end of a person, an annihilation. God keeps a memory of all things and at the point of resurrection will restore a person to the full vigor of existence. In this way, an accurate Biblical understanding of the nature of death takes the sting away out of death, and offers believers hope beyond death.

In light of his detailed discussion of terms in his introduction, his sharp exegesis of 2 Corinthians 5:1–10, and his pastoral application in his conclusion, I wholeheartedly recommend this work. It deserves to be a landmark study in discussions of death.

—Kim Papaioannou

Preface

I WAS BORN IN a family with a monist conception of human being, but a dualist background. Even the common family expressions denoted that dualistic background. My environment and high school education was under the common dualistic conception of human being, proper of popular religion in Christian countries. During my theological bachelor degree I realized that concepts and biblical support in that matter were not as clear and plain as I would like them to be. Soon I saw that serious biblical studies supporting dualistic views were based on few passages, among those 2 Corinthians 5, and especially the word "naked," was one of the most important.

Perhaps the other passage broadly used to strengthen the dualistic view is the parable of the rich man and Lazarus. However, being a parable, it is subject to speculations and personal interpretations. Biblical exegesis in this parable does not give conclusive inputs to the discussion.

In my master studies I found a tension on what I thought the Bible teaches as a whole regarding the nature of the human being and some specific passages interpreted in a dualistic way. My fundamentalist background on the conception of revelation and inspiration forces me to see coherence and unity in biblical teachings. The Scriptures teach anthropologic dualism as a whole, or with monism; and every passage should fit in this scheme.

Later I spent four years doing my PhD in biblical studies in the Philippines, an important Christian (mainly Catholic) country in Asia with strong dualistic practices. I focused my efforts there in anthropological biblical studies, especially regarding death. Death is the "state" which more clearly defines the ultimate composition on human being. This book is the result of those studies. I hope the reader will find sincere and open exposition of what I found regarding theme and how Bible remains as a unity even in this matter of the nature of human being.

Acknowledgments

To GOD BE GLORY, honor, and my deepest gratitude. Through this book He has showed me how to depend on Him and to hope for that great day when I can see Him face to face, if possible, without experiencing death.

A special acknowledgement to my dear wife Mary Rodriguez, for her support, love, and patience in this process. Mary, and my children, Jafeth and Yameli, did important contributions while they listened to my deliberations. I owe them too much.

I would like to thank Richard Sabuin for his friendship, advice, patience, support, and good suggestions in this book. Thanks also to Kim Papaioannou, my friend, for his contributions and friendly advice. I give also thanks to Mrs. Elsie de la Cruz and her team for their help and patience during the editing process.

Chapter 1

Introduction

HAVING A DUALISTIC UNDERSTANDING of the nature of human being, perhaps inherited from our Greco-Roman background, most Christians think that "something" left the human body at the moment of death. This "something," which sometimes is called "soul" represents the real person, or at least, links the person before death and after it.

Laid on this understanding, many other concepts that, in my opinion, can modify our beliefs regarding salvation, future rewards, and the hope of eternal life, are affected. In this book the reader will not find a general study on the theological or philosophical issue of life after death; instead I would like to tackle one of the main passages used in this discussion: 2 Corinthians 5, especially the concept of nakedness found in verse 3.

The reader will notice that the book is quite technical, although I have transliterated Greek and Hebrew terms. I try to use simple and plain language, first, because I would like everyone to be able to read the book, and second, because English not my mother tongue and I would not like to confuse things that are not very clear.

The Greek term γυμνός (*gymnos* from now on) commonly translated as "naked" in 2 Cor 5:3 has been understood to refer to the state of the human being between death and resurrection. The nature of the human being in the NT, and especially in relation to what happens between death[1]

---

1. Unless it is specified, the term *death*, in this book, refers to "the cessation of [physical] life and the state that follows." I will not discuss here other uses, such as the "penalty of sin . . . (Rom 6:23; Rev 2:11; 20:14; 21:8)," the "spiritual death 'in trespasses and sins,' the condition of those who have never accepted Christ, or who, having accepted him, fall away (Rom 8:6; Eph 2:1, 5. 6; Col 2:13; 1 Tim 5:6)"; and "death to sin, which accompanies

and resurrection, has been the object of more philosophical argumentation than of exegetical study. For some the doctrine of resurrection, which includes what happens between death and resurrection, "has not received as much philosophical attention as some other aspects of Christian theology."[2] Moreover, the passages used have been largely interpreted "through conceptual schemes borrowed from Greek philosophical traditions"[3] according to Oscar Cullmann, even to the point of negating biblical truths on behalf of philosophical heritage.[4]

Congruent to a correct understanding of *gymnos* are some other Greek terms, the meaning of which is sometimes overlapping or seemingly ambiguous.[5] Examples of these are (a) those used to refer to the human nature or some dimension of it, such as *psychē* ("soul"), *pneuma* ("spirit"), *sōma* ("body"), and *sarx* ("flesh"); and (b) those used to refer to the span between death and resurrection, such as *koimaomai* ("to sleep").[6] Of such terms, the one most strongly used by dualists, and less explained by monists, is *gymnos* in 2 Cor 5:3 and its inferences in the rest of the chapter, as I will show later. It seems that, generally speaking, there is no clear interpretation of the state of nakedness in this passage that can be consistent with

---

the new birth (Rom 6:2–11; Gal 2:20; Col 2:13; 1 Peter 2:24; 1 John 3:14)." Neufeld, *Seventh-Day Adventist Encyclopedia*, s.v. "Death."

2. Baker, "Death and the Afterlife," 389.

3. Kesley, "Human Being," 168. See also Martin, *The Corinthian Body*, 7, 8; and Cullmann, *Immortality of the Soul or Resurrection of the Dead?*, 6, 7, and 15. An excellent survey of how body-soul dualism has contributed to the rise of modern secularism and the distinction between secular and spiritual or religious life is found in Walsh and Middleton, "The Development of Dualism," 107.

4. Cullmann, *Immortality*, 8. On this point, Martin Heidegger argues that for Christians, Greek philosophy has to be foolishness according to Paul in 1 Cor 1:20. Heidegger, *Pathmarks*, 288. See also Westphal, "Continental Philosophy of Religion," 485.

5. See for instance, Gundry, "Human Being," 411; and Martin, *Body*, 7. Regarding this misinterpretation of terms, Cullmann underlines that, although the same words are used for NT anthropology as for Greek philosophy, "they mean something quite different, and we understand the whole New Testament amiss when we construe these concepts only from the point of view of Greek thought." Cullmann, *Immortality*, 31, 32.

6. I will consider some of the scholars who use them in that sense. Although the focus of this book is *gymnos*, I will refer frequently to the other terms because, due to the nature of *gymnos*, it can be explained in the context of 2 Cor 5:3 by its relation with them, especially in reference to 1 Cor 15:35–55 which uses these other terms clearly. The use and comparison with *koimaomai* will be strongly prominent in the quest for the meaning of *gymnos*, although it is not the focus of this book.

Introduction

the other terms and the general concept of the Bible. So, the whole concept of death has an exegetical void.

The Corinthian correspondence, especially 1 Cor 15:35–55 and 2 Cor 4:7–5:10, have been the most frequently used NT passages to approach the issue of the nature of the human being between death and resurrection.[7] Scholars have seen them as parallel passages due to their similarities in language, subjects, and theme.[8] These passages have to be considered together due to the fact that they are the only ones that use *gymnos* in the context of the nature of the human being at death.

Due to the language of these passages, such as *skēnos*, "tent," *oikia*, "house," *oikodomē*, "building," *ependyō*, "to be clothed with," and *gymnos*, some interpreters "feel" that Paul is "referring to an intermediate body, which already exists in heaven, to be put on at death."[9] The literalism of the imagery, and some comparison with its use in Greek philosophy,[10] has led some scholars to see some kind of human existence between death and resurrection;[11] although others recognize that this teaching is not explicit in NT but has to be inferred.[12] David Hocking, after stating that "the soul represents the real person, but without a body," says that there is even the possibility that "God has some sort of intermediate body which we take on between the time we die and the time when our bodies are resurrected."[13] Nevertheless, Hocking maintains that in 1 Cor 15 there is no body in the intermediate state. He explains this clear contradiction by saying that

---

7. Baker, "Death," 368. There are many other passages used outside the Corinthian correspondence, but these two, in my opinion, seem to focus on this specific issue. These are the larger passages on the topic and speak clearly of physical resurrection and the nature of the body, as it will be shown. On the contrary, other NT passages (with the exception of 1 Thess 4:13–18) have a different focus; they mention death or resurrection in a secondary frame without explaining what happens.

8. See for instance, Gillman, "A Thematic Comparison: 1 Cor 15:50–57 and 2 Cor 5:1–5," 439–54, and MacGant, "Competing Pauline Eschatologies," 23–49.

9. Ladd, "Eschatology," 2:140. Ladd, however, sees a relationship on language between 1 Cor 15 and 2 Cor 5 that makes it difficult to arrive to that conclusion.

10. See Osei-Bonsu, "Does 2 Cor 5:1–10 Teach the Reception of the Resurrection Body at the Moment of Death?" 89, 90.

11. This implies the duality of the human being, having an immortal soul independent of the body, a concept taken from Greek though in contrast to Paul's Jewish inheritance; see McCasland, "The Basis of the Resurrection Faith," 213.

12. Helm, "Intermediate State," 1:1043.

13. Hocking, *Who Am I and What Difference Does It Make?*, 139.

"While God can make some of the dead appear in a body, it is not their normal condition."[14]

Others tend to spiritualize the terms and imagery in 2 Cor 5:1–10 leading the discussion away from the field of anthropology[15] towards soteriology,[16] taking expressions regarding human existence and turning them into expressions regarding spiritual or moral experiences.[17] Thus, according to Bruce R. Reichenbach, Pauline anthropology "is not developed philosophically."[18] Paul's concern was to develop a theology in relation to the redemption of man, "not to present a coherent anthropology in consonance with or contrast to Hellenistic thought."[19] Reichenbach sees Paul as a monist[20] and says that any hint of dualism[21] in Paul is only apparent, because he has been read with the eyeglasses of Greek philosophy.[22]

---

14. Ibid., 141, 142.

15. Although anthropology has many subdivisions and covers different aspects of the human being, due to the nature of this book, here anthropology will address to what Millard J. Erickson calls "the constitutional nature of the human." See Erickson, *Christian Theology*, 537.

16. Soteriology (the study of salvation) covers Jesus' work to finish the sin problem and restore the image of God in humanity. Nevertheless, for the purposes of this book, the term here focuses on the Christian experience after accepting Jesus as saviour. It includes justification and sanctification. The final eradication of the sin and the physical changes on humanity due to this is referred to here as eschatology, together with the events related to the Parousia (the second physical coming of Jesus).

17. See the section on Salvific Experience on p. 13.

18. Reichenbach, "Resurrection of the Body, Re-Creation and Interim Existence," 36.

19. Ibid.

20. *Monism*, in contrast to dualism, stands for the view of the human being as an indivisible entity with different dimensions. Then, the person dies as a whole or lives as a whole. Only anthropological monism in this sense will be referred in this book with this theological term. See my sections Dualism (p. 5) and Monism (p. 13).

21. In this book, *dualism* refers to the "view of human beings as constituted of two irreducible elements (as matter and spirit)." See *Merriam-Webster's Collegiate Dictionary*, s.v. "Dualism." The term will be used here exclusively for anthropological dualism; the conception of the composition of human being as having a body and a soul (or spirit), which can exist separated from the body. Dualism here does not necessarily include the acceptance of eternal hell or punishment neither the conscious state of the soul when separated from the body. See the definition of anthropological dualism and monism in Cairus, "The Doctrine of Man," 212.

22. Reichenbach, "Resurrection," 36. Greek philosophy in this book stands for Platonism, which sees the body as a prison of the soul. It includes positions such as those of Philo and Pythagoras. See Myers, s.v. "Dualism," on this regard. Nevertheless, dualism of the human being is not exclusive to Greek philosophy, but is present with some

Introduction

It is fair to say that most of the studies of these images in the Corinthian correspondence either: (a) assume a kind of dualism in relation to human nature after death and before resurrection; or (b) avoid an anthropological interpretation of passages such as 1 Cor 5:1–10. Moreover, there is only one study made specifically on *gymnos*.[23] Other discussions of the term appear in theological discussion or biblical commentaries with little detailed exegesis. Theological presuppositions lead scholars to understand *gymnos* as inferring dualism.

Most theological discussion in relation to the state of the dead in the Corinthian correspondence has revolved around the issue of wether the soul is mortal or immortal. The real issue, however, with images such as *gymnos* is not the immortality or non-immortality of the soul, but whether dualism or monism is implied. Dualism anticipates that the person is a compound entity made up of the body, plus an immaterial soul or spirit, and that this soul/spirit has some form of innate immortality. By contrast, monism sees the human being as an indivisible entity. When the body dies, the person dies.

The focus of this brief review is not the state of the dead per se, but how the image of *gymnos* has been understood to support different approaches to the state of death in the Corinthian correspondence.[24] The only two passages that use *gymnos* in a clear reference to this state are 2 Cor 5:3 and 1 Cor 15:37. Therefore, it is impossible to separate the consideration of 1 Cor 15:35–55 and the other images used there, such as κοιμάομαι, to refer to the same state.

Dualism

According to Tony Walter, in a study published in 1996, 71 percent of Americans believe in some form of conscious existence after death,[25] either under the scheme of dichotomism (the person is made up of body and

---

variations in almost every religion aside from biblical monism.

23. This work is, Sevenster, "Some Remarks on the Γυμνός in II Cor. v. 3,", 202–14.

24. For a historical approach to the different perspectives on the issue of the end of life, see the brief summary in Beck and Demarest, *The Human Person in Theology and Psychology*, 46–54. For a review of traditional Christian perspectives see Cooper, *Body, Soul and Life Everlasting*, 7–35.

25. Walter, *The Eclipse of Eternity*, 32, quoted in Bacchiocchi, *Immortality or Resurrection?*, 10.

soul),[26] or thrichotomism (body, soul, and spirit).[27] Dichotomism, which is also referred to as Dualism, is by far the most common view. In another study published in 2007, the percentages were 83 for Catholics and 86 percent for Protestants.[28] Many place the origin of belief in the immortality of the soul as coming from Plato's *Phaedo*.[29] Some believe that the evolution of this idea precedes Plato,[30] and forms the basis of paganism and animist beliefs.[31]

A person is, according to dualism, an immaterial soul, which can exist apart from the body,[32] but that is temporarily imprisoned in the body. The soul then is spiritual and good, and the body evil and earthly. In this context, death is liberation from the prison of the body into the freedom of disembodied existence. Even scholars, who see a necessary link between soul and brain, accept the continuing existence of the soul without a body. An example is Richard Swinburne, who says that, "Indeed, the soul is the necessary core of a person which must continue if a person is to continue."[33] Others, such as Joseph Osei Bonsu, arguing for eschatological

---

26. See Erickson, *Christian Theology*, 540–42. One clear example of this view is Clarke, *An Outline of Christian Theology*, 182, 188. He holds that the body dies and the spirit continues living (ibid., 449). See also DeWolf, *A Theology of the Living Church*, 150, 151, who has the same argument. Both see the resurrection of the body as the final state of the immortal soul.

27. See Delitzsch, *A System of Biblical Psychology*, 116, 117. Louis Berkhof says that, although thrichotomism was popular among some of the early fathers, it was decreasing in strength; but it was revived in the nineteeth century. See Berkhof, *Systematic Theology*, 191, 192.

28. B. A. Robinson registered 83 percent among Catholics and 86 percent among Protestants in 2007. Robinson, "Religious Beliefs of Americans, About Ghosts, Satan, Heaven, Hell," etc.

29. Baker, "Death," OHPR, 366, 367.

30. Jaeger, "The Greek Ideas of Immortality," 97. Also the mere prohibition given to Israel about consulting the dead, which was a practice of the surrounding cultures (Deut 18:11, 12), speaks of some kind of belief in the immortality of the soul outside Greek philosophy and predating it. Claudia Setzer points out some archaeological discoveries which parallel the belief in an afterlife of the Egyptian and Ugaritic graves; see Setzer, *Resurrection of the Body in Early Judaism and Early Christianity*, 6, 7. Nevertheless such "evidences" may only highlight pagan influence on Israel.

31. See Handy, "Serpent (Religious Symbol)," 5:1114.

32. Wolfson, "Immortality and Resurrection in the Philosophy of the Church Fathers," 21, 22.

33. Swinburne, *The Evolution of the Soul*, 146.

Introduction

bodily resurrection, use 2 Cor 5:1–10[34] to imply an intermediate existence of a disembodied soul/spirit with the Lord before the resurrection at the Parousia.[35]

When it comes to the state of death and the interpretation of 2 Cor 5:1–10, two main possibilities have developed. The first entails a conscious existence in death; the second, an unconscious state between death and the resurrection, sometimes called *soul sleep*.[36]

Conscious immortality of the soul.

The understanding of the imagery of the Corinthian correspondence to support the conscious state of the human being after death is not new. Already in the third century, Methodius, discussing the meaning of the expression "made with hands" and "not made with hands" in the context of 2 Cor 5:1–10,[37] upheld that, after the earthly life, souls will have a "habitation which is before resurrection." He inferred that such a state is "the other life."[38] Clement of Alexandria used the same text to refer to the spirit which "will dwell in heaven above," while the pious in dying is present with God.[39]

Following Aristotle's view of the soul as the "agent intellect," Thomas Aquinas saw the soul as "subsisting" on its own when separated from the body during the so-called "intermediate state." During this state, the individual does not exist as such, but only the soul as a separated entity. At

---

34. The limits of the pericope are 2 Cor 4:7—5:10, as will be shown later in this book; however, for a majority of scholars the images regarding human nature at death are placed in 2 Cor 5:1–4 or 2 Cor 5:1–10. I will use their limits when I discuss others's views.

35. See for instance Barnett, *The Second Epistle to the Corinthians*, 262–63; Martin, *2 Corinthians*, 106. Osei-Bonsu, "Resurrection Body," 92–95. Peterson, *Hell on Trial*, 185.

36. A third view sees the resurrection taking place immediately after death in which case there is no intermediate state or span between death and resurrection; this view will not be considered here. Some scholars say that such a view is a misunderstanding or misinterpretation of 2 Cor 5:1–10; e.g., Bracken "Bodily Resurrection and the Dialectic of Spirit and Matter," 782. Others see an allusion to resurrection at death in 2 Cor 5:1–10, in contrast with 1 Cor 15 where Paul speaks about resurrection at Parousia. See Bruce, "Paul on Immortality," 469–72; Bruce, *1 and 2 Corinthians*, 200–206; Bruce, *Paul*, 309–313; Harris, "2 Corinthians 5:1–10: Watershed in Paul's Eschatology?" 32–57; Harris, "Paul's View of Death in 2 Corinthians 5:1–10," 317–28.

37. All Bible quotations are from *The New American Standard Bible* (NAS), (1995), unless otherwise noted.

38. Methodius, *From the Discourse of Resurrection* V.

39. Clement of Alexandria, *The Stromata or Miscellanies* XXVI.

resurrection, when the soul is reunited with the body, the human being as an individual is fully restored. According to Aquinas, being an agent intellect, the disembodied soul is the part of the person that thinks and wills, but can neither sense nor feel.[40] Commenting on 2 Cor 5:3, John Calvin also said that the clothes of "immortal glory" are received at death,[41] inferring a state between death and resurrection.

Matthew Henry's Commentary calls this state, the "other life." It is acquired "immediately after death, so soon as *our house of this earthly tabernacle is dissolved.*"[42] Then it explains that the soul, which is divested from the body, goes to Christ to be dressed with an immortal body. This state is called "a happy life after this present life," which infers a conscious state, but in some sense, an embodied one, since the "naked" soul puts on "the robes of glory."[43] Is this a kind of resurrection body received upon death?[44] Some scholars have argued against such a view.[45]

Although traditionally the conscious state after death has been a Catholic interpretation of these images, most evangelicals also hold this position.[46] Perhaps one of the best representatives is the Westminster Confession of Faith that presents the conscious immortality of the soul separated

---

40. Baker, "Death," OHPR, 372.

41. Calvin, *Calvin's Commentaries: 2 Corinthians*, s.v. "2 Cor 5:3."

42. Henry, *Matthew Henry's Commentary on the Whole Bible*, s.v. "2 Cor 5:1–11" (italics are his). Cullmann says that, "Karl Barth considers it to be the New Testament interpretation that the transformation of the body occurs for everyone immediately after his individual death—as if the dead were no longer in time." Cullmann, *Immortality*, 49. This also makes death a conscious state in agreement with H. Matthew.

43. Henry, *Commentary*, s.v. "2 Cor 5:1–11." See also Price, "Personal Survival and the Idea of Another World," 364–86, who sees the afterlife as one of disembodied consciousness.

44. Cf. the discussion of Brunner, *Eternal Hope*, 101.

45. See the list of objections provided by Harris, *Raised Immortal*, 255; and Ladd, *A Theology of the New Testament*, 599.

46 In the volume of the evangelical conference held in 1989, John Ankerberg argues that, "the denial of eternal punishment is tantamount to a denial of the deity of our Lord and Savior." Ankerberg, "Response to J. I. Packer," 139. In addition, Nicholas Thomas Wright, in an interview with David Van Biema for *Time* Magazine, said, "We know that we will be with God and with Christ, resting and being refreshed. Paul writes that it will be conscious, but compared to being bodily alive, it will be like being asleep." Biema, "Christians Wrong About Heaven, Says Bishop," 2008, under the question, "Is There Anything More in the Bible About the Period Between Death and the Resurrection of the Dead?" This position is also common among Protestants.

Introduction

from the body waiting for resurrection. The Westminster Confession uses also 1 Cor 15 and 2 Cor 5, among others, as a basis for this position.[47]

Charles Hodge says that the heavenly tent of 2 Cor 5 is heaven itself, and in support cites John 14:2.[48] He says that, "The body is compared to a house in which the soul now lives; heaven is the house into which it enters when this earthly house is destroyed."[49] For him, Paul "says in effect that the destruction of the body does not destroy the soul or deprive it of a home. His consolation was that if unclothed, he would not be found naked."[50] Hodge then links this experience with Matt 22:31, 32 saying that Jesus was speaking about the existence of spirits when quoting Exod 3:6, 15, and 16, and inferring that "Abraham, Isaac, and Jacob, therefore, are living and are not in a dreamy state of semiconscious existence."[51]

Hodge's view seems to be built on the idea that a body is needed if bliss is to be reached.[52] In this respect he differs from Greek dualism. Others, by contrast, see no need for an intermediate body and speak of a disembodied consciousness in the afterlife.[53] Millard Erickson also points to the Pauline expression of being away from the body and at home with the Lord of 2 Cor 5:8, and the state of nakedness in 5:3 as arguments to doubt the validity of monism.[54]

---

47. Williamson, *The Westminster Confession of Faith for Study Classes*, XXXII, 1. 0

48. Hodge, *2 Corinthians*, s.v. "2 Cor 5:2," compare also with his arguments for verse 3 where *nakedness* means *homelesnesss* for him. See also the affirmation of souls dwelling in heaven after death in Owen, *Body and Soul*, 29, 98.

49. Hodge, *2 Corinthians*, s.v. "2 Cor 5:2."

50. Ibid.

51. Ibid. Although Hodge sees the need of a body in 1 Cor 15:35–55 and sustains the truth of resurrection, I do not see the case for resurrection if souls can already enjoy the mansions Jesus went to prepare (John 14:2) before resurrection.

52. See MacArthur, *2 Corinthians*, 165; Sevenster, "Some Remarks," 208; and Barclay *The Letters to the Corinthians*, 204, 205.

53 See Criswell, *The Believer's Study Bible*, s.v. "2 Cor 5:3." The conception of disembodied consciousness is more philosophical than exegetical. See for instance Price, "Personal Survival," 364–86, who shares the same conception of an afterlife as a disembodied consciousness.

54. Erickson, *Christian Theology*, 546. He uses also the parable of the Rich Man and Lazarus, the words of Christ to the thief on the cross, and the distinction between body and soul in Matt 10:28.

Soul sleep.

Soul sleep is another possible modality that can be discussed under the concept of the immortality of the soul. It can be seen as either (a) a clear dualist view that does not infer resurrection, or (b) a more discreet dualist view inferring resurrection. Differently, to the traditional immortality of the soul, according to soul sleep, the soul is unconscious once the person dies. It can also be impersonal. There is an understanding of soul sleep that does not take the Bible as a basis, and is more akin to Pantheism or some variations of Gnosticism that see the soul as simple energy, spirit, or light liberated from the body to be reunited to the universal energy.[55] Biblical scholars also hold to soul sleep. The difference is that while, in the former case, there is no resurrection for the unconscious immortal soul, in the latter there is.

Soul sleep has been seen at least in two ways that are sometimes confused, though distinct. The first sees an existence or entity, which sleeps during death. The core of the human being, which bears its identity, *exists* with the Lord in some degree of unconscious state (sleeping) awaiting its reunion with the body, either the same as before or a glorious immortal one. It implies that some part of the individual survives death, though is unable to interact with others. The second view sees a complete absence of existence at death. If this is the case, the state of sleep does not refer to death, but it is a metaphor for the unconsciousness that is implied in a time of nonexistence. This second view will be considered under the category of monism below.

Soul sleep is sometimes called psychopannychism. This word infers that there is an entity (soul) that sleeps in death. It sees "the soul [as] an immortal substance that is unconscious in some obscure place until it is reunited with the body at the General Resurrection."[56] In Reformation times one of the greatest holders of soul sleep was Luther. The view was also "espoused by Tyndale, Frith, and perhaps William Tracy."[57] In modern times Cullmann is one of its best-known advocates. He assures that immortality of the soul is not compatible with resurrection of the body. He highlights that

---

55 For an extended discussion of Gnosticism, see Logan and Wedderburn, *The New Testament and Gnosis*, 21–186; Roukema, *Gnosis and Faith in Early Christianity*, 13–68; Layton, *The Gnostics Scriptures*, 5–462; Hendrick and Hodgson, *Nag HammadiGnosticism, and Early Christianity*, 1–307.

56. Burns, "Tradition of Christian Mortalism in England, 1530–1660," 170–171.

57. Ibid.

the "soul is not intrinsically immortal, but rather became so only through the resurrection of Jesus Christ, and through faith in Him."[58] Contrary to Greek philosophy, he points out the fact that it "is death and not the body which must be conquered by the Resurrection,"[59] since the body is not evil but also created by God. Nevertheless, though Cullmann recognizes that genuine life cannot exist apart from the body, he still suggests a kind of "shady existence without the body, like the dead in Sheol according to [his understanding of] the Old Testament."[60] Thus, while fighting against the misunderstanding of the meaning of terms used by both Greek philosophy and the NT, and while building up a case against the immortality of the soul, he still uses this unclear concept of a kind of existence apart from the body. There is no intention here to demerit his work since he attempted to show a monist view of the human being; however, when he arrives to the condition between death and resurrection, his language suggests a dualistic understanding in favor of some kind of unconscious state of the soul at death.[61]

For him, sleeping is a "*condition* of the dead before the Parousia"[62] (italics in the original) and related to the "repose" of Rev 14:13. This is an "'interim condition': (1) that exists; (2) that it already signifies union with Christ,"[63] and in which the dead are waiting. He interprets 2 Cor 5:1–10 affirming that, though the dead do not have a body while they are sleeping they are in "special proximity with Christ."[64]

Cullmann defines flesh and spirit, on the basis of his understanding of these terms in Pauline theology. He maintains that these "are two *transcendent* powers which can enter into man from without; but *neither is given*

---

58. Cullmann, *Immortality*, 17.

59. Ibid., 26.

60. Ibid., 33. However, scholars recognize that "the idea of immortality of the soul is foreign to the Old Testament which teaches the belief in the resurrection of the bodies." Papademetriou, "The Human Body According to Saint Gregory Palamas," 2. See also on this point Romanides, "Man and His True Life According to the Greek Orthodox Service Book," 64; and Bultmann, *Primitive Christianity in Its Contemporary Setting*, 46. See also a good summary of the OT belief on life and death, which called "traditional anthropological conception by the people of YHWH" in Martin-Achard, "Resurrection," 5:683.

61. Reichenbach also sees this contradiction in Cullmann's argument. See Reichenbach, "Resurrection," 38, 39.

62. Cullmann, *Immortality*, 51.

63 Ibid.

64. Ibid., 53.

with human existence as such"⁶⁵ (italics in the original). The body is the "locus, from which point it [flesh] affects the whole man."⁶⁶ Paul sometimes speaks of body instead of flesh. Nevertheless, flesh is less connected with the inner man. On the other hand, the spirit, for Cullmann, is the power of life given through the Holy Spirit and contrary to sin and death. It affects in a greater degree the inner man. The issue is that the inner man, because he is "transformed by the Spirit (Rom 6:3), and consequently made alive, continues to live with Christ in this transformed state, in the condition of sleep."⁶⁷

Although Cullmann recognizes in his view a "certain analogy to the 'immortality of the soul,'"⁶⁸ he says that this condition differs from immortality of the soul because this state of nakedness, or sleep, is an imperfect condition awaiting the resurrection. In other words, the inner man is not a complete or real person as the soul in Greek philosophy. On the other hand, this state is not a "natural essence of the soul" as in the immortality of the soul view, but rather it is "the result of a divine intervention from outside."⁶⁹ Thus, indirectly, he proposes another kind of unconscious state under the category of duality of the being. This duality is seen in the expressions "outer" and "inner" in 2 Cor 4:16. In this sense, in the state of death the person is an incomplete being.

Edmund Hill summarizes his concept of the unconscious state, saying that the dead are "incommunicado" because all human communication is through the body, and since the soul lacks a body, it lacks also the ability to receive impressions and to give impressions.⁷⁰ Nevertheless, he says, this isolation from senses and the body does not apply to the relation with God. The dead believers are not isolated from God.⁷¹ Hill explains that putting the souls with Christ in heaven "leaves the body almost entirely out of account."⁷² This is the very issue Cullmann argues against; he says that this contradicts the resurrection of the body; however, Hill's isolated condition in essence is the same as Cullmann's sleep.

65. Ibid., 33.
66. Ibid., 34.
67. Ibid., 56.
68. Ibid.
69. Ibid.
70. Hill, *Being Human*, 119.
71. Ibid., 120.
72. Ibid., 273, 274.

Introduction

Anthony Hoekema argues that soul sleep is indeed a dualist view, since such a view implies "that there is a soul which continues to exist after death, but in an unconscious state."

The great majority of modern scholars see the state of the dead as some kind of disembodied intermediate state before resurrection, either conscious or unconscious.[73] This is the existence of a so-called soul, which represents the real person and lives independently from the body. As such, soul sleep perpetuates the concept of the immortality of the soul.

Monism

Monism "was popular in neoorthodoxy and in the biblical-theology movement. Their approach was largely through a word-study method."[74] John A. T. Robinson, following the thoughts of H. Wheeler Robinson, has more emphatically presented monism as the biblical conception of death.[75] The monist interpretation of death includes (a) one soteriological view, called here "salvific experience," and (b) two anthropological views, which include "Christian annihilation" and "monist-mortalism."

Salvific experience.

This view is not a view of death, but rather an interpretation of the images in 2 Cor 4:7—5:10 in order to make them fit into a monistic view of death as it avoids the anthropological, dualistic tension some see in the passage. Since this study focuses on this passage, I will discuss "Salvific experience" as a view.

Those who take this approach see the Christian experience of salvation in Christ rather than the physical nature of a person.[76] Hodge, for instance,

---

73. Owen, *Body*, 27.

74. Erickson, *Christian Theology*, 543.

75. See Robinson. *The Body: A Study in Pauline Theology*, 11–33, and Robinson, "Hebrew Psychology," 361–66. Baker has made a good summary of the different approaches to the monist view but on a philosophical-biblical approach. See Baker "Death," 366–91. In relation to the constitution view, see Baker, *Persons and Bodies*, 167–227. See also Zurchier, "The Christian View of Man I," 156–68; Zurchier, "The Christian View of Man II," 66–83; and Zurchier, "The Christian View of Man III," 89–103.

76. Cf the Valentinian interpretation of resurrection of 1 Cor 15 in Pagels, "'The Mystery of the Resurrection': A Gnostic Reading of 1 Corinthians 15," 276–88; especially 283, 284. For them, death, as synonymous to sleep, means being under sin; and resurrection

quotes "Calvin among the older commentators, and Usteri and Olshausen among the modern," who hold the view that the words *endysamenoi*, "clothed," and *gymnos* in 2 Cor 5:3 "must be understood to refer to the moral or spiritual state of the soul, to its being clothed with righteousness or being destitute of that clothing."[77]

Horst Robert Balz sees a relationship between *gymnos* and "a daily renewal of the inner person through the power of God" in 2 Cor 4:7–18 (cf. 5:6, 8). The "life in Christ" (4:11) works in the inner man, providing it with clothes from heaven (5:1) and glory (4:17). The "daily renewal" "corresponds to the continual dying of the earthly body."[78] At the end, although dying, believers are found not naked, but clothed with heavenly glory. He sees the anthropological implications as being subject to the primary soteriological focus of the pericope, in demerit of "Gnostic demands for liberation from the earthly body."[79]

Another example of this approach is Samuele Bacchiocchi. He sees 2 Cor 5:1–10 as referring to two different modes of existence, a heavenly one and an earthly one. But he sees the passage as soteriological rather than anthropological. "The heavenly dwelling place is Christ himself and the gift of eternal life He provides to believers,"[80] the new life in Christ and his righteousness accepted at baptism. Thus, to be found naked stands in contrast to being clothed with Christ and his Spirit. It "stands not for the soul stripped from the body, but for guilt and sin which result in death."[81]

---

means to receive the power of the Spirit.

77. Hodge, *2 Corinthians*, s.v. "2 Cor 5:3." This, however, is not the view of Hodge who sees the heavenly house as referring to the house Jesus promised in John 14:1–3.

78. Balz, "γυμνός," *Exegetical Dictionary of the New Testament*, 1:266.

79. Ibid.

80. Bacchiocchi, *Immortality*, 185. Bacchiocchi uses "dwelling places" for houses (οἰκία) used in 2 Cor 5:1. He does not mean that "dwelling" carries the idea of something or somebody living in it as this could give the sense of dualism. I prefer the simple term "houses" as physical matter, and used by Paul to avoid that misunderstanding. Walter Bauer shows that the primary meaning of οἰκία refers to a "structure"; although in few instances it refers to "the social unity within a dwelling." Bauer, *A Greek-English Lexicon*, s.v. "οἰκία." On the other hand, the term οἶκος, has a broader significance. It is a place to live in, a home, a palace, a family, the whole tribe, or a property or possession. Ibid., s.v. "οἶκος." It seems that the former emphasizes a physical structure without necessarily implying that someone dwells in, and the late emphasizes more the "dwelling" sense of the house.

81. Ibid., 186.

Introduction

This interpretation of the images fits with biblical monism and eschatology. It states that the imagery of *gymnos*, houses, or clothes, do not have anything to do with the physical nature of the human being. On the other hand, this interpretation avoids the nature of the language and imagery in the context and Pauline use in general. It takes for granted, on the basis of theology instead of exegesis, the soteriological intention of the passage as the primary meaning.

Christian annihilation.

In a secular environment, death is defined as annihilation, the cessation of life. The death of the body is the death of the individual. It means the total destruction or extermination of the individual without anything that survives.[82] This is a naturalistic view of death and has been avoided as an option to interpret the imagery of death in the Corinthian correspondence, because naturalistic annihilation denies the possibility of resurrection. But it has been used by the opponents of monism or soul sleep as an argument against the views that categorize them as non-biblical views, especially with reference to the death of believers. For instance, Paul Helm mentions that Calvin, in his controversy against some of the Anabaptists, used this term to define the view of soul sleep as inferring the disappearance of the person during death and the downplaying of the power of Christ to rule over the dead before resurrection. Helm said that Calvin's view agrees with Paul in Rom 8:35, 39—that nothing can separate the believer from the love of God,[83] not even death.

In a Christian context, however, annihilation "is the doctrine that the souls of the wicked will be snuffed out of existence rather than be sent to an everlasting, conscious hell." It is applied to what is called "the second death."[84] It speaks about the wicked rather than the righteous, since only the wicked will undergo the second death. This view was better known among

---

82. "No more could a rational soul exist apart from the body whose form it was than could the shape of a particular axe exist apart from that axe. The soul is the form of the body. So, Aristotle had no place for an afterlife." Baker, "Death," 372. This statement contradicts Baker's previous one that Aristotle saw the soul as agent intellect which "subsists" on its own (see p. 7).

83. Helm, "Intermediate State," 1:1043.

84. Geisler, *Baker Encyclopedia of Christian Apologetics*, 22. Geisler does not hold this position; he only mentions it.

its defenders as conditional immortality, biblical mortalism, or Christian conditionalism.[85]

Richard Bauckham mentioned in 1978 that "no traditional Christian doctrine has been so widely abandoned as that of eternal punishment. . . . The alternative interpretation of hell as annihilation seems to have prevailed even among many of the more conservative theologians."[86] Nevertheless, in 1990 Pinnock suggested that "the annihilation of the wicked . . . is the view of a minority among evangelical theologians and church leaders."[87] What is clear by the comparison of these two perspectives of the impact of this view is that annihilation is seen for some as a valid view of death.

However, this doctrine traditionally has been used to speak against the unconditional immortality of the soul rather than the nature of the human being. The use of soul, if not explained, would lead to a dualist conception of man even though, at the end, it can be annihilated. The main problem with the Christian annihilation view of death is that it speaks mainly of the eternal fate of wicked,[88] but fails to clearly explain the nature of death, before resurrection, either for the wicked or for believers. If before the resurrection the anthropological natures of people "good and evil are alike" and sleep is "the beautiful euphemism of Death,"[89] Christian annihilation could imply two different kinds of death: one before resurrection, and another after the second death. And only the second, that applies only to the wicked, will mean annihilation.

---

85. There is a confusion of terms here. Sometimes terms such as conditional immortality, biblical mortalism or Christian conditionalism are used to infer a soul that dies after the resurrection. In that case, the terms have been used like the soul sleep view, in a dualistic way, and they have been considered in the previous section. Here they are seen as representing the view of death as total cessation of life. When this nomenclatures refers specifically to the immortality that it is not inherent to human being but only to God and that death means cessation of life, then some scholars have put the Seventh-day Adventists under these views. See Hoekema, *Major Cults*, 136.

86. Bauckham "Universalism: A Historical Survey," 47. See also Smith, *Here and Hereafter or Man in Life and Death*, especially 138–146; Froom, *The Conditionalist Faith of our Fathers*, 29–498, especially 79–81; 313, 314 and 324–47; Fudge, *The Fire That Consumes*, 33–252; especially 116–34; Edwards and Stott, *Essentials*, 313–20; Pinnock, "The Destruction of the Finally Impenitent," 243–59; among others.

87. Pinnock, "Destruction," 248.

88. "This supposition has had a considerable number of advocates. It was maintained, among others, by Arnobius, at the close of the third century, by the Socini, by Dr. Hammond, and by some of the New England divines," Alger, *The Destiny of the Soul*, 546.

89. Froom, *Conditonalist Faith*, 79.

Introduction

If the intention of *gymnos* in 2 Cor 5:3 is to point to what happens between the earthly existence and the heavenly and the implied judgment, it is easy to understand why the traditional Christian annihilation view has not been used in interpreting this passage. The passage is speaking of the first death, and an explanation of what happens in the second death does not fit here unless the same concept of death applies to both, the first and the second deaths. In such a case, the use of the nomenclature "Christian annihilation" could lead to misunderstanding since it has not been used traditionally to speak of the first death; however, I include this interpretation of death here to show the ideological relation that it has with the meaning of *gymnos*, as it will be shown. On the other hand, the use of annihilation, assuming monism, is well linked with monism-mortalism, which will be discussed in the next section.

Terms such as conditional immortality, biblical mortalism, or Christian conditionalism, which speak of this kind of Christian annihilation, already have a lot of meanings that express divergent points of view. A clear definition of what they hold in relation to death in general is not an easy task. When these terms emphasize only the total extermination of the soul after the resurrection (second death), the first death is diffuse and could imply dualism, following the concept of the soul sleep view. But, if these terms emphasize the total cessation of human being at death, regardless of the time it happens—first and second death alike—then they can be considered as monist views.

The issue these terms emphasize is immortality versus conditional immortality, and the focus is the nature of God in punishing sinners rather than the nature of human being. To avoid confusion and misunderstanding, it is necessary to use different nomenclature to speak of anthropological death as cessation of life whenever it appears.

Monist-mortalism.

Although a variety of ideas have been covered by the term sleep, and some of them stand in close relation to the belief in the unconscious state of an immortal soul or dualism, there is another view that contrasts with the immortality of the soul, and thus, it sustains the monist interpretation of the images and its corollary of mortality of the individual. This view sees the image of sleep as simply a metaphor for unconsciousness and does not imply any entity surviving death, but sees death as a cessation of existence.

Historically such a view has been called thnetopsychism. It considers the soul to be "the insubstantial 'breath of life' of a living creature or the 'whole man'; they said that the soul dies but, confident of the General Resurrection, they sometimes spoke figuratively of its 'sleep.'"[90] Norman Burns concludes that, "When young Browne, Milton, Overton, and Hobbes adopted thnetopsychism the idea was not at all novel. It had become an integral part of the creed of a number of Adventists, General Baptists, millenarians, Socinians, and Independents."[91]

At the core of the idea of the nature of death, the foundation similarity with the annihilation view[92] is that they both see death as final and total. The difference is that, for Christian monism, resurrection breaks death, bringing persons again to life, while for secular annihilation death is irreversible whenever it occurs. Furthermore, for monism, the concept of death seems to apply to both the first and second death, which is not the case with Christian annihilation.

Thnetopsychism has been strongly linked to the soul sleep view. The use of the word soul to define the person who dies could be interpreted in a dualistic way, since the terminology has been used with that purpose. These facts show the need of caution in using the term as representative of the monist view. In addition, thnetopsychism emphasizes the unconscious state of the dead without explaining their nature.

Another term used sometimes as representative of biblical monism is Christian mortalism. For Erickson, it is the belief that the Bible does not teach the existence of a separate immaterial or immortal soul. Erickson defines this view as follows: "A form of the doctrine of annihilationism: Human life is so closely identified with the physical organism that the death of the body results in the cessation of life."[93] Louis Berkhof says, "The Bible does not know the distinction, so common among us, between a physical, a spiritual, and an eternal death."[94]

Nevertheless, Christian mortalism has not only been interpreted as Erickson does, but it has been also strongly linked to soul sleep, psychopannychism, and thnetopsychism. The boundaries of these terms are not very

---

90. Burns, "Tradition," 170–71.

91. Ibid.

92. Thomson, *Bodies of Thought*, 42. See also Garber and Ayers, *The Cambridge History of Seventeenth-Century Philosophy*, 383; and Hick, *Death and Eternal Life*, 211.

93. Erickson, *The Concise Dictionary of Christian Theology*, 163.

94. Berkhof, *Systematic Theology*, 258, 259.

Introduction

clear and, instead of clarifying the concept of death, their use as representative of the monistic view of death could bring ambiguities. Therefore, in this book, to avoid misunderstandings, I will use the terminology monist-mortalism as representative of my understanding of biblical monism and its relation with death.

Monist-mortalism in this book stands for the concept of person as an indivisible unit (as it will be discussed, the Bible sometimes calls this unity "body," or "soul," though the same terms sometimes reveals different dimensions of this unit) that completely stops living at death without anything that survives. Thus death is a period of nonexistence. The representative of this unit is the living body. When it dies and disintegrates, it is indeed the person who dies and disintegrates in all dimensions. The "spirit" that returns to God is only an expression to refer to life, since God is the source of all life. The implication is that, at the eschatological resurrection, the whole person is recreated with the same identity but with an imperishable physical nature. Thus the images of *koimaomai* (to sleep) and *gymnos* (naked) do not attempt to describe the state of death, but are metaphorical biblical expressions that refer to the link between the person before death and after resurrection, as it will be shown in this book.

In recent years, an increasing number of scholars have interpreted the Corinthian correspondence, to hold the view of a spiritual or glorious body given to believers at the time of Christ's second coming.[95] While, for dualists, the soul of the person is awaiting that body-soul reunion, monist-mortalism sees the body as the person indeed that vanishes at death. The person does not exist at all until resurrection comes, at which point the person comes to existence again but with an immortal body, which represents an immortal existence.[96] Even defenders of dualism have begun to see that biblical monism appears to be more soundly based in Scripture than dualism. John Cooper, for instance, recognizes that "historical Christianity has really just read anthropological dualism into Scripture where it is not present at all."[97] Dualism is beginning to be seen as a non-biblical tradition.

---

95. Travis, *I Believe in the Second Coming of Jesus*, 198. They refer especially to 1 Cor 15:35–55 and 2 Cor 5:1–10.

96. See Bacchiocchi, *Immortality*, 185. Although Bacchiocchi does not support this view as his interpretation of 2 Cor 5:3–10 he presents it as an option. The reason is that he sees the passage focusing not on a kind of body but on a spiritual experience of salvation.

97. Cooper, *Body*, 35. Cooper wrote his book with a view to defend dualism, scholarly (5); he presents the option of "holistic dualism" to conciliate the clear monistic anthropology of the Scriptures (36–57) and the dualistic philosophical implication of the

Biblical monism implies some change of the traditional paradigms in anthropological views. For instance, (a) theologically speaking, it questions the validity of traditional interpretations of anthropological terms and passages; (b) practically speaking, if souls cannot exist separately from bodies, then "we do not actually exist between death and resurrection, either with Christ or somewhere else, either consciously or unconsciously."[98] This thought, notes Cooper, can bring "some level of existential anxiety"[99] due to the lack of a link between the person before death and after resurrection. The question thus turns to the issue of the continuity of identity between death and resurrection, if death means nonexistence. It seems that this continuity of identity has not been satisfactorily explained among monists.[100]

Here is where some see the metaphor of sleep as a proper reference to unconsciousness implying nonexistence between death and resurrection. Although the main and clearest references to death as sleep are in John 11:1–44 and 1 Thess 4:13–18, some scholars use the inferences in 2 Cor 5:1–10 to build a case. Niels-Erik Andreasen, for instance, sees *gymnos* in 2 Cor 5:1–10 as referring indeed to a second "phase" of human existence which occurs between the end of the present life, the first phase, and the beginning of life after the resurrection, the third phase.[101] Although the condition of death in this phase, *gymnos*, is not completely clear for him, it seems to refer simply to a state of unconsciousness, which he compares to sleep. He says, "Paul refers repeatedly to death as a sleep, confirming that death represents an inactive period of waiting," but "not yet enjoying the presence of his Lord."[102] This "inactive" period of waiting not in the "presence" of the Lord, seems to suggest a period of nonexistence. Although the period of nonexistence is not very clear, it is more obvious if it is compared to Andreasen's own statement that "death does not divide body from soul so as to permit the soul to continue existing."[103]

Similarly John C. Brunt uses the image of sleep as a reference to the unconsciousness of death and not to an entity that remains.[104] He uses the

---

existence during death that he assumes (58–80, especially 78).

98. Ibid., 3.
99. Ibid., 194.
100. Ibid., 193.
101. Andreasen, "Death," 327.
102. Ibid.
103. Ibid., 317.
104. Brunt, "Resurrection and Glorification," 348, 349.

sleep imagery from 1 Thess 4:13–18, and its comparison with 2 Cor 4:14 ("knowing that He who raised the Lord Jesus will raise us also with Jesus and will present us with you"), to explain the state of the dead who will be resurrected in 1 Cor 15:52–58 and to link it with 2 Cor 5:1–5.[105] In this context he says that the expression "God will bring with him those who have fallen asleep" (1 Thess 4:14) "refers to bringing these deceased believers to life through the resurrection in the same way that Jesus died but rose again."[106]

Nevertheless, it has to be recognized that those who hold what here is called the monist-mortalism view, do not elaborate it clearly, but they only infer it from the texts. Thus, they do not solve the issue of the continuity of the identity of human identity before death and after resurrection. It waits to be resolved biblically.

Summarizing, the image of *gymnos* has been interpreted under the umbrella of dualism as referring to a supposed disembodied state of the human self, either conscious or unconscious, during death. It has been strongly linked to κοιμάομαι as referring to the same state between death and resurrection. Conversely, under the umbrella of monism, *gymnos* has been interpreted in two ways. The first way sees *gymnos*, soteriologically, as spiritual nudity, the rejection of the robe of Jesus' righteousness. The second sees either (a) death as the final fate of the wicked and no direct relation to *gymnos* in that eschatological frame, or (b) *gymnos* as a metaphor for the condition of the human being at death without implying any kind of dualism. In such a case, the relation to κοιμάομαι is strong. On one hand, the implications of the interpretation of *gymnos* challenges monism if some entity survives death. On the other hand, it challenges the continuity of the identity if nothing survives death.[107]

---

105. Ibid., 350–351.

106. Ibid., 350. He says that in contradiction to the disputed suggestion that God will bring "souls with him from heaven to be reunited with bodies at the resurrection" which supports the immortality of the soul view.

107. Here U. Smith goes farther than others trying to explain the issue of identity in a monist view of human being, though more in philosophical way than an exegetical. See Smith, *Here and Hereafter*, 224–32.

The Naked State of Human Being

The Problem

The image of *gymnos* in 2 Cor 5:3, due to its relation to the language in the context and the broad context,[108] has been used anthropologically to refer to a part of the human being—an incorporeal entity that has an existence between death and resurrection.[109] This understanding has led the theological use of the text in a dualistic definition of the human being. On the other hand, monists have avoided the interpretation of this image, or interpret it soterilogically to refer to the spiritual condition of being without Christ. Others have seen it simply as a metaphor of death. Even more interesting is the fact that the same term and relationships with other images have been used by both dualists and monists. And all this is done without a detailed exegetical basis.

In light of this, there are two questions to be answered in this study: (a) Is *gymnos* in 2 Cor 5:3 referring to soteriological or anthropological issues? And (b) what is the significance and theological implications of *gymnos* in that context if an anthropological is chosen? The implications of this discussion are twofold. On one hand, if this imagery speaks of an entity waiting for the resurrection, consciously or not, then some kind of duality of the human being can be sustained. On the other hand, if there is no such existence, then, how is the continuity of the identity of the human being maintained until the resurrection after a period of nonexistence?

Then, the purpose of the study in this book is to analyze the significance of the use of the Greek term *gymnos* to refer to the state of the human being between death and resurrection in 2 Cor 5:3. It endeavors to show that the Greek term is used here to refer to anthropological issues rather than soteriological. It also endeavors to show a monist OT mindset as a background of the meaning of the image and a strong relation to 1 Cor 15:35–55 and the images of the nature of the human being at death. I will argue that the image of *gymnos* speaks of the emptiness or nonexistence of life, highlighting the continuity of identity, despite death.

As a result, I hope to strengthen the exegetical biblical basis of the monist view of the human being, and to help the understanding of the

---

108 Such as "tent," building" and "to be clothed with" in 2 Cor 5:1–4 and in relation to *gymnos* in 1 Cor 15:37 and *koimaomai* (to sleep) in 1 Cor 7:39; 11:30; 15:6, 18, 20 and 51.

109. They take the figurative sense of *gymnos* in Greek literature. Oepke, "Γυμνός," *Theological Dictionary of the New Testament*, 1:173. Others use "*koimaomai*" as a reference to the state (or fate) of the believers after death and before resurrection. See Friedrich Hauck, "κοιμάομαι," 3:789; and Vine and Bruce, *Vine's Expository Dictionary*, 2:81.

continuity of the identity of persons despite the dissolution that death means. Also, the practical issues related to the discussion regarding dualism versus monism will be seen in clearer light through an emphasis on the indivisible nature of the human being. I see *gymnos* and the images related to it in the passage as anthropological images in harmony with the majority of scholars. The difference, however, is that I will interpret these images from a monistic view. I found that most monists have not held an anthropological approach to 2 Cor 5:3.

The common images used to refer to death, such as "sleep," "to be gathered with the ancestors," and "to be in the dust" (or the grave), do not explain the state of the dead. A study on the image of *gymnos* will enlighten the meaning of death as lack of existence.

Other theological issues are closely related to the implications of this study, such as the nature of the resurrection, the continuity of the identity from the life before death to the life after resurrection, the validity of the covenant of God with dead people, and the judgment of God.

Presuppositions

Before going on, I have to recognize some presuppositions, although someone can call them "bias." It is clear that no one writes something without a platform of knowledge and worldview. It is not my intention to "force" anyone to accept them, but to recognize that they are part of the worldview that this study is based on.

This study accepts the unity of the two Corinthian epistles and their Pauline authorship. It takes for granted the biblical conception of death as the result of sin and the last enemy to be destroyed.[110] It holds also the monist view of the constitution of humans, death as monist-mortalism,[111] and bodily resurrection as the eschatological reality on the Parousia.[112]

The ideological background of this study holds the unity, consistency, and divine inspiration of the Bible. This study recognizes that, outside of the Bible, dualism is preeminent among almost every culture and religion

---

110. See Cullmann, *Immortality*, chapters I and II, and Cairus, "Man," 217, 218.

111. I use this nomenclature in order to differentiate it from other views.

112. See for example Dewart, *Death and Resurrection*, 25–35; Reichenbach, *Is Man the Phoenix?* 180–82; Simpson, *The Theology of Death and Eternal Life*, 11–28; Petavel, *The Problem of Immortality*, 117–43; Cairus, "Man," 205–32; Andreasen, "Death," 314–46 and Brunt, "Resurrection," 347–74.

around the globe. Even within the Bible, the testimony of the OT and archaeology proves that the Israelites fell many times into the practices of their neighbors, including communication with the supposed spirits of the dead. Nevertheless, the OT reflects a monist view of the human being as a growing number of scholars seems to accepts,[113] and its message is not a reflection of human thought (though expressed in human words), but a message from the Holy Spirit to humanity. In this sense, the core of the theology of the OT is not only consistent and steady but also relevant and transcendent to the NT.

Some Delimitations

The focus of this study is the significance of *gymnos*, in the specific context of 2 Cor 5:3, and its relation to some other anthropological terms used in the same context of death in the Corinthian correspondence. Thus, this study will avoid a historical-theological approach to the issue, and the systematic-theology approach of the theme in the Bible. Only those discussions that can be used as background of the passage will be considered.

Since the focus of this study is the nature of the human being between death and resurrection by the use of terms in the Corinthian correspondence, other meanings of *gymnos* will receive consideration only if they contribute to the anthropological discussion in the context of death.

---

113. As this study progresses I will introduce some holders of OT monism. Also the treatment of the terms between OT Hebrew and LXX in chapter 2 supports this suggestion. See also Robinson, *The Christian Doctrine of Man*, 5, 21, and 69. Dahl, "The Semitic Totality View," 59. Niebuhr, *The Nature and Destiny of Man*, 1:13. Ladd, *Theology*, 457. Reichenbach, *Phoenix?* 176, 180–86. Perhaps one of the most relevant expositions of OT monism, due to his dualistic background, is Cooper's book, *Body, Soul and Life Everlasting*, quoted earlier. He wrote his book to defend dualism, but recognizes that scripturally the anthropological view of man is monist. Cooper, *Body*, 36–57, especially 47–49. He defines monism as the Israelite view of "human nature as a 'unity' of personal and bodily existence. Soul and body, the mental, physical, and spiritual are so essentially tied together that when they somehow separate, a human being would not only cease in every way to function, she would actually cease to exist. In fact, body, soul, and spirit do not refer to mere parts at all, but in different ways connote the whole human person" (ibid., 38); however, he sees some biblical allusions to persons "held in existence without fleshly bodies until resurrection" (253, cf. 58–59, 63, and 77). In order to make the two views agree, he proposes the "holistic dualism" view (78–80, 252, 253), which shows the need of a proper terminology to refer to the biblical perspective of the nature of the human being. It seems to me that his view could need a concept such as the concept of "ideological presence" I will propose in chapter 4 to avoid such inconsistency.

INTRODUCTION

Although the study of 2 Cor 5:3 is the main focus of this book, some other texts will be considered as they are closely related. This is especially true speaking of 1 Cor 15:35–55.

This study will explore the OT use of the relevant terminology, but will not venture into extra-biblical literature. While extra-biblical literature is valuable in understanding the milieu in which Christianity developed, the biblical data is more than sufficient in establishing a valid context against which to understand the terms in view.

Speaking about the span between death and resurrection, Hill, with reason, frames the discussion in a temporal setting of our own human experience subjected to time.[114] It means that the way time works outside our world, and in God's view, is something unknown. The Bible states that for God, time is not the same as for humans.[115] Therefore the discussion of the human state between death and resurrection will be made from the human perspective of the sense of time and taking into account the limitations of human language. Also, Jesus' death, his incarnation, and eternity are out of the scope of this book.

---

114. Hill, *Human*, 118, 119.
115. See Ps 90:4; 2 Pet 3:3.

Chapter 2
Literary Background

As the discussion in the introduction demonstrated, the issue of the state of the human being between the moment of death and the moment of resurrection lies on the interpretation of some Greek terms related to death or human existence. The first issue to clarify is that Greek terms, as is the case with any other language, beyond their plain and literal meaning may have another metaphorical meaning based on context. Thus, determining the context and background helps to determine the meaning of the term itself. So, what is the background of the issue discussed by Paul when he uses the term *gymnos* in 2 Cor 5:3? This chapter deals with the specific background of the passage.

The passage uses the verbs *ependyō*, "put on," and *ekdyō*, "put off," that would imply clothes; but rather than clothes, the context applies these verbs to earthly or heavenly habitations (2 Cor 5:1–2). There is an implicit change from one habitation to another. Moreover, 5:4 seems to parallel the habitations with death or life, in this case death being swallowed by life, as inferring that one garment or habitation is being changed for another. The question then arises, what is the issue here? Is Paul talking about spiritual experiences in the Christian life, such as conversion or new life in Christ? Is he talking about human physical existence? If that is the case, is he inferring a change of body? Does he speak with a dualistic perception of the human being, or with a monist one?

In this passage Paul gives a clue to identify the background that can clarify how to interpret the passage. The point of departure is the expression *oidamen gar*, "for we know," in 2 Cor 5:1, which introduces the issue to

LITERARY BACKGROUND

be discussed as something already spoken of.[1] This formula links the issue discussed with the immediate context of the passage, since the use of the conjunction *gar*, "for," presupposes the continuation of a theme and with a broad context, since *oidamen*, "we know," presupposes a previous common knowledge the Corinthian readers have already had on the issue.

The first step of the analysis of the background is to explore the immediate context referred to by *gar*. It includes the chapter and the letter of 2 Corinthians itself. The second step is to explore the broad context that can infer a previous knowledge that Paul alludes to by the term *oidamen*. It includes the consideration of Greek philosophy, the OT, and the first letter to the Corinthians. Derived from the second step, the third step will consider 1 Cor 15:35–55 as the nearest background referred to by *oidamen*. The study of the anthropological Greek terms used there, as the way the anthropological Hebrew terms in the LXX have been translated, will show its anthropological concern of the body change and an ideological OT background. It will set also the background for 2 Cor 5:1–10, where the same issues are considered.

Gar, the Immediate Background

The issue of *gymnos* in 2 Cor 5:3 is introduced in 2 Cor 5:1 with the conjunction *gar*, which is used to "express cause, inference, or continuation."[2] It initiates an explanation[3] or clarification.[4] This means that in 5:1 Paul is continuing an argument he started earlier, and he now intends to give further explanation.[5] A review of the context of 2 Cor 5, which should include 2 Cor 4 and the role of the whole pericope in the letter's message, will therefore enlighten the meaning and application of the images used in the pericope. After showing the importance of determining the theme and first concern of the context, this section shows the whole message and fluency of the letter, determines the limits of the pericope, and shows its role within the letter's message. Then, through the language of the pericope itself, it displays the primary concern on Pauline exposition of the images

1. Plummer, *A Critical and Exegetical Commentary*, 141.
2. Gingrich, *Shorter Lexicon of the Greek New Testament*, s.v. "γάρ."
3. Friberg and Miller, *Analytical Lexicon of the Greek New Testament*, 96.
4. Bauer, BDAG, s.v. "γάρ."
5. David Lowery also sees this relation with γάρ with the immediate previous context. See Lowery, "2 Corinthians," 2:565; and Martin, *2 Corinthians*, 102.

of houses as clothes in 1 Cor 5:1–4 to determine the nature of his concern: anthropological, soteriological, or both.

Some commentators see a spiritual meaning in the references to earthly tent, heavenly house, to be clothed and unclothed, and the consequent nakedness Paul uses in 2 Cor 5:1–4.[6] From such perspective, earthly and heavenly houses are sinful or sinless natures respectively, and the change from one to the other represents a spiritual new life in Jesus Christ. In this case, the issue at hand would not be anthropological but moral issues when referring to houses; subsequently, nakedness would mean to be without the righteousness of Christ. Others see these buildings or houses as earthly or heavenly, literal homes.[7] Nevertheless, most commentators see clearly an allusion to the nature of human existence. These approaches, and the evidences their holders see, would suggest more than one application of what Paul attempts to say; however, if the context reveals that Paul's primary concern is anthropological, then the other approaches need to be taken as secondary ones, as homiletic applications.

The concerns of Paul, after three possible previous letters,[8] are the accusations against his ministry and the tribulation and necessities the members of the church are facing. Some of the Corinthians apparently were taking this situation as proof against the legitimateness of Paul's ministry and message.

Before Paul tackles the issue of the offering for the saints (8:1–9:15), and the specific mention of the accusations against him and his consequent defense (10:1–12:21), he prepares the ground by presenting and justifying his ministry and apostleship (1:12–7:16). In this section he uses two main arguments: (a) The believers, which are a product of his ministry, are the clearest evidence of the authenticity of his ministry (2:14–4:6); and (b) the sufferings and tribulations he is facing are not evidence of weakness in his ministry or lack of faith in God (1:9), but part of the reality of a life of faith which gives him reason to groan for the consummation of the hope in the change of the body, either by resurrection, if he dies (4:7–17), or transformation, if he is still alive at the Parousia (5:2–10). As a result of his ministry,

---

6. See among others Robinson, *The Body*, 96, and Ellis, "The Structure of Pauline Eschatology (2 Cor. 5.1–10)," 147–65.

7. See for instance Hodge, *An Exposition of the Second Epistle to the Corinthians*, 107–28 also Wall, *Going for the Gold*, 44–48.

8. See the reference to them in 2:3, 4 cf. 1 Cor 5:9–11. See also as examples of this position Belleville, *2 Corinthians*, s.v. "2 Cor 1:1"; Barnett, *The Message of 2 Corinthians*, 12; and Martin, *2 Corinthians*, xxxiv.

LITERARY BACKGROUND

he has the authority to call them to a new life in Christ and to care for the whole church.

From the beginning of the letter, Paul justifies his ministry by saying that the love for the church was always the motivation of his ministry;[9] thus the church is the best witness of the authenticity of his ministry.[10] This ministry goes beyond the local church (8:1–9:15). This love and care for the life of the believers, both eternal and present, is an argument on which he requests respect and recognition from them (10:1–12:13). Paul's ministry was marked by his own sufferings, which he uses as one of the strongest arguments for the authenticity of his apostleship, his love for the church, his hope for a better reality, and even his glory. Suffering is an important theme throughout the whole letter.[11] The context seems to focus on earthly challenges that believers, including Paul, may have to face daily while ministering for the church.

The letter shows the relation between ministry and tribulations. It is arranged to show that tribulations in the life of the apostle do not demerit the authority of his apostleship and ministry. I propose the following annotated outline in order to highlight the key elements of the Pauline discussion, to show how he develops this issue, and to see how the pericope 4:7–5:10 fits in the letter.

> 1:1–4   Preface. Paul begins with a salutation and a doxology, and then anticipates one of the principal concerns of the letter: *consolation* in *tribulations* (1:4).
>
> 1:5–11   The purpose of the *tribulations*. It is to build trust "in God who raises the dead" (1:9). Paul is pointing to the life after the present *tribulations* (i.e. after or beyond death) as a hope beyond the reality of bodily *sufferings*.
>
> 1:12–9:15   Presenting his *Ministry* and Apostleship.
>
> 1:12–3:4   His *ministry*. Paul speaks about his behavior and testimony among the Corinthians (1:12–14, 23, 24; 2:14–17), explains the reason why he did not visit them on a previous occasion

---

9. E.g. 2 Cor 1:6, 7, 14; 2 4; 5:14; 7:3; 11:7–8, 11; 12:15.

10. E.g. 2 Cor 3:1–3; 10:13–17. Tthe authenticity of his ministry is an important theme in the letter as can be seen in 4:15–5:4; 6:4–13; 7:5; 11:23–30; and 12:10.

11. E.g. 2 Cor 4:15–5:4; 6:4–13; 7:5; 11:23–30; 12:10.

The Naked State of Human Being

(it does not mean weakness 1:17 cf. 1:20), the purpose of the previous hard letter (2:3, 4), and the relation with the offender (2:5–11). The result of his preaching, the Corinthians, is the recommendation for his ministry, though it is a work of God (3:4–6).

3:5–4:6 The basis of his *ministry*. Paul underlines the validity of his ministry through the fact that he is a holder of the new covenant which is superior to the covenant held by Moses (3:7–15). This *ministry* is better than the previous one because it is about Jesus, who is the basis of the gospel (3:18–4:6).

4:7–5:10 The holder of the *ministry* (treasure). The nature and purpose of the holder, compared to a vessel (7–12), is presented; and the process of change of this nature is discussed (4:13–5:5). Given the hope of being with the Lord (5:6–8) the present vessel is not relevant; what is important is what is done through that vessel 5:9, 10).

5:11–7:1 *Ministry* of reconciliation. Paul introduces and justifies this ministry and his role in it (5:11–6:2). He presents the role of his endurance in the midst of sufferings as evidences of how he embraces this ministry (6:4–13). Paul calls his readers to be separated for that ministry (6:14–7:1).

7:2–16 *Ministering* by letter. Paul explains that a previous hard letter fulfilled its purpose in bringing them to repentance; and it was part of his *ministry* and his care for them.

8:1–9:15 *Ministering* through an offering. Paul uses the good attitude of the Macedonians, even in the midst of tribulations (8:2), and the gift of Jesus (8:9) to appeal to his readers to fulfill their good intentions (8:10–11) of helping according to their capability (8:12–15). Paul explains something about the process (8:16–9:5) and the future rewards (9:6–13). The conclusion of this section is 9:15.

10:1–12:21 Defense against his opponents.

10:1–18 The accusations. Paul walks according to the flesh (10:2). Paul is not from Christ (10:7). Paul boasts about his *authority*

LITERARY BACKGROUND

(10:8). He is strong only by letter but weak in presence (10:9–11). Paul commends himself (10:12–18).

11:1–12:18   A little foolishness (the presentation of Paul's credentials). Paul presents the reason (11:1–4) and some arguments (11:5–11) for his pride. Paul reveals the real nature of his opponents (11:12–15) and boasts about his roots and *sufferings* (11:16–12:11). Then, he mentions wonders and signs of his *apostleship* (12:12), and his financial independence (v 13–18).

12:19–21   Conclusion of the defense.

13:1–10   Conclusion of the letter. The coming visit will solve the problem of weak presence (1–4). Paul makes an appeal to the Corinthians to examine themselves (5) and his intention (6); expresses the desire of find them doing well (7–9); and confirms his *authority* (10).

13:11–14   Salutations and Doxology. Some final recommendations and the summary of the source (grace, love, and communion) of the principal elements of the ministry he has mentioned.

As this outline shows, the pericope of 2 Cor 4:7–5:10[12] is inserted as an explanation of the holders of the ministry (*diakonia*). In 2 Cor 4:7 Paul calls the ministry a treasure (*thēsauros*), and the people who hold it, earthen vessels (*ostrakinos skeuos*). Paul introduced the ministry he holds in 2 Cor 3:7. A comparison with 3:7 shows that he parallels this ministry with the covenant (*diathēkē*). He introduced himself as a minister (*diakonos*) of that covenant in a kind of contrast with Moses, who was the holder of the previous covenant (3:13). Paul says that "having" this ministry (4:1) they do not lose heart. This ministry, that includes the new covenant, is a "ministry of reconciliation" (*diakonia tēs katallagēs*)—a ministry that reflects the work of Jesus in favor of sinners (5:18, 19). Paul calls it the gospel (*euangelion*, 4:3,4). In this sense, the treasure that is contained in earthen vessels is the ministry he is called to perform in the name of Jesus and, at the same time, the gospel it represents. The same verb "to have" (*echo*), used in 4:1 to refer to the ministry is used in 4:7 to refer to the treasure.

He explains that the nature of the vessel, or holder, of the ministry shows "that the surpassing greatness of the power may be of God and not

---

12. Cf. Metts, "Death, Discipleship, and Discourse Strategies," 62, 63.

from ourselves." Thus, the apparent degrading external condition of the vessel (4:8–11, cf. 6:8–10) does not demerit the value of the treasure it holds. The earthen condition of the vessel, then, is related to physical sufferings and problems. The nature of the earthen vessel, the holder of the ministry, and its purpose, already introduced in the same verse,[13] are explained in the rest of the pericope. In 4:7 it is clear that the image of earthen vessels refers to "ourselves": "But we have this treasure in earthen vessels, that the surpassing greatness of the power may be of God and not from ourselves." Then, the discussion goes to the physical nature of the holder by using the specific term *sōmati*, "body" (4:10).

The expression "earthen vessels" makes reference to the apparent frail character of the holder of the treasure.[14] At the same time, the same characteristic makes it possible to preserve the content of the vessel, the ministry. Furthermore, the humble and frail characteristic of the vessel does not affect its content. This distinction between what is external and what is internal is notable when Paul speaks about physical difficulties

(4:8–11, cf. 6:8–10); he presents a series of external adversities and contrasts them with their internal significance. Thus, he can be "afflicted in every way, but not crushed; perplexed, but not despairing; persecuted, but not forsaken; struck down, but not destroyed" (2 Cor 4:8, 9). The physical dimension of the person is decaying while the hope in future eternal realities (4:18) renews his spiritual dimension (4:16).

Even though a different term is used, the earthly vessel is related thematically, according to the context, with the earthly (*epigeios*) tent (5:1).[15] This relationship responds to their relationship with earth. The earthly tent in 5:1, which may be torn down, refers to the same body, which is subject to sufferings (4:8–11), death (4:12), decay (4:16), and resurrection (4:14). At the same time the term refers to the positive characteristics of the earthly vessel presented by Paul in this contrast. Thus, the conjunction *gar* introduces an explanation of how the "momentary, light affliction" (4:17), will "produce an eternal weight of glory far beyond all comparison" (4:17).

---

13. In 4:7 the purpose of the earthly vessel is "that (ἵνα) the surpassing greatness of the power may be of God and not of ourselves."

14. It denotes breakableness. Bauer, BDAG, s.v. "ὀστράκινος." It also speaks of the humble nature of the holder. See 2 Tim 2:20 where it contrasts with silver and gold vessels. See also Kleine, "ὀστράκινος," 2:537.

15. Zodhiates, *The Complete Word Study Dictionary*, "ὀστράκινος," compares the symbolical meaning of ὀστράκινος with ἐπίγειος, due to their earthly character (made from earth).

Literary Background

The anthropological stress of this term, in addition to *thanaton*, "death," (4:11, 12), *thnētēi sarki*, "mortal flesh" (4:11), and *egeirō*, "resurrection" (4:14), in the context of Jesus' resurrection, makes clear the physical concern of Pauline. The theme of bodies goes until 5:10, where the expression in the body (*dia tou sōmatos*), introduced by wherefore (*dio kai*) in 5:9, serves as conclusion for the section. Thus the complete pericope is 4:7–5:10, which must be completely considered in order to get the meaning of the images and terms involved in it.

The main theme presented by Paul in this pericope is that the earthly tribulations do not reduce the worth of the ministry (treasure)[16] due to the faith in the purpose of God. This purpose of God is that they may have the life that comes from Jesus.[17] This life will come to the vessels through resurrection (4:14), which will solve the problem of the earthly body that is torn down (5:1). This life is manifested in the body (4:10) and not out of the body. It means that both the death and life of Jesus can be manifested in the bodies of believers.

The context—physical tribulations—are the physical implications of being "delivered over to death for Jesus' sake" (4:11); the death (*thanatos*) and life (*zōē*) working (*energetai*) in Christians (4:12); and the kind of life or death. This context infers an anthropological setting. Thus, the process of receiving this new life, despite death acting in Jesus' people, is presented from 4:14 to 5:4. Here Paul retakes the resurrection of Jesus as a warranty of the saints' resurrection (4:14), which he has introduced already in 1:9. This hope of the resurrection is the motivation for endurance (4:16) despite the decay (4:16) of their body. The emphasis is not what will happen to the body or with this present life, which is obvious, but what will happen with them because of resurrection (4:14), which is not visible now, but eternal (4:18).

The following explanation in 5:1 is closely related to what was expressed in 4:7–18. The BKC points that "few chapter divisions are more unfortunate than this one, since what follows (5:1–10) details the thought expressed in 4:16–18."[18] From 5:1 Paul contrasts the temporariness of the present earthly

---

16. Barton and Osborne, *1 & 2 Corinthians*, 342.

17. The "purpose" of God is highlighted by the use of the conjunction ἵνα (2 Cor 4: 7, 10, 11 and 15). The expression τοῦ Ἰησοῦ in 4:10 should be understood as a genitive of source as a derivation of a genitive of possession, see Wallace, *Greek Grammar*, 108. In this way the life belongs to Christ and comes from him to the saints: "life which comes from Jesus." Paul then puts all under the condition of faith according to 4:13.

18. Lowery, "2 Corinthians," 2:565.

tent with the lastingness of the heavenly house. He emphasizes the process of change from earthly to heavenly, and the desire of having that change of nature without experiencing nakedness (5:2–4). This image of nakedness infers that the earthly tent is not torn down (5:1) which points to resurrection in the context of 4:14 to 4:18. Then, Paul introduces in 5:2 another kind of process in order to change from one nature to the other without experiencing death.

Paul retakes the argument of the purpose of the vessel (5:5–10), concluding that since the earthen holders have the hope of eternal life, they must live to please the Lord (5:9). That way of living is the basis for their judgment (5:10). Thus the earthly body is not an excuse for earthly sinful deeds.[19]

Therefore, the authenticity of the ministry of Paul is presented as valid despite the earthly tribulations he and the other believers experienced. Paul argues about the nature of the holder of the ministry in the view of the eternal life coming from Jesus. What is important is not the present nature of the holder, but the hope for the change of nature and the deeds he performs while he is in the earthen vessel condition. For these deeds he will be judged. Paul presents in 5:10 the reason for taking the present deeds seriously and opens the door for his following presentations.

Once the apparent tension between tribulations on the body and the purpose of God is resolved, Paul continues to talk about the ministry he holds, which the recipients of the letter should also have. This explanation prepares the audience to receive the following exhortations about reconciliation ministry, holy life, the petition of the special offering, the purpose of Paul's ministry, and the exposition of the fallacies of his opponents, in the rest of the epistle.

Summarizing, the location of our pericope in the letter shows its role in explaining why physical sufferings are not important in view of the future life after the earthly vessel is transformed. The thematic unity and the issue which opened the Pauline exposition—the earthly vessel—places the discussion in an anthropological setting in which the images of the pericope refer to the physical conditions of the holders of the "treasure" or ministry. Therefore, this background of change of nature and the hope of physical resurrection sets the platform for finding the background referred by *oidamen* in 5:1.

---

19. See for example 5:17; 6:14 ff; 10:3.

Literary Background

Oidamen, the Broad Background

The explanation Paul introduces in 5:1, regarding the hope beyond the earthly nature of the vessel, is based on some common knowledge. Paul uses the expression *oidamen gar*. Although it could be possible that the first person plural that Paul uses as the subject of this verb includes his readers (inclusive we), the other uses of *we* in the same context suggest that Paul was not necessarily including them (exclusive we). In 4:5 Paul uses an exclusive we to speak of *doulos*, "servant." This sense is clear by the use of *hymōn*, "of you," there. Paul and his companions[20] are servants of them, the readers. The preaching of Paul includes the presentation of Jesus as the Lord and the preachers as servants of the hearers.

In 4:12 again Paul shows a distinction between the first person plural and the readers who are presented in the second person plural: "So death works in us [*hēmin*], but life in you [*hymin*]." This reference alludes to the physical tribulations for the sake of Jesus in 4:8–11. In 4:14 Paul assumes that those represented by the first person plural (*hēmas*), will be gathered at the resurrection with the readers, represented by the second plural (*hymin*). Paul and the other ministers and servants suffer all the physical difficulties for the sake of the readers (4:15). This distinction between the first and second person plural points to the exclusive we. The reference to the outer man in 4:16 points back to the mortal flesh in 4:11. It refers to the physical experience of the writers excluding the readers. These physical experiences are irrelevant in the view of the hope they have. Therefore, the logical argument in 5:1 using a basis knowledge should also use an exclusive we.

In 5:9 Paul says, "We have as our ambition . . . to be pleasing to God." This is something Paul could ask also from the readers, but the present tense of the verb makes the readers the possessors of that present ambition. Paul goes back to the point that he is not taking the main role in this ministry—but that Jesus is (4:5)—by saying, "Therefore, we are ambassadors for Christ, as though God were entreating through us; we beg you on behalf of Christ, be reconciled to God" (5:20). There again is a clear distinction between the first and second person plural.

Having showed the exclusiveness of the first person plural in 5:1, we can say that the knowledge Paul is referring to with οἴδαμεν comes not from the Greek background of the readers. The knowledge that serves as a basis for Paul's hope beyond death is found in the background of Paul and

---

20. Perhaps Timothy, as he was introduced as cowriter in 1:1.

his companions as ministers of the covenant and the Gospel. It includes the knowledge that Paul shared with them while he was teaching them the gospel personally, and in previous correspondence.

Another consideration is the Pauline use of the expression *oidamen* itself. He uses it eleven times in his writings.[21] In all of these instances the expression refers to the common knowledge of believers, perhaps extracted from the general OT teachings or from oral teachings.[22] For example, Paul reminds the Roman believers that "we know" (Rom 2:2) that the judgment of God is against those who practice things that were common in a Greek and Roman setting, but worthy of death in Hebrew law; things such as idolatry (Rom 1:23, 25), extra-marital and non-natural sexual intercourse (Rom 1:26, 27), and several other practices (Rom 1:29–31). Many of the sins listed there, such as hating God and disobedience to parents (Rom 1:30), together with idolatry and sexual immoralities, are explicitly mentioned as worthy of death in the OT,[23] but not in a Greek or Roman context. Paul tells Corinthians that we already know that an idol is nothing in the world (*oidamen*, 1 Cor 8:4), perhaps echoing Isa 44:9 and other similar OT knowledge.[24]

In 2 Cor 5:1 Paul uses also the expression *oidamen* to point to a common knowledge[25] the readers already have in regards to the change in the nature of the body. The lack of specific information in 2 Cor 5:1 regarding a specific background in the OT, suggests another source for that common knowledge. The possibilities are the common Greek background, the general OT background, and a common knowledge in a previous letter to the same readers, 1 Cor 15:35–55.

A short review of a possible Greek background shows the non-Hellenistic background of Paul's *oidamen*. In the same way, a section on OT background shows that, although no specific information can be referred to with *oidamen*, there is still some general knowledge there. The study of the parallel passage of 1 Cor 15:35–55 shows that it is the most adequate background of the knowledge Paul refers to through οἴδαμεν. This passage stresses the anthropological background of the Pauline discussion in 2 Cor

21. Romans 2:2; 3:19; 7:14; 8:22, 26, 28; 1 Cor 8:1, 4; 2 Cor 5:1, 16; and 1 Tim 1:8.

22. Cf 1 Cor 8:4; Deut 6:4; Ps 115:4–8; Isa 44:8, 9; Jer 10:14.

23. E.g. Exod 21:15, 17; 35:2; Lev 20:2, 9; Num 16:13; 35:16–30; Deut 17:12; 22:21, 25.

24. E.g. Deut 6:4; Ps 115:4–8; Isa 44:8; Jer 10:14.

25. Shillington, *2 Corinthians*, 108.

LITERARY BACKGROUND

4:7–5:10 by speaking about physical eschatological resurrection and body change. The presentation of resurrection as a new creation tied to a body, and the necessary change of the nature of the body of those who are alive in 1 Cor 15:35–55, speak of a monist composition of the human being. This passage sets the basis for the analysis of 2 Cor 4:7–5:10.

Paul also uses *oidamen* to point to knowledge, which does not derive from a clear OT scriptural source, but might be implicit in the teachings of the Bible, or known from nature. Paul says, *oidamen* (we know) that the law speaks for those who are under the law (Rom 3:19), that the law is spiritual (Rom 7:14), and that creation suffers (Rom 8:22). Paul declares to the Corinthians, "we know that we all have knowledge" (1 Cor 8:1), and to Timothy that the law is good (1 Tim 1:8).

Paul also uses the verb to express knowledge that he expected the readers to already have, and to expand it. Thus he poses the rhetorical question in a negative stress: *ouk oidate*, "do not you know?" Paul uses this formula twelve times, twice in Romans and ten times in 1 Corinthians. Although few times it seems to refer to simply common knowledge,[26] or common Christian knowledge,[27] most of the time it refers to OT knowledge.[28]

The verb *oida*, "to know," is used in 2 Corinthians eleven times in different forms. It refers to a conviction or hope that Paul has,[29] a personal knowledge regarding someone,[30] or intellectual information.[31] In the case of 5:1 it could refer to a hope or conviction Paul and the other ministers have that is based on knowledge he had shared with his readers.

Since there is no clear reference to a specific OT verse that can be used as a direct source for the *oidamen* in 1 Cor 5:1, the common knowledge about this hope of the change of the body might be drawing from some other source. First I will show here the incongruence of taking the Greek background as a source of the Pauline teachings in 2 Cor 5:1–10. After this, I will suggest some general knowledge from the OT that can serve as a source; if not as the direct source of the images, at least as general

---

26. Rom 6:16; 1 Cor 5:6; 9:24.

27. 1 Cor 6:3 (cf. Jude 1:6); 6:15.

28. Rom 11:12 (cf. 1 Kgs 18:4, 13; 19:10); 1 Cor 3:16 and 6:19 (cf. Num 11:17; Ezek 11:19; 36:26, 27); 1 Cor 6:2, 3 (cf. Ps 149:5–9; Dan 7:18, 22); 1 Cor 6:9 (cf. Deut 25:13–16; Prov 11:1; 22:8; Isa 10:1; Zech 5:3); 1 Cor 6:16 (cf. Gen 2:24; Judg 16:1); and 1 Cor 9:13 (cf. Lev 6:16, 26; 7:6; Num 5:9; 18:8).

29. 2 Cor 1:7; 4:14; 5 6.

30. 2 Cor 5:16; 12:2, 3.

31. 2 Cor 5:11; 9:2; and 11:11, 31 (both verses speak of God's knowledge).

background. Finally the similarity to the previous Pauline teachings in 1 Cor 15:35–55 will show it as the most clear exposition of the knowledge Paul has in regard of the topic, and of what he already has shared with his readers.

Greek Background

The language Paul uses in 2 Cor 4:7–5:10 can also be found in Greek philosophy;[32] however, a dualistic Greek platonic background does not fit with Paul's view of man.[33] The first fact is that Paul never used *oidamen* to refer to a knowledge that infers a Greek or Roman background contrary to the OT. Moreover, when he uses some source outside of the common OT or Christian knowledge he makes it clear. For instance, when Paul was in Athens he contextualized the gospel to them by using an inscription he saw on an altar, "to an unknown god." Hence, quoting and using their own knowledge Paul said, "Some of *your* own poets have said" (Acts 17:28, the emphasis is mine). Thus, even in that circumstance Paul was clear about the source of that thought, "your own poets." Paul does not say "our own poet" even though he was acquainted with that knowledge. In contrast, in 2 Cor 5:1 he says, "we know," which could refer to a Christian knowledge he is part of, rather than a Greek background.

By the first century AD, Greek mythology and its anthropomorphic deities had influenced the early animistic religion of the Romans.[34] Roman religion became weak and gave opportunities for new forms of religion, such as mystery religions, to flourish.[35] For pagans, and even among some Jewish sects, resurrection was seen as impossible.[36] In general, while the Greeks believed in an immortal soul, the Jews believed in bodily resurrection.[37] Therefore, if Paul were arguing in favor of resurrection, he would

---

32. For instance, Simon J. Kistemaker says that "Greek philosophy taught that this earthly life is comparable to living in a tent" but he sees more OT background in this allusion. Kistemaker and Hendriksen, *Exposition of the Second Epistle to the Corinthians*, 167. See also Wisdom 9:15.

33. Barton, *1 & 2 Corinthians*, 341, 343.

34. See Niswonger, *New Testament History*, 83.

35. Ibid., 88.

36. Wright, *The Resurrection of the Son of God*, 83.

37. Ibid., 129. Nevertheless he recognizes the difficulty of categorizing all views included in Greek thought in only one general statement. Regarding the belief on immortality of the soul see also Rohde, *Psyche*, 3–40 and 253–79.

LITERARY BACKGROUND

have used images taken from a background that he has in agreement with, not from one he was opposed to. Even if some kind of resurrection occurred in Greek mythology,[38] the whole picture in the passage that includes the desire to avoid nakedness, the process of putting on the heavenly dwelling, the mortal swallowed up by life, and the judgment seat of Christ, do not fit with the Greek conception of resurrection or death.

Greek thought had a wide variety of views on death and the afterlife, but all of them included an implicit or explicit dualist view of the human being.[39] On Greek dualism the state of the soul without the body is referred to as nakedness and the interest of the Greeks was "entirely concentrated on the contrast between body and soul."[40] On the contrary, Paul is focusing on the change from one existence into another, through the hope provided by the resurrection of Jesus. Nakedness for him is an undesirable absence of a house.

Some see in Paul an attempt to combine both Greek and OT teachings into one; however, a comparison with Philo, who indeed tried to do it, reveals the opposite. Robert H. Gundry says that, "The distance of Paul from Philo, who attempted to combine Jewish theology and Hellenistic philosophy, clearly shows the comparatively un-Hellenistic character of Pauline anthropology."[41]

Summarizing, the words Paul uses to speak about death, especially in 2 Cor 5, have "no real similarity in background to Plato"[42] or any other Greek philosopher. They can be explained "without recourse to Hellenistic

---

38. See Martyr, 1 *Apol.* 21, who says, "When we say . . . Jesus Christ, our teacher, was crucified and died, and rose again, and ascended into heaven, we propose nothing different from what you believe regarding those whom you consider sons of Zeus." See also the reaction of the Athenians in Acts 17:30, 32 when Paul spoke about resurrection.

39. Gundry says that, "The anthropological dualism in Greek tradition is so well known," that requires little discussion. Gundry, *Soma in Biblical Theology*, 85. See also Bedard, "Hellenistic Influence on the Idea of Resurrection," 176, 177. Bedard sees a strong link between Hellenistic (and even Egyptian, p. 188) thought and Jewish thought by comparing some images superficially and out of their context, such as stars in Dan 12:2, 3 representing the resurrected ones (ibid., 182), a supposed pantheon in Ps 82 (ibid., 183), and Jesus' reference to resurrected ones being like angels in Mark 12:25 (ibid., 184). Sevenster, "Some Remarks," 207, says that sometimes when speaking of comparison and parallelism "the agreement is limited to terminology. At closer investigation it appears that the parallel in words does not at all imply an agreement in ideas."

40. Sevenster, "Some Remarks," 209. Sevenster sees in the similitude of terms no affinity of ideas between Greek concepts of *gymnos* and Paul's concept.

41. Gundry, *Soma*, 83. See also Stacey, *The Pauline View*, 215–22.

42. Sevenster, "Some Remarks," 213.

sources."[43] These images seem to be closer to OT background than to any other.

Old Testament Background

Many scholars think there was dualist anthropology in the Judaism of the NT times, and, although it was slightly different from Greek dualism, it was still present;[44] however, when the anthropological terms are seen in their context, the OT seems to remain monist.[45] In this section the OT allusions to tent and its destruction are briefly considered, as well as allusions to resurrection and eternal house referred.

Tent.

The term *skēnē*[46] translates the Hebrew *'ōhel* of the OT to refer to a temporary or mobile tent. It is permanent in the sense that it serves as home or house, but not in its material structure. This is especially true when it is compared to *baît*, "house," which primarily has the meaning of home or family, but, when it refers to a physical dwelling, it denotes a building that is made of more durable materials than a tent.[47] Paul may have used the reference to a tent having in mind the Feast of Tabernacles, "during which the Jews lived in temporary shelters for seven days."[48] The temporal character of these tents was not comparable with their permanent houses (buildings).

The word *katalyō*, "to destroy," is only linked to *skēnos*, "tent," in 2 Cor 5:1. It is used in connection to *oikia*, "house," only in Josh 2:1 but with the meaning of "to lodge"; however, the image of a tent being torn down

---

43. Davies, *Paul and Rabbinic Judaism*, 314.
44. Gundry, *Soma*, 87.
45. Ibid., 119. Gundry calls it holistic anthropology; however, despite the evidences for "holism" he presents, he tries to show some kind of dualism that he calls "dichotomy within the unity of man's constitution" in the OT (122, cf. 127). His dualist view of the OT, that is discrete at the beginning, becomes bold at the end when he says that the dualism of the OT can be compared to the dualism of Homer (133, 134). With regards to OT monism, see the section Presuppositions in this book (p. 23).
46. In 2 Cor 5:1 the word is *skēnos*, however, the semantic relation between *skēnos* and *skēnē* is strong. The masculine version (*skēnos*) is used only in 2 Cor 5:1 and 4, and seems to refer more to the temporariness of the tent than the tent itself.
47. E.g. 2 Sam 7:6; 1 Chr 17:5; Ps 84:10; Jer 42:7.
48. Kistemaker, *Second Corinthians*, NTC, 167.

appears in the OT using the verb *kathaireō*, "to take down," (Num 1:51, and 10:17) and *seiō*, "to shake."

There are also allusions to the body using the image of a tent. Job 19:12 says, "His troops come together, and build up their way against me, and camp around my tent." There, "me" seems to parallel "my tent." In Job 29:4, speaking about his youth, and the times of the favor of God upon him, Job says, "When the friendship of God was over my tent." The context refers to his person. Perhaps the clearest allusion is Isa 38:12. There Isaiah speaks of his own death saying, "Like a shepherd's tent my dwelling is pulled up and removed from me; as a weaver I rolled up my life. He cuts me off from the loom; from day until night Thou dost make an end of me."

Ecclesiastes also uses a house language to speak of the body approaching death. It says, "In the day that the watchmen of the house tremble . . . and those who look through windows grow dim; and the doors on the street are shut as the sound of the grinding mill is low" (Eccl 12:3, 4). The context has some similarities with 2 Cor 4:7–5:10. Both passages describe physical difficulties that lead to death (Eccl 12:3–5 cf. 2 Cor 4:11,16). Death is the destruction of the body, represented as a dwelling place (Eccl 12:6, 7 cf. 2 Cor 5:1). They both include an eternal house (Eccl 12:5 cf. 2 Cor 5:1); although in a different sense. Ecclesiastes uses *baît* (*oikos* in LXX) with the sense of habitation or place to stay and 2 Cor 5:1 uses *oikia* with the sense of structure. The sense of this dwelling place in Ecclesiastes reminds of the image in the OT of joining the dead ancestors at death. "Eternal home" is a euphemism to speak of the total dissolution of the body, which is clearly the case in 12:7: "Then the dust will return to the earth as it was, and the spirit will return to God who gave it." The reference to the creation of Adam as described in Gen 2:7, but in a reverse way, is clear; as Adam did not exist before God breathed into his nostrils the breath of life, likewise when the spirit/breath of God is removed, the person ceases to exist.

Eccl 12:7 is part of the conclusion of the book. It shows that human life is *hăbēl*, "a vapor," which is dissolved with the sun (12:8). That is the reason why, what is done in life is the subject of what will be judged at the end. The ultimate focus of life is to prepare for judgment (Eccl 12:13, 14 cf. 2 Cor 5:10). In this conclusion, again the text is like 2 Cor 5:10, which concludes in the same way.

Job 4:19 is another example of the use of a house as an image for a person. It also speaks about the temporariness of men in contrast with God, using a metaphor of houses of clay. It says, "'How much more those who dwell in houses of clay, whose foundation is in the dust, who are crushed before the moth!" (Job 4:19). Although the metaphorical use of a tent as a body, and the comparison of death with the process of tearing it down are not frequent in the OT, the few occurrences could lead the disciples to understand the comparison Jesus made between his body and the temple building (John 2:19, 21), and perhaps also Paul's usage.

There is another dimension, however, of this comparison between a tent and a building. Exodus 25:40; 26:30; and Num 8:4 compare the tent (the tabernacle of God) which was made with hands from a model that was shown to Moses on the mountain.[49] This model building, according to Heb 8:5, was not made with hands (Heb 9:11) and it is in heaven. The expression "not made with hands" is only used in these two verses. This connection sees the reality of the present tent as a shadow of the perfect reality of the heavenly one. In this case, both the earthly tent and the heavenly existed at the same time. In contrast, for Paul, the earthly tent must to be destroyed before the heavenly one appears (2 Cor 5:1).

In conclusion, as Sevenster says, the way Paul uses the terminology appears "still more striking against the background of platonic use" but in agreement with "the Semitic line of the Old Testament."[50] Before we proceed to examine the immediate background of 2 Cor 5, it is worth examining briefly the concept of resurrection in the OT and in the NT understanding of the OT, since the relevant discussion in Paul revolves around resurrection.

Resurrection.

The extent to which resurrection was anticipated in the OT has been discussed at length. What is important for our purpose is not only to what extent OT writers believed in resurrection, but, more importantly, how Paul, the other apostles, Jesus, and their contemporaries understood OT texts as referring to resurrection.

According to Jesus[51] the OT teaches the doctrine of resurrection beyond the clear passages that present it, such as Dan 12:2, 3; Ps 16:8–11;17:15,

---

49. Clarke, *Clarke's Commentary*, s.v. "2 Cor 5:1."

50. Sevenster, "Some Remarks," 210.

51. Luke 20:37, "but that the dead are raised, even Moses showed, in the passage about the burning bush, where he calls the Lord the God of Abraham, and the God of Isaac, and the God of Jacob."

LITERARY BACKGROUND

Isa 26:19; and Job 19:25, 26. The fact is that, in the OT, a living being is the result of a body made alive by the power (breath) of God[52] in a monist view of the human being. And death represents the end of life.[53] Thus, to be conscious again, or to receive any kind of reward after death[54] (which implies a body), resurrection is required. That is the implication of Jesus' argument in favor of resurrection based in Exod 3:6,15, when he answered the question of the continuity of the covenant and resurrection in Luke 20:37. "For the patriarchs to receive the land personally as an everlasting possession, however, would presumably require their eventual resurrection."[55]

Thus, writers of the NT imply a teaching of resurrection in the OT. An example is Heb 11:19, which explains Gen 22:5 in that way; it shows that Abraham believed in resurrection. The idea of resurrection was so common that when Jesus asked, "who do people say that the Son of Man is?" (Matt 16:13) the disciples answered, "some say John the Baptist; and others, Elijah; but still others, Jeremiah, or one of the prophets" (Matt 16:14). Jesus, being in his human physical condition, was linked with the dead prophets, which means that they expected their bodily resurrection.

Davies understands the doctrine of resurrection as scriptural on the OT basis; he quotes the Mishnah Sanhedrin (10. 1) and says that, "Proof texts from the Law, the Prophets and the Hagiographa were adduced in support of the doctrine."[56] The Mishnah says, "All Israel have a portion in the world to come"; they shall inherit the Promised Land forever, except "he who maintains that resurrection is not a biblical doctrine"[57]

Perhaps the closest passage with the same theme that Paul infers in 2 Cor 5:1, is Job 19:25–27. It reads, "And as for me, I know that my Redeemer lives, and at the last He will take his stand on the earth. Even after my skin is destroyed, yet from my flesh I shall see God. Whom I myself shall behold. And whom my eyes shall see and not another. My heart faints within me." The mention of flesh (h) and the eyes which are needed to see the Lord suppose a bodily resurrection if the skin ($'ôr$) is destroyed, which means

---

52. Gen 2:7, see the section "Pneuma and Its Implications" ahead in the book.

53. Gen 3:19; Job 7:9, 10; Ps 103:14–16; 146:4; Eccl 12:7.

54. Psalm 6:5; 88:10–12; and 115:17 speak of no hope at death. At death also there is no remembrance (Ps 6:5), no praise (Ps 30:9; 88:10; 115:7), and no reward (Eccl 9:5, 6) Compare with Isa 38:18, 19.

55. Trick, "Death, Covenants, and the Proof of Resurrection in Mark 12:18–27," 252

56. Davies, *Rabbinic Judaism*, 300.

57. Ibid., 300. Davies compares both conceptions of resurrection, pharisaic and Hellenistic, and for him, Paul undoutably has a pharisaic conception (ibid., 303).

death. There is also a strong emphasis on the continuity of the identity with a body after the destruction of the visible (skin) person, and an allusion to resurrection. The contrast between the temporal skin and the more permanent flesh could be a basis for the Pauline use of materials with different durability, tent and building. Paul says, "For we know that if the earthly tent which is our house is torn down, we have a building from God" (2 Cor 5:1).

The common knowledge referred to by the expression "we know" in 2 Cor 5:1 can be based in these OT assumptions; however, it appears that the specific field of knowledge Paul is referring to when he says, *oidamen* in 2 Cor 5:1 has to be found not only in the OT, but specifically in the Corinthian correspondence.

Corinthian Correspondence

Background

The concern of the earthly vessel that carries the treasure of the ministry in 2 Cor 4:7, the mention of resurrection in 2 Cor 4:14, and the change from the earthly realm to heavenly in 2 Cor 5:1 set the anthropological theme that helps to relate the expression *oidamen* with 1 Cor 15:35–55. The truth about resurrection and the change of the body is clearly taught there. Since this letter is addressed to the same readers and is written by the same author, it is the best and logical source for this common knowledge.[58] Thus, "the confident assertion, *we know*, was based on the argument set forth in 1 Cor 15."[59] In his first letter (1 Cor 15:1–55) Paul recalls all of the teachings he gave them about resurrection, body change, and the Second Coming, making an echo not only of the first letter to Thessalonians, but of what was already exposed regarding this concept in the OT.

---

58. Although most scholars agree that this letter is the fourth addressed to the Corinthians (2 Cor 2:3, 4 cf. 1 Cor 5:9–11), some do not place the letters in chronological sequence, as Harris explains (see Harris, "Watershed," 32); but relations between these two letters, and specifically between these two passages, are very strong, and this clue could help to see some chronological sequence. These two passages have been compared by many, as Gillman shows; see Gillman, "Thematic Comparison," 439; and MacCant, "Pauline Eschatologies," 23–49.

59. Lowery, "2 Corinthians," 2:565, emphasis is his.

LITERARY BACKGROUND

In 1 Cor 15, Paul deals with the topic of resurrection, which was a core of the gospel for Paul[60] and the disciples.[61] Contextual evidence supports the fact that Paul in this chapter is speaking about physical resurrection, arguing against deniers of resurrection or at least using their questions to build his own case.[62] Whatever applications to spiritual life in general are secondary.[63]

The first argument Paul uses is the physical resurrection of Jesus, which is proof for the eschatological resurrection of the saints. He refers to the scriptures and the presence of eyewitnesses to Jesus' resurrection, who confirm the historicity of the event (15:4–11). Then he draws the logical salvific implication, namely that if resurrection does not occur then faith is in vain and salvation means nothing (15:13–19). The chapter then continues with an exposition of theological support for resurrection (15:20–28), and a last argument that baptism means little if there is no resurrection (15:29–33). Having defended the truth of the resurrection, Paul leads the discussion to another related issue: how resurrection affects the present nature. From verse 35 onwards he clarifies it.

The leading question of the new, but related theme in the chapter is, "how are the dead raised?" (15:35). The nature of the body of the resurrected ones takes the discussion from 15:35 to 15:58, with verses 55–58 forming the conclusion of the whole chapter. Talking about the physical resurrection of Jesus and the saints, the question on the nature of the body is a key point that helps to unveil the state of the human being during the lapse between the moment of death, and the eschatological resurrection, and the inferred link between the present existence and the existence after resurrection.

There is some common language in 2 Cor 4:7–5:10 and 1 Cor 15:35–55. For instance, the adjective *thnētos*, "mortal," in 2 Cor 4:11 is used also in 1 Cor 15:53, 54 with the same sense of physical subjection to death.[64] In

---

60. E.g. 1 Cor 15:3, 4, 13, 14, 15, 19; cf. 1 Thess 4:14; Acts 23:6; Rom 6:4; 14:9; Gal 1:1.

61. E.g. 1 Cor 15:11, cf. Acts 2:32; 4:2, 10, 33; 1 Pet 1:21.

62. E.g. 1 Cor 15:29, 33, 35, 36.

63. E.g. 1 Cor 15:17, 31, 56, 57.

64. This physical realm of the terms does not affect the spiritual or moral implication. The effect of sin is shown not only in the anthropological realm but also in the soteriological. This can be seen in the use of the same adjective in Rom 6:12 where the death and resurrection of Jesus, represented by baptism, affects the consequence of sin in both areas.

the same verse (2 Cor 4:11) the mention of flesh also relates the discussion to a physical realm as the term flesh also does in 1 Cor 15:39. Another example is the image of wearing a human existence that emerges from 2 Cor 5:2–4 and 1 Cor 15:53, 54. Both passages speak about the change from one nature to another. These natures are referred to as earthly (2 Cor 5:1 and 1 Cor 15:47–49) before the change, or heavenly (2 Cor 5:2 and 1 Cor 15:47–49) after the change. The image of one existence swallowed by another is unique to the Corinthian correspondence. In both 2 Cor 5:4 and 1 Cor 15:54 the image of swallowing the existence is associated to the image of putting on something.

In 2 Cor 5:3 Paul wants to avoid nakedness. This image is repeated in 5:4 using the image of being unclothed. This is a state between the two existences, the earthly one and the heavenly one. The same happens in 1 Cor 15:51, 52, where Paul puts himself in the group of those who will skip the sleeping state. The element of desire is not present in the first letter, perhaps because Paul considered the possibility that he would be alive at the Parousia more real than in the second letter. Nevertheless, both letters include the concept of some people skipping nakedness or sleep and being translated alive. Even though the relationship between these two images will be considered in the next chapter, here they stand as points of reference for the background of the discussion.

All in all, the Pauline presentation in 1 Cor 15:35–55 stands as the logical and closest background for the *oidamen* of 2 Cor 5:1. If the issue of the change of the body has an anthropological concern in 1 Cor 15:35–55, then 2 Cor 5:1–10 should display the same concern; however, since there is no contradiction between the Corinthian background and the OT information on the issue, the next section and the following discussions will demonstrate that the OT references to the topic could also be considered as a broader background of 2 Cor 5:3.

The Background on First Corinthians 15:35–55

Of the possible background that Paul took as basis for his discussion in 2 Cor 5:1–10, the passage of 1 Cor 15:35–55 seems to be the one that fits best, as it was explained in the previous section. Scholars who have used this passage to discuss bodily eschatological resurrection present two main views. At the point of resurrection, Dualists see one supposed part of the human being, the soul, receiving another part, a visible body.⁶⁵ In this view, the soul is the link between the two existences, the earthly existence before death, and the existence after the resurrection. The Monist view sees the present body as an important element in the resurrection; it is necessary as a link between the present identity and the identity after resurrection.⁶⁶ But, what does the text itself say on this issue?

In order to understand this passage, there are two issues to be discussed. The first is the anthropological use of some terms in the passage and their relation to the OT. The aim is to indicate how Paul uses Greek terms with an OT mindset in an anthropological framework. This will be done by considering how the LXX translates anthropological terms from the OT into Greek and how the context determines their significance. This comparison allows the reader to find the proper meaning of the terms in the context of resurrection, and gives assurance that the interpretation is not forced, but supported by some other uses of the same terms. The second issue relates to the nature of the body at resurrection taking into account the meaning of the language used by Paul. It shows a total change of individual nature that can be called a re-creation, achieved either through resurrection or through a change, while the believer is yet alive at the Parousia.

The Significance of Anthropological Terms

Anthropological terms could be misinterpreted if taken out of their context. Before we analyze the nature of the body in 1 Cor 15:35, there are some terms that have to be defined, namely, *sōma*, *pneuma*, *psychē*, and *sarx*. They have been used in both a spiritual and anthropological sense. Depending on how they are interpreted, they determine the anthropological or spiritual understanding of the discussion. That interpretation reinforces either a monist or dualistic approach to the issue of resurrection and the nature of the body. There has been considerable discussion in the scholarly world regarding the use of these terms in Pauline writings.⁶⁷ It seems that some see a strong soteriological implication, while others see just a plain

---

65. Henry, *Commentary*, s.v. "1 Cor 15:51–58."

66. Taking the analogy of the seed and the plant, some say that even though the body after resurrection is different from the body before death, the first is the base of the second in order to preserve identity, see Barclay, *The Letters*, 157.

67. See for example Gundry, *Soma*, 3–158, and Jewett, *Paul's Anthropological Terms*, 49–460.

anthropological sense. I will show here that these terms, especially as used in 1 Cor 15:35–55, have primarily an anthropological function.

Sōma *and its significance.*

Of the 91 occurrences (in 75 verses) of the Greek term *sōma* in Pauline writings, it occurs 46 times in 1 Corinthians, primarily to refer to a physical body as the visible physical structure of the human being.[68] It appears in the context of sexual immorality,[69] resurrection,[70] the habitation of the Holy Spirit (6:19), and as metaphor for the church.[71] In 1 Cor 11:24 *sōma* refers to the bread of the Lord's Supper as a symbol of the physical body of Christ. So, even there, the term alludes to a physical body. The only uses, perhaps where there is a spiritualizing tendency, is when *sōma* refers to the church as a body of believers.[72]

In 2 Corinthians, *sōma* appears only ten times. It emphasizes the visible physical structure of the human being. It is the receptacle of the life or death of Christ (2 Cor 4:10), the expression of life (2 Cor 5:6, 8, 10), and the physical presence in contrast with the presence through letters (2 Cor 10:10) or through a vision (2 Cor 12:2, 3).

In the LXX the term *sōma* translates a variety of Hebrew terms. For example, it can translate *pegel*, which literally means "corpse" or "carcass" (Gen 15:11). The same Hebrew term is elsewhere translated with the Greek terms *kōlon*, "corpse,"[73] *nekroi*, "dead,"[74] *skylon*, "booty" or "spoils" (2 Chr 20:25), among others. The combination of (Hebrew) *pĕgārym mētîm*,

---

68. See 1 Cor 6:18, 20; 7:4; 9:27; 11:27, 29; 12:12, 18; 13:3; and 15:35, 37, 38. See also the definition in Bauer, BDAG, s.v. "*sōma*." 1 Cor 5:3 and 7:34 link the body with the spirit as dimensions of the person. This issue will be discussed in the section "Pneuma and Its Implication with the Text." See also Rom 4:19; 12:1; Gal 6:17; 5:28; Phil 1:20; 3:21; Col 1:22; and 2:17, 23. In 1 Thess 5:23 it seems to refer to a specific dimension of the human being in the same way. Only in Romans (6:6, 12; 7:24; 8:10, 13) the word seems to have a moral meaning; and in Col 2:11 it seems to refer to the spiritual meaning of circumcision.

69. 1 Cor 6:13; 6:15, 16. Cf Rom 1:24.

70. 1 Cor 15:40, 44. Cf. Rom 7:4, 8:11, 23.

71. 1 Cor 12:12, 14, 15, 16, 17, 19, 20, 22, 23, 24. In these texts *sōma* refers to the physical body and the church is compared to it. Cf. Rom 12:4, 5.

72. 1 Cor 10:17; 12:13, 25, 27. Cf. Eph 1:23; 2:16; 4:4, 12, 16; 5:23, 30; Col 1:18, 24; 2:19; 3:15.

73. E.g. Lev 26:30; Num 14:29, 32, 33; 1 Sam 17:46; Isa 66:24.

74. 2 Chron 20:24; Isa 34:3; Jer 33:5.

LITERARY BACKGROUND

"dead bodies," has been translated with the Greek *sōmata nekra*, "dead bodies" (2 Kgs 19:35; Isa 37:36)—a very literal view of the body. Sometimes the Hebrew *peger* is rendered by a personal pronoun (Jer 41:9), indicating that the whole person is in view. The use of the Greek *traumatias*, "wounded" (Nah 3:3), *phonous*, "murder" (Ezek 43:9), and *peptōkōs*, "the fallen" (Amos 8:3), corroborates this. The Hebrew *nĕbēlāh* has been translated in the same way, referring to dead bodies/persons.[75] Another Hebrew word translated as *sōma* is *gĕwiyâ*, "corpse,"[76] or living "body."[77]

The Hebrew *bāśār*, "flesh," referring to the whole physical organism is also translated with *sōma*.[78] Job 41:23 (LXX, 41:15 in MT[79]) reads, "the folds [*sarkes*, "flesh"] of his flesh [*sōmatos*] are joined together, firm on him and immovable." Here *sōma* translates *bāśār* and *sarx* translates *mapĕlê*, "hanging parts." This text emphasizes the idea of flesh in the OT, the physical organism. Even the Hebrew term *nepheš*, which is frequently translated into English as "soul," has been translated into Greek as *sōma* as in Gen 36:6. The KJV translates it as "all the persons." This use strengthens the idea of the whole person referred to by *sōma*. In addition, sometimes *sōma* appears in Greek without translating any specific Hebrew term, but just to give the idea of a (whole) person.[80]

Sōma also refers to "the whole person" when Paul asks the question asked by opponents of resurrection: "With what kind of body do they [the resurrected ones] come?" (1 Cor 15:35). The idea of the question is, "What physical nature will they have at resurrection?" The interrogative pronoun *poios*, "what kind of," used here forces the readers to choose from at least two different possibilities: the same they have before they die, or a different one. The resulting explanation of kinds of bodies, fleshes, and glories seeks to demonstrate that, in resurrection, there will be a different kind of nature, represented by a different body.

---

75. 1 Kings 13:22, 29 as *sōma* and 1 Kgs 13:30 and Isa 26:19 as the whole person referred in the conjugation of the verb. But most of the times it has been translated by *thnēsimaios*, carcase, dead body (Lev 5:2; 7:24; 11:8, 11; Ps 79:2; Isa 5:25).

76. Also translated *ptōma* (corpse), Judg 14:8; Ps 109:6, and *thnēsimaion* (carcase) Ezek 4:14, 31.

77. E.g. Gens 47:18; 1 Sam 31:10; 31:12; Neh 9:37; Ezek 1:11, 23; Dan 10:6; and Nah 3:3.

78. Lev 6:10; 14:9; 15:2, 3, 13; Job 7:5.

79. MT stands for the Masoretic Text.

80. E.g. Gen 34:29, 47:12; Lev 15:11, 21; Job 6:4; 33:24; 40:32.

The Naked State of Human Being

Paul answers the question about the kinds of bodies at the resurrection by comparing them with different kinds of bodies that exist in nature: The grain that dies in the ground is different from the plant that will grow up; the bodies of animals are also different among them. Paul uses the Greek term *sarx* (15:39), which emphasizes the physical composition of the body to speak about differences in the nature of animals: "One flesh of men, and another flesh of beasts, and another flesh of birds, and another of fish" (1 Cor 15:39). In this context he mentions in 15:40 *kai sōmata epourania, kai sōmata epigeia*, "and heavenly bodies and earthly bodies," as part of the explanation of the kind of flesh that the saved will have, (15:35) as opposed to their current one. Paul also brings into the equation the different glory or shine of different celestial bodies, such as the moon, sun, and stars (15:40–41).

After Paul explains the different kinds of physical compositions he compares them with resurrection. 15:42 reads: "So also is the resurrection of the dead. It is sown a perishable body, it is raised an imperishable body." The comparative sentence in verse 42, *houtōs kai hē anastasis tōn nekrōn*, "so also is the resurrection of the dead," relates the examples with the resurrection, differentiating between the bodies before death and after resurrection.

He concludes with a conditional sentence, *ei estin sōma psychikon, estin kai pneumatikon*, "If there are natural bodies then, there are also spiritual bodies," (15:44). He infers that in the resurrection the raised will have a different kind of body from the one they had before death. There is no other occurrence of the phrase "spiritual body" in the Bible. We will revisit this expression in the next section.

Summarizing, in the quest of the meaning of the term *soma*, the immediate context should be taken into account. We noted that the term can be used metaphorically, as when applied to the church, or the bread of the Lord's Supper, which symbolizes the physical body of Christ, which was broken for the salvation of humanity; however, the most common use of *sōma* refers to the physical human body, and usually as a synecdoche to refer to the whole person. In 1 Cor 15:35–55, *sōma* is linked to the resurrection and refers to the characteristics of the visible physical structure of the human being in its entirety, either before or after the change of nature. Its use is anthropological.

Literary Background

Pneuma and its implication in the text.

Perhaps the hardest of the anthropological terms to be translated and interpreted is *pneuma*. The lexical meaning of the term is "air in movement."[81] In a biblical setting, it has a wide variety of senses. It means the wind,[82] the breath of life,[83] a state of mind or disposition,[84] or behavior.[85] It is also a way to call beings that cannot be seen in their natural form, such as God,[86] angels[87] or demons,[88] which are fallen angels; however, the most challenging meaning is when it refers to the so-called inner man,[89] or that part of the character or personality that is not physical or touchable and related to morality.[90] A dualistic reading of *pneuma*, especially in this last use, could lead to a misunderstanding of the term, but a brief study of how this word is used in the OT can clarify its monist meaning.

The equivalent of *pneuma* in the OT is the Hebrew *rûaḥ*. There are few exceptions in the LXX when *pneuma* translates words other than *rûaḥ*. Three times[91] *pneuma* translates the Hebrew *nĕšāmāh*, "breath," and the meaning is "life." In Isa 38:12, the Hebrew *ḥayyay*, "my life," is translated into Greek by *to pneuma mou*, "my spirit," and it again means "life."[92] In

---

81. Bauer, BDAG, s.v. "πνεῦμα"; derived from πνέω (*blow*) according to Friberg, *ANLEX*, s.v. "πνεῦμα"; see also Liddell et al, *A Greek-English Lexicon*, s.v. "πνεῦμα."

82. Although the Greek term *anemos* is the common word in the NT to refer to wind, in some instances *pneuma* is used (e.g., 2 Thess 2:8 and John 3:8 and also the use of *pneuma* to translate *rûaḥ* in the LXX (e.g., Gen 8:1; Exod 15:10; Num 11 31; Ps 10:6; Ezek 1:4). Cf. the discussion below.

83. E.g. Matt 27:50; Luke 8:55; 23:46; Acts 7:59; Js 2:26; 2 Thess 2:8; Rev 11:11; 13:15. Cf. the LXX of Gen 6:17, 7:15, Judg 15:19 among others.

84. Matt 5:5; Luke 13:11; Rom 8:15; 11:8; Gal 6:1; 2 Tim 1:7; Gen 45:27; Num 5:14.

85. Luke 1:17; 1 Cor 2:12; 1 Cor 14:32.

86. E.g. 1 Cor 2:11; 2 Cor 3:17; 1 John 4:8.

87. Heb 1:7, 14; 12:9, 23; 1 John 4:1; Rev 4:1.

88. E.g. Matt 10:1; 12:45; 5:13; Luke 20:20; Acts 16:16; 1 Tim 4:1.

89. Rom 7:22; 2 Cor 4:16; Eph 3:6.

90. Matt 26:41; Mark 2:8; 8:12; Luke 1:47, 80; 2 Cor 4:13; Eph 1:17; 4:23; 1 John 4:5.

91. 1 Kings 17:17; Dan 5:23; 10:17.

92. There is one more instance in the LXX, but it is not considered here because it does not correspond to the MT. It is Job 7:15 the LXX renders: *apallaxeis apo pneumatos mou tēn psychēn mou apo de thanatou ta osta mou* (ἀπαλλάξεις ἀπὸ πνεύματός μου τὴν ψυχήν μου ἀπὸ δὲ θανάτου τὰ ὀστᾶ μου, You will remove my soul from my spirit, and yet my bones from the death). Here, even a superficial reading would take *pneumatos* as the person paralleling "bones," and *psychēn* as life contrasting (δὲ) death. Thus *pneumatos* is "person."

Ps 118:131[93] the Hebrew *šā'ap*, "to pant after," is translated *heilkysa pneuma*, "I dragged the spirit," meaning to pant in longing for the commandments of God: "I opened my mouth wide and panted, for I longed for Thy commandments." Finally, in 1 Kings 20:4, the LXX reads, "*kai egeneto to pneuma Achaab tetaragmenon*," "and the spirit of Ahab became troubled." In the Hebrew (21:4 in MT) there is no reference to "spirit," only the name Ahab. *Pneuma* could thus refer either to the state of mind of Ahab, or to Ahab as a person, "and Ahab became troubled."

The rest of the 287 occurrences of *pneuma* in LXX translate *rûaḥ*. The relationship between *pneuma* in the LXX and *rûaḥ* in the MT helps to clarify their significance. It also enlightens the use of *pneuma* in 1 Cor 15:35–55, if it is used based on its OT meaning. A brief overview of its use will help inform the discussion of Paul in 1 Cor 15:35–55. I have grouped the use of *pneuma/rûaḥ* in three categories. Uses that (a) carry the meaning of air, sometimes with the meaning of life, (b) suppose a dimension of the person, and (c) refer to non-human beings.

The first category includes a wide variety of senses and implications, which make it difficult to relate each other. The first thing to note is that, of 394 occurences of *rûaḥ*, 287 are translated by *pneuma*. Other words used, however, share a common outlook. For instance, in a few cases, *rûaḥ* is translated by the Greek *osphrainomai*,[94] which carries the sense of receiving a feeling or smell,[95] once of the burning on fire,[96] and once to convey the meaning of separation.[97] *Rûaḥ* is also translated twice (Esth 4:14; Isa 31:3) by the noun *boētheia*, which has the meaning of "help." Other Greek words used to translate *rûaḥ* are *anapausōmai* "to feel relief" or "to breath" (Job 32:20; *diastēma*, "an interval" (Gen 32:17); *rhipista*, "ventilated," (Jer 22:14); and *anepsychen*, "refreshed," (1Sam 16:23).

Some presence of air is the common element implied in these uses of *rûaḥ* and its translations. It may be introduced to the body through smell, or may be implied in the concepts of refreshment, or life. Air or space is also implied in the idea of separation, or in the burning of a fire.

93. Psalm 119:35.

94. The verb *osphrainomai* appears twelve times in the LXX, eleven of them as translation of *rûaḥ*.

95. Gen 8:21; 27:27; Exod 30:38; Lev 26:31; Deut 4:28; Job 39:25; Ps 115:6 (113:14 in MT); 134:17; Amos 5:21.

96. Judges 15:14. It is also used in 16:9 but there it translates the Hebrew *baar* (to consume) instead of חור.

97. 1 Sam 26:19.

LITERARY BACKGROUND

As noted earlier, the most common rendering of *rûaḥ* and the most important for our purposes, is *pneuma*. As used in the LXX, it often carries the literal meaning of air in motion, "wind"[98] though this sense is better expressed by the use of the Greek *anemos*, "wind."[99] Metaphorically, *pneuma*, with the meaning of wind, can also refer to the cardinal directions;[100] although *anemos* more commonly translates *rûaḥ* with that sense.[101] In general, *rûaḥ*, related to *pneuma*, shares part of its meaning with *anemos*, perhaps with a different stress in literality.

Another meaning of *rûaḥ* when translated by *pneuma* is breath, respiration, blowing.[102] The LXX gives this meaning by using the Greek *pnoē*, "breath" even in instances where *pneuma* would be expected. For instance, Prov 1:23 says, "Turn to my reproof, behold, I will pour out my spirit [*pnoēs*] on you; I will make my words known to you." Usually this meaning of breath has the sense of life, as it expresses the ability to breathe in and out, or the air coming into the body to preserve life. This aspect of רוח is shown also when the LXX uses "blood" (*haima*) instead of "spirit" or "air" as in Job 6:4, and *pnoēs* with the sense of breath (Isa 32:16), and breath of life (*pnoēn zōēs*) in Gen 7:22. The same link between life and breath is present when life (*ḥayyîm* in Hebrew and *zōēs* in Greek) modifies breath differentiating the common breath with a person's life. Hence "breath of life" (*rûaḥ ḥayyîm*) is translated using *pneuma zōēs*.[103] The *pneuma* is not a separate component of the human existence as in the dualistic view, since the same Hebrew expression is translated as *pnoēn zōēs* in Gen 7:22.

---

98 Nums 11:31; 1 Kgs 18:45; 19:11; 2Kgs 3:17; Job 1:19; 8:2; 15:2; 30:15; 41:8; 48:3; 103:16; 104:4; 107:25; 147:18; 148:8; Eccl 1:6; 8:8; 11:5; Isa 7:2; 25:4; 26:18; 27:8; Jer 4:11, 12; Ezek 1:4; 5:2; 13:11; 27:26; Hos 4:19; 12:2; Amo 4:13; Jon 1:4; 4:8; Mic 2:11; Hab 1:11; Zech 5:9.

99. Exod 10:13; 10:19; 14:21; 2 Sam 22:11; Job 21:18; 28:25; Ps 1:4; 11:6; 18:11; 18:43; 35:5; 83:14; 104:3; 135:7 Prov 11:29; 25:14; 23; 27:16; 30:4; 5:15; 11:4; Isa 17:13 41:16; 57:13; 64:5; Jer 5:13; 13:24; 14:6; 18:17; 22:22; 49:32; 51:1; Ezek 5:10, 12; 12:14; 17:10; 19:12; Hos 8:7; 13:15.

100. Jer 49:32 (30:27 in LXX) and Ezek 37:9.

101. 1 Chron 9:24; Jer 49:36 (25:16 in LXX); Ezek 17:21; Dan 8:8; 11:4; Zech 2:10.

102. Joshua 2:11; 5:1; Judg 15:19; 1 Sam 30:12; 2 Sam 22:16; Job 4:9; 17:1; 19:17; 32:8; . Job 32:20 Ps 3:5; 75:13 78:39; 104:29; 135:17; 146:4; Eccl 3:19, 21; 12:7 Isa 42:5; Jer 10:14; 51:17; Lam 4:20; Ezek 37:6 (translated into Greek as *pneuma mou* which can infer the Holy Spirit); Ezek 37:8; 37:10; Hab 2:19. In Job 9:18 *anapneusai* translates the Hebrew with the same significance.

103. Gen 6:17; 7:15 Job 7:7; Job 10:12; 27:3 Ezek 37:5.

Isaiah 42:5 is a good example of the use of *pnoē* (as translation of *nĕšāmāh*, "breath") and *pneuma* (as translation of *rûaḥ*) as life. The text reads, "thus says God the LORD, Who created the heavens and stretched them out, Who spread out the earth and its offspring, Who gives breath [*pnoēn*] to the people on it, And spirit [*pneuma*] to those who walk in it." Speaking about God's creative power, the text presents a parallel between "the people on it" who have breath, and "those who walk in it" who have received "spirit", i.e., the breath of life. The context makes it clear that in both cases the terms refer to life.

With this sense, *rûaḥ* and *pneuma*, with the meaning of life or breath, could also refer to the whole person. For instance, in 2 Chr 36:22 God stirred up (*hē'îr*) king Cyrus to write a letter. But the text literally says, "The LORD stirred up the *rûaḥ* [*pneuma*] of Cyrus."[104] Another example is Ps 32:2 (LXX Ps 31:1), where the expression *bĕrûḥô rĕmîyāh*, "deceived spirit," is translated as "deceived mouth" in the LXX. There, perhaps the inference of deceived air producing sounds from the mouth would imply a deceived person.

These comparisons indicate the understanding of *rûaḥ* as air, and the implication of its motion regarding life. It means that, although literally *rûaḥ* (and *pneuma* by implication) is an independent element, and in relation to men or God, it can be a separable element as well (breath); it is not the immaterial component of human nature as dualists want to understand it. In all the examples noted here, *rûaḥ* can be translated as air or life without any manipulation.

The second category of the use of *pneuma* as a translation of *rûaḥ* denotes a mental or moral dimension, character, disposition of mind, or just the mind.[105] These uses do not suppose a separable element as air does in the cases considered before, but still they can share this metaphorical meaning. Some other uses of *rûaḥ* corroborate this sense. For example, sometimes when *rûaḥ* is linked to a word expressing mood or mental disposition, the LXX uses only one Greek word to substitute two Hebrew words. It means that the LXX takes *rûaḥ* as reference to mood or disposition, and uses an equivalent of the compound expression. Some examples are: when *rûaḥ*

---

104. Compare with Ezra 1:1 and 1 Chr 5:26 among others.

105. Num 14:24; Deut 2:30; Judg 8:3; 1Kgs 21:5; 1 Chr 5:26; 1 Chr 28:12; 2 Chr 36:22; Ezra 1:1; 1:5; Job 32:18; Ps 34:19; 51:12, 14, 19; 77:74; 78:8; 106:33; 142:4; 143:4, 7; Prov 15:4; Eccl 1:14, 17; 2:11, 17, 26; 4:4,6, 16; 6:9; 7:8, 9; 10:4; Isa 4:4; 11:3; 19:3, 14; 26:9; 28:6; 29:10, 24; 57:16; 61:13; 65:14; Jer 51:11; Ezek 11:19; 18:31; 21:12; 36:26; Dan 2:3; Hos 4:12; 5:4; 9:7; Hag 1:14; Zech 12:10; Zech 13:2 Mal 2:16.

LITERARY BACKGROUND

qqōṣer, "shortness of air or breath," is translated by *oligopsychia*, "loss of heart,"[106] or when *phronēsis*, "sense," is a translation of *'ôd rûaḥ*, "breath long," in Josh 5:1.

Another related phenomenon is when the LXX avoids the translation of *rûaḥ* and only translates the adjective that qualifies it;[107] the adjective implies a mood, which makes the translation of *rûaḥ* unnecessary. One example is the use of the Greek adjective *lypēros*, "distressing," in Prov 17:22 to translate the adjective *nāka'*, "stricken," that qualifies *rûaḥ*, leaving *rûaḥ* untranslated. Sometimes *rûaḥ* simply means anger.[108] These examples could infer that *rûaḥ* refers simply to the person or to character.[109] *Pneuma* in these examples can denote attitudes, responses to life, and even practical performances. In this last sense, the talents or abilities are also *pneuma* or *rûaḥ*.[110]

Furthermore, the LXX in Ps 31:2 translates *rûaḥ* as *stomati*, "mouth", in Prov 25:28 as *boulēs*, "will"; in Isa 40:13 as *noun*, "mind"; and in Job 15:13 21:4, and Zech 6:8 as *thymon*, "wrath." These specific uses agree with the idea of *rûaḥ* as one non-independent dimension of a person, a part of the individual. The LXX translates *rûaḥ* sometimes by a reflexive pronoun,[11] giving the idea of the whole person, since one part cannot subsist independently. Gen 41:8 and Exod 35:21 render it *psychē* with the meaning of "mind or disposition." In this case the implication is that the dimension in view itself dies when the person dies.[112]

---

106. See Exod 6:9; Prov 14:29; Isa 57:15. The word *oligopsychia* (ὀλιγοψυχία) comes from ὀλίγος (small, short or little, See Bauer, BDAG, s.v. "ὀλίγος") and ψυχή (life in its physical aspect, see Gingrich, *Lexicon*, s.v. "ψυχή"). Here *qōṣer* (shortness) equates ὀλίγος and *rûaḥ* equates *psychē*; however, the compound word gives an idea of discouragement that is slightly different from the literal meaning of its components.

107. Prov 16:18, 19; 17:22, 27; 23; Isa 66:2; Dan 2:1. Prov 15:13 supplies the word σκυθρωπάζει (countenance) to give clarity to the sentence but omits the translation of *rûaḥ*.

108. Prov 29:11, Isa 59:9.

109. Even when translated by *pnoē*, such is the case of Prov 11:13, where 'aman rûch (*aman*, "trustworthy," *ruach*) is translated as *pistos pnoēi* (faithful wind), referring to "he who is trustworthy," as the English renders.

110. Exod 31:3; 35:31; 2 Kgs 2:9, 15.

111. Translated in 1 Kgs 10:5 and 2 Chr 9:4 as ἑαυτῆς (oneself); in 2 Chr 21:16 it refers to the self; and in Ezek 13:3 translated as *kardias autōn* (own heart).

112. Ezek 18:4, 20. These are the only two instances *psychē* translates *rûaḥ*, since *psychē* usually translates the Hebrew *nepheš*. *Pneuma* in the LXX never translates *nepheš*, which suggests some more specific meaning of this term.

Although moods, states of mind, or character are not material things, they can be referred to through a material concept, such as air (*pneuma* or *rûaḥ*), since they share the same sense. It means that their influence and results can be seen; although the "thing" itself cannot be. Therefore the same words are used for the moods, state of mind, life, and air. Sometimes the word has literal meaning; sometimes it has a metaphorical one.

The third category refers to beings that are not human. Sometimes these beings act as an external influence on humans.[113] The primary use of the word here is in relation to God, his breath, or his Spirit;[114] however, sometimes it refers to independent beings apart from God. An example is Job 4:15, "then a spirit passed by my face; the hair of my flesh bristled up." Job 4:16 says that this spirit had an unrecognized appearance and it spoke to Job; the verses that follow present his message. It is clear that the reference is to an intelligent being, apart from God, since he speaks about Him in third person.[115]

In another example *rûaḥ* is translated by *anemos*, but seems to imply a being. Zechariah 6:5 reads: "These are the four spirits [*rûaḥ/anemos*] of heaven, going forth after standing before the Lord of all the earth." Although the texts can be translated as winds, their behavior is more likely to point to intelligent beings, and they can be compared to the beings (*zōiōn*) in Ezek 1:5, 15, and in Revelation.[116] What is clear is that they are not human beings. The term *rûaḥ* can even refer to evil beings.[117] Beings are persons. Thus *rûaḥ* and *pneuma* refer to persons.

To bring this discussion together, I consider that one of the most enlightening passages for the use of *rûaḥ* is Ezek 37:8, 9. The term is used

---

113. Exod 28:3; Deut 34:9; 1 Kgs 22:23; Num 5:14, 30; Job 20:3.

114. Gen 1:2, 6:3, 8:1; 41:38; 45:27; 15:8; 15:10; Num 11:17, 25, 26, 29 (Holy Spirit?); Num 24:2; 27:18 (HS); Judg 3:10; 6:34; 11:29; 13:25; 14:6, 19; 15:14; 1 Sam 10:6, 10; 11:16, 13, 14; 10:20, 23; 2 Sam 23:2; 1 Kgs 18:12; 22:24; 2 Kgs 2:16; 1 Chr 12:19; 2 Chr 15:1; 18:23; 20:14; 24:20; Neh 9:20, 30; Job 26:13; 33:4; Ps 18:16 (breath of God); Ps 33:6; 51:13; 139:7; 143:10; Isa 11:2, 4, 15; 30:1; 30:28; 32:15; 34:16; 40:7; 42:1; 44:3; 48:16; 59:21; 61:1; 63:10; 63:11, 14; Ezek 2:2, 12, 14, 24; 8:3, 11:1, 5, 24; 20:32; 36:27; 37:1; 37:14; 39:29; 43:5; Joel 3:1,2 (2:28,29 in English), Mic 2:7; 3:8; Hag 2:5; Zech 4:6; 7:12, as examples.

115. Cf. 1 Kgs 22:21, 22 (compare with the deceiving spirit in 1 Kgs 22:23); 2 Kgs 19:7; 2 Chr 18:20, 21, 22; Isa 37:7; Ezek 1:12, 20, 21 (could mean *motion* or *strenght*); and 10:17.

116. Rev 4:6ff; 5:6, 8, 11, 14; 6:1, 3, 5ff; 7:11; 14:3; 5:7; 19:4.

117. Judges 9:23; 1 Sam 16:15, 16, 23 (twice); 18:10; and 19:9. It is clearer in the NT. See Matt 12:43; Mark 1:23, 26; 3:30; 5:2, 8; 7:25; 9:25a; Luke 8:29; 9:42; 11:24; and Rev 18:2 as examples.

LITERARY BACKGROUND

five times in these verses; four times the LXX translates it as *pneuma*, and the fifth is obviated. Nevertheless they belong to the different categories mentioned before.

The passage reads:

> And I looked, and behold, sinews were on them, and flesh grew, and skin covered them; but there was no breath [*rûaḥ, pneuma*] in them. Then He said to me, "Prophesy to the breath [*hārûaḥ, to pneuma*], prophesy, son of man, and say to the breath [*hārûaḥ, tōi pneumati*], 'Thus says the Lord God, "Come from the four winds [*rûḥôt, pneumatōn*], O breath [*hārûaḥ*, no Greek], and breath [*ûpĕḥî, emphysēson*] on these slain, that they come to life."""[118]

The first mention of *rûaḥ* is in 37:8, which, according to the context, refers to the breath of life. It is not present in the dry bones even though they were provided with sinews, flesh, and skin. They are dead, they do not breathe. The second and third instances in 37:9 will be considered below. The fourth *rûaḥ*, due to its relation with *mē'arba'*, "from the four," clearly has the literal sense of winds, and idiomatically refers to the four cardinal directions. The fifth *rûaḥ* is asked to blow to the dead so they can live. The LXX omits it and infers it by the subject of the verb "to breathe." In this case, it points back to the third *rûaḥ* who is coming from the four cardinal directions. It can be identified with the Spirit of God, the Holy Spirit. This is a different person from God, since he is commanded in the name of the Lord God to blow. The same words used for "to blow" in both Greek and in Hebrew, are used in Gen 2:7 when God blew life into the first man.

If the command is given to the fifth *rûaḥ* and the prophecy is given to the second and third *rûaḥ*, they all are the same entity. The text could therefore be rendered as follows: "He said to me, 'prophesy [speak in the name of the Lord] to the Holy Spirit.... The Lord God says [to the Holy Spirit]: blow to the dead.'" Another option (in the MT but not so much in the LXX) is that the second and third *rûaḥ* refer to the breath of life, which is lacking in the bones in 37:8, and the rest of 37:9 shows the procedure to get it by the Holy Spirit (the fifth *rûaḥ* of the verse). A third option is that all *rûaḥ* refer to the wind where life comes from; although this does not fit with the image of wind coming from the four winds to blow (wind) into the dead.

---

118. The Hebrew and Greek words do not appear in the English version (*NAS*); they were added to see the original Hebrew term used in the passage and their translation into Greek in the LXX in order to illustrate what is discussed in this section. The quotation marks are in the original.

Since the Hebrew uses only one word for all of them, it is preferable to do the same as the LXX does, and use *pneuma* for all. The question is: what word should be used in English? The NAS quoted above uses "breath" for all of them except for the wind referring to the cardinal directions. Despite the incongruence of a breath blowing a breath, the KJV translates 37:9 as follows: "Prophesy unto the wind . . . and say to the wind, Thus saith the Lord GOD; Come from the four winds, O breath, and breathe upon these slain, that they may live." The Spanish version Reina Valera translates all instances except the fourth as *espíritu*, spirit.

These translations, used as a sample, appear to indicate that, in modern thinking, to choose only one word to translate *rûaḥ* in this text, when the context requires more than one meaning, will cause problems of understanding; however, it is clear that for a Hebrew mentality this was not the case. The inherent meaning of *rûaḥ* as something that cannot be seen, and yet exists, allows them to use it as the only word in this text. In light of this, *pneuma* can be used in the same sense if the meaning is the same as *rûaḥ*.

The conclusion of the comparison between *pneuma* and *rûaḥ* is that they show the same adaptability to the context. It seems that *rûaḥ* is used whenever something invisible or subjective, but real, is alluded to. Sometimes it is used as a dimension of a whole or even as the whole entity. Sometimes it refers to beings that do not have the known human nature. Only the context can determine the specific meaning. In accordance, it seems that the plain and simple meaning of the Greek term, *pneuma*, is air; nevertheless, it can also apply to something that, while cannot be seen, exists and can be perceived.

In light of this review of the use of *pneuma* and its relationship with other Greek terms in the LXX, and with the Hebrew *rûaḥ*, the platform is set to appreciate the meaning of *pneuma* in 1 Corinthians. There, *pneuma* has the same adaptability to the specific context as it does in the OT. In 1 Corinthians it is used mainly to refer to the Holy Spirit, a divine entity who possesses personality.[119] The term also refers to a dimension of the human

---

119. 1 Cor 2:4, 10, 11b, 12b, 13, 14; 3:16; 6:11; 6:19; 7:40; 12:3, 4, 7, 8, 9, 11, 13. Since the nature of the Holy Spirit is not the focus of this study, it will not be discussed at length. But it is clear that these verses refer to another personality not to a part of the human being. On the issue of the Holy Spirit see Whidden et al, *The Trinity*.

LITERARY BACKGROUND

being alluded to by its relation with *sōma*,[120] by the adjective *pneumatikos*,[121] and by the adverb *pneumatikōs*, "spiritual manner,"(1 Cor 2:14).

Another use is found in 1 Cor 4:21 where *pneuma* includes a mood, spiritual state, state of mind, or disposition.[122] This is the only use in this sense in this letter, although it occurs in a few other instances beyond the letter,[123] which makes it a non-common usage not only within the letter but also in Pauline writings. There is also another use that is distinctive in this letter. In 1 Cor 2:12 τὸ *pneuma* τοῦ κόσμου, "the spirit of the world," refers to "everything that characterizes this age or the finite world."[124] These two uses of the term can be related to each other. They are not physical entities, nor independent entities, but just subjective dimensions that cannot be seen—the character.

In the specific context of 1 Cor 15, the word *pneuma* is used only once (15:45) and it refers to Jesus after his resurrection, in contrast with Adam when he was created. Adam is called *psychēn zōsan*, "living soul," while Jesus is *pneuma zōopoioun*, "life-giving spirit." The context and the discussion of the adjective related to the nouns *psychēn* and *pneuma* suggest that they refer to the nature of a living being, in this case, Jesus. This concept will be further considered in the next section: The Change of Nature.

The adjective *pneumatikos* is related to the noun *pneuma* and has the same implications. The adjective modifies a noun, putting it in the realm of a specific dimension. It is used in the NT nineteen times by Paul[125] and once by Peter.[126] In almost every instance it refers to the dimension of the life that links the Holy Spirit to the Christian experience. For W. David Stacey, "Spirit stands for the divine life and power as manifested to men. . . .The flesh stands for the weakness and frailty of man which entertains evil

---

120 There are two instances in 1 Corinthians (5:3 and 7:34) where *sōma* is syntactically related with *pneuma*. In 1 Cor 7:34 *body* refers to the physical dimension of a woman as can be seen by the context of marital physical relationship, while *pneuma* refers to her dedication to God's things. In 5:3 Paul can be united with the Corinthians in his ideological conceptions while he is physically absent (see the use of *pneuma* in Phil 1:27, 1 Thess 5:23 and Heb 4:12 in footnote 140 on p. 63).

121. 1 Cor 2:13, 15, 3:1; 9:11; 10:3, 4; 12:1; 14:1, 37.

122. Bauer, BDAG, s.v. "πνεῦμα" (833).

123. Rom 11:8; Gal 6:1; Eph 1:17; 4:23; 2 Tim 1:7; 1 Pet 3:4.

124. Bauer, BDAG, s.v. "πνεῦμα" (835).

125. Rom 1:11; 7:14; 15:27; 1 Cor 2:13, 15; 3:1; 9:11; 10:3f; 12:1; 14:1, 37; 15:44, 46; Gal 6:1; Eph 1:3; 5:19; 6 12; Col 1:9; 3:16.

126. 1 Pet 2:5.

The Naked State of Human Being

and so separates from God and leads to death."[127] Nevertheless there are two exceptions.

The first is Eph 6:12, which reads, "For our struggle is not against flesh and blood, but against the rulers, against the powers, against the world forces of this darkness, against the spiritual [*pneumatika*] *forces* of wickedness, in the heavenly *places*" (cursives in the original). In this verse the adjective works as noun. The word "forces" used in English does not appear in Greek. It is supplied to complete the idea of the adjective, since the adjective in English requires a noun. The genitive *ponērias*, "of wickedness," qualifies the "spirituals" ones. The context does not allow the reader to see *pneumatika* as related to the Christian life. The *pneumatika* are spiritual forces, not blood and flesh, and they are "rulers of this darkness." They are in the heavenly places or in the air.[128]

If *pneumatika* is not the dimension of Christian life, the other possibilities of interpretation are mood or state of mind, literal air, breath, or a person (being). The context leads to see *pneumatika* as referring to a being, and to its invisible nature in contrast to the earthly visible nature.

The second exception emerges in the context of resurrection in 1 Cor 15:44, and it modifies the noun *sōma*: *sōma pneumatikon*, "spiritual body." It is a *hapax legomenon*. The passage compares Jesus after his resurrection to Adam after his creation (15:45–49). Both were alive, Adam (*zōsan*, alive) and Jesus; the latter also capable of giving life (*zōiopoioun*). In addition, according to the context, both of them have a body.[129] Jesus is presented as *pneuma*, while Adam is presented as *psychē*. The bodies are either *sōma psychikon* (natural body) or *sōma pneumatikon* (spiritual body) (15:44). This verse follows the theme of 1 Cor 15:36, 37 that expresses the change in nature experienced at the resurrection. Answering the question of Paul in 15:35 about the nature of the resurrection bodies, the spiritual body refers to a kind of body that humans will have at the resurrection. Thus, the nature or essence will be different from the one before resurrection.

---

127. Stacey, *View of Man*, 174–78.

128. Heavenly is related to air in Eph 2:2 since the evil beings once were inhabitants of the heavens according to Jamieson et al, *Comentario Exegetico y Explicativo de la Biblia*, 491.

129. The term *zōopoieō* in the Bible, which infers resurrection or living experiences, always includes a body. See Judg 21:14; 2 Kgs 5:7; Neh 9:6; Ps 70:20; Eccl 7:12; Job 36:6; John 5:21; 6:63; Rom 4:17; 8:11; 1 Cor 15:22, 36, 45; 2 Cor 3:6; Gal 3:21; 1 Pet 3:18. BDAG translates it as "make alive," "give life to" (John 5:21; 1 Cor 15:22, 36, 45; 2 Cor 3:6; 1 Pet 3:18); "bring to life" (Rom 4:17). Bauer, BDAG, s.v. " ζωοποιέω."

Literary Background

The similarity with 15:39, 40,[130] the specific mention of kinds of flesh, and the contrast between the adjectives *epigeia* (earthly) and *epourania* (heavenly) gives a clue of what the theme of the discussion is, the nature of the body. It seems that this use of the adjective *pneumatikos* in this passage follows the third category of the uses of *pneuma*: It refers to an intelligent being that does not have a mortal human nature. In this case the person has an immortal nature at resurrection.

Psychē *in First Corinthians.*

The term *psychē* occurs 103 times in the NT and 739 in the LXX. Its frequent use and its "multivalent" character make it hard to define in a simple way;[131] however, a brief consideration of its use, especially in 1 Corinthians, where it is used only three times, shows its relationship with the nature of the body before its change.

The term is most frequently used in the Bible to refer to an individual person. It infers life. "Without ψ. a being, whether human or animal, consists merely of flesh and bones and without functioning capability."[132] *Psychē* dies (Ezek 18:4, 20) because it is not eternal. The term also emphasizes human fragility and vulnerability more than sinfulness.[133] Even in the OT, *nepheš* translated as *psychē* denotes man as a living being, after the breath of life has entered into his physical body that was formed from the elements of the earth (Gen 2:7). This process of creation is the background of Paul in 1 Cor 15:45.

The word *nepheš*, translated to Greek as *psyche*, has been translated into English as *life*. Leviticus 17:11 says that that *nepheš* is in the blood, but the context clearly refers to an animal, explaining why the Israelites and aliens among them should not eat blood. Then *nepheš* means not only life, but what this life represents in the sight of God, including animals's life.

---

130. "All flesh is not the same flesh, but there is one flesh of men, and another flesh of beasts, and another flesh of birds, and another of fish. There are also heavenly bodies and earthly bodies, but the glory of the heavenly is one, and the glory of the earthly is another."

131. Bauer, BDAG, s.v. 'ψυχή."

132. Ibid.

133. Weiss. *Paul of Tarsus*, 106–107.

The Naked State of Human Being

Only four times the term *psychē* is used as a complementary term to *sōma*.[134] The rest of the instances refer to the whole person, physical life, or mental dimension.[135] Eric C. Rust contrasts the conception of *psychē* in the Bible, especially in the OT with the pagan Greek conception. He says, "'Soul' means 'mind' or 'reason' for the Greek and this alone is by its nature immortal; whereas, in the biblical understanding, the fundamental usage of the term soul is to describe a personal whole, conceived realistically in bodily form."[136]

Coming to the Corinthian correspondence, the only three occurrences of *psychē* refer to the whole person.[137] In this context, body or flesh is used to point towards different aspects of human existence,[138] and contrast the present existence with the existence after the resurrection; the adjective *psychikon* for the present, and the adjective *pneumatikon* for the one after resurrection (1 Cor 15:44, 46). The noun *psychikon* is related to *psychē*, as *pneumatikon* is to *pneuma*. The adjective *psychikon* is used only six times in the NT,[139] five times making a contrasting with *pneuma* or *pneumatikōs*, and one contrasting with *anōthen*, "from above"(Jam 3:15). In all instances *psychikon* refers to something physical, natural or earthly, in contrast to *pneumatikōs*, which refers to non-physical or heavenly-related issues.

Paul contrasts the heavenly bodies with the earthly ones. Expressions such as corruption (1 Cor 15:42), weakness (15:43), from the earth (47), earthly (48, 49), flesh and blood (50), perishable and mortal (53, 54), and *psychikon* (44, 46), are representative of earthly bodies. They are characteristics of the body subject to death in its stage before death. Paul uses the noun *psychē* as the earthly characteristic of Adam (15:45) between two uses of the adjective *psychikon*. This parallel puts the noun and the adjective on the same side as synonymous, contrasting them with the heavenly and spiritual characteristics. Therefore, *psychē* has the same meaning of self

---

134. Matt 6:25–26, 10:28, and 1 Thess 5:23, 7.

135. Physical life (Matt 6:28; Acts 20:10); true life as distinguished from mere physical life (Mark 8:35); whole person (Matt 11:29; Acts 2:4, 27,31; 7:14; 27:37; Rom 2:9; 13:1); the inner man in terms of the place of decision (John 10:24; Acts 14:2; 15: 24; Col 3:23; Eph 6:6) or experiences of joy, sorrow, love (Matt 12:18; Mark 14:34; Luke 12:19). See also Schweizer, "ψυχή in the NT," *TDNT*, 9:654–56; and Reichenbach, "Resurrection," 36.

136. Rust, "Interpreting the Resurrection," 25.

137. 1 Cor 15:45; 2 Cor 1:23; 12:15.

138. Brunt, "Resurrection," 361.

139. 1 Cor 2:14; 15:44 (twice); 46; Jas. 3:15; and Jude 1:19.

as it has in Gen 2:7 (with the same expression in the LXX), which is the background of the Pauline argument, and not a separated entity from the body.[140] Figure 1 shows these contrasts.

Earthly body			Heavenly body		
v.	Translation	Greek	Greek	Translation	v.
42	corruption	φθορᾷ	ἀφθαρσίᾳ	incorruption	42
43a	dishonor	ἀτιμίᾳ	δόξῃ	glory	43a
43b	weakness	ἀσθενείᾳ	δυνάμει	power	43b
44	natural body	σῶμα ψυχικόν	σῶμα πνευματικόν	spiritual body	44
45	living soul	ψυχὴν ζῶσαν	πνεῦμα ζῳοποιοῦν	life-giving spirit	45
46	natural	ψυχικόν	πνευματικόν	spiritual	46
47a	from earth	ἐκ γῆς	ἐξ οὐρανοῦ	from heaven	47b
47b, 48, 49	earthly	χοϊκός	ἐπουράνιος	heavenly	48, 49
50	flesh and blood	σὰρξ καὶ αἷμα	ἀφθαρσίαν	imperishable	52
53a, 54a	perishable	φθαρτὸν	ἀφθαρσίαν	imperishable	53a, 54a
53b, 54b	mortal	θνητὸν	ἀθανασίαν	immortality	53b, 54b
54b	death	θάνατος	νῖκος	victory	54b

Figure 1. Anthropological characteristics in 1 Corinthians 15:35–55.

140. Paul uses the noun *psychē* thirteen times and in NO instance does he refer to an entity separated from the body. Rom 2:9; Rom 13:1; 1 Cor 15:45; 2 Cor 1:23; 2 Cor 12:15; Eph 6:6 (heart, mind or self); Phil 1:27 (one mind, will or self); and Col 3:23 (heart, mind, self or strength) are used to refer to the self. And Rom 11:3; Rom 16:4; Phil 2:30; and 1 Thess 2:8 are used to refer to life. 1 Thess 5:23 is the only place in the Bible where *psychē* appears together with *sōma* and *pneuma* as dimensions of the whole individual. The use of *psychē* and *pneuma* occurs twelve times. In most of the cases *psychē* can stand for the self, while *pneuma* stands for breath (Eccl 6:9; Isa 26:9), wind (Isa 7:2), the Holy Spirit (Isa 42:1; Matt 12:18) or another kind of self (1 Cor 15:45). Two times *psychē* can be translated as life, while *pneuma* stands for wind (Jonah 4:8) and breath (Job 12:10) in this case, the LXX includes the same pattern in Job 7:15. Although in Hebrew only *nephesh* is used, the word *pneuma* is only supplied for clarity. The last three instances are Phil 1:27, 1 Thess 5:23 and Heb 4:12. These refer to dimensions of the person. In Phil 1:27 Paul desires to find the believers completely united. He uses the adjective *eis* (one) But they cannot have only one body (*sōma*) physically speaking, so he omitted it and only includes *psychē* and *pneuma*. The other two instances clarify what these dimensions are. Hebrews 4:12 uses the same dimensions but includes "joints and marrow" for body. then, in a parallelism he uses thought (*enthymēseōn*) and intentions of the heart (*ennoiōn kardias*). These two dimensions can supply the meaning of these terms in 1 Thess 5:23 and Phil 1:20.

The relationship between sarx *and* sōma.

The noun *sarx*, "flesh," is used many times in the Bible with the same meaning as *sōma*.[141] For instance, *sarx* is understood by synecdoche as a physical body, the whole body or in relation to it, but especially in the earthly realm.[142] In this sense "the destruction of the flesh can hardly mean anything else but death"[143] since the entire person is destroyed.

Other significant uses of these terms as synonymous are when they refer to the union of a man and a woman. Man and woman became one *sarx* in some verses, and one *sōma* in others, with the same meaning and OT background.[144] In this context the use in 1 Cor 6:16 presents a parallel of both body and flesh, making them synonymous terms. The text reads, "Or do you not know that the one who joins himself to a harlot is one body [*sōma*] with her? For He says, 'The two will become one flesh [*sarx*].'"

The use of these terms in an interchangeable way can also be seen in the context of being physically absent. The expression in 1 Cor 5:3 is similar in words and sense to Col 2:5, the difference being that the first Paul uses *apōn tōi sōmati*, "absent in body" while in the second he uses flesh: *tēi sarki apeimi*, "absent in flesh."[145]

Another common meaning that these terms share is in relation to sinful nature in contrast to life under the guidance of the Holy Spirit.[146] It

---

141. Alexander Sand arrives to the same conclusion using different comparisons. Sand, *Der Begriff "Fleisch" in den Paulinischen Hauptbriefen*, 129, 144f. See also Schweizer, "σάρξ in the Greek World," *TDNT*, 7:104.

142. John 1:14; Acts 2:26, 31; 1 Cor 7:28; 15:39b [with]; 2 Cor 7:1, 5; 12:7? Luke 24:39; John 3:6; 6 63; Rom 7:18, 25; Gal 4:13 [see 14]; Eph 5:29; Col 2:5; Heb 9:10, 13; 10:20; Jam 5:3; 1 Pet 3:18; Jude1:7, 8, 23; Rev 17:16; 19:18, 21. See also 2 Cor 10:3a Gal 2:20; 4:14 (see 4:13); 6:12, 13; Eph 2:14; Phil 1:22, 24 Col 1:24; 2:1; 1 Ti 3:16; Phm 1:16; Heb 5:7; 1 Pet 4:2; 1 John 4:2; 2 John 1:7.

143. Conzelmann, *1 Corinthians*, 97, in relation to 1 Cor 5:5. The same conclusion is shared with many other scholars. See on this footnote 29 in Garland, *1 Corinthians*, 169.

144. It happens usually when *sarx* follows the preposition *eis*; see Matt 19:5,6 Mark 10:8; 1 Cor 6:16; and Eph 5:31. Compare them with the use of *sōma* in 1 Cor 6:15, 16. The background is Gen 2:24 where *sarx* is used in the LXX.

145. The English translation renders "body" in both texts. I translate "flesh" directly from the Greek. The verb in both verses is *apeimi*; participle present active nominative masculine singular in 1 Cor 5:3 and indicative present active 1st person singular in Col 2:5. The syntactical construction in each verse demands this difference but the sense of the verb is the same.

146. Matt 26:41; Mark 14:38; John 1:13; Rom 6:19; 7:5, 14; 13:14; 1 Cor 3:1; Gal 3:3; 5:13, 16, 17, 19, 24; Eph 2:3b; 1 Pet 3:21; 4:1,2; 2 Pet 2:10; 1 John 2:16; possibly also Rom

LITERARY BACKGROUND

refers to the core of human nature after the entry of sin; hence, being mere human means "a disappointing level of behavior or characteristics."[147]

Another example is in connection to *haima*, "blood." Sometimes this connection only speaks of two different parts of the organism, especially referring to the symbol of the body and blood of Christ. In this context of the last supper, 1 Cor 10:16, and 11:27 refer to the breath as a symbol of the body of Christ and the wine as a symbol of his blood. Besides that, in John 6:53–56 Jesus speaks of eating his flesh and drinking his blood.

However, most of the times that *sarx* is used in connection with *haima*, the construction refers to the earthly physical and mortal condition of the human being, and it specifies its corruptible or degradable nature. It is sometimes translated as human being.[148] In these occasions the expression *aima kai sarka* constitutes a formula for this meaning. Thus flesh and blood cannot inherit the kingdom of God (1 Cor 15:50),[149] while non-earthly beings do not have flesh and blood (Eph 6:12). In contrast, *sōma* in itself lacks the intrinsic earthly characteristic, unless it is specified (1 Cor 15:44).

In its literal meaning, *sarx* means the muscular part that "covers the bones of a human or animal body,"[150] In this sense it cannot share the significance with *sōma*, which never means only the muscular part of the organism, but the whole.

When *sarx* is used after the adjective *pasa*, "all," it generally refers to humanity as a whole (all flesh).[151] When blood is the link in a group, *sarx* preceded by preposition *kata*, "according to," seems to be the more appropriated term. Then it refers to a lineage or family.[152] Because the relationship

---

8:8, 9, 12a; Gal 6:12 Eph 2:3a; Col 2:18, 23; 2 Pet 2:18.

147. Bauer, BDAG, s.v "σάρκινος."

148. Matt 16:17; 1 Cor 15:50; Gal 1:16; Eph 6:12; Heb 2:14.

149. The expression "inherit the kingdom of God" appears four times in the Bible, one in Galatians (5:21) and three in First Corinthians (6:9, 10; 15:50). The context in Galatians and 1 Cor 6 is the wicked people that, because of their immorality, will not enter into heaven. The context is soteriological, while the expression refers to their physical inheritance in heaven. In the same way in 1 Cor 15 Paul speaks about the physical entrance into heaven, while by the expression he can allude the moral issues linked to the earth; however, the moral implications are only a secondary application under the main anthropological context.

150. Bauer, BDAG, s.v. "σάρξ." See for instance, 1 Cor 15.39, Luke 24:39.

151. Matt 24:22; Mark 13:20; Luke 3:6; John 17:2. Acts 2:17; Rom 3:20; 1 Cor 1:29 (1 Cor 15:39a); Gal 2:16; 1 Pet 1:24.

152. John 8:15, Rom 1:3; 4:1 Rom 9:3, 5; 1 Cor 1:26; 10:18 2 Cor 11:18; Gal 4:23, 29; Eph 6:5; Col 3:22.

kata + *sarx* is related to this earth, it is also linked to an earthly nature.[153] On the contrary, *sōma* refers to a specific group emphasizing unity, as the "body of Christ" or "the church,"[154] especially considering that this group does not have "blood" or family links. The lack of blood links makes this kind of group a spiritual body.

The distinction between the two terms *sarx* and *sōma* is emphasized when they are used in combination with *pneuma* in the same clause. The reference to *sarx* and *pneuma* is more frequent than the reference to *sōma* and *pneuma*. There, two dimensions of human nature are considered, the spiritual and the physical dimension. The spiritual dimension is represented by *pneuma* while the physical is represented sometimes by *sōma* and sometimes by *sarx*.[155]

When *sarx* is used with *pneuma*, *sarx* refers to the earthly aspect of the human body, the earthly material it is made from, and the earthly implications.[156] Conversely, when *sōma* is used with *pneuma*, *sōma* emphasizes the unity of the physical body,[157] or is used as a dimension,[158] but emphasizing its counterpart, the spiritual dimension. In other words, the spiritual dimension is emphasized by contrasting *pneuma* with *sōma*, which is a general term; while by contrasting *sarx* with *pneuma*, the earthly dimension is emphasized independently of the spiritual.

I agree with A. Robinson's explanation, who says that *sarx* can refer to the whole human person, but with some difference in emphasis. It can emphasize human mortality in contrast with immortality, or it can denote sinfulness.[159] On the other hand *sōma* could be equivalent to "personality."[160]

---

153. Rom 8:4, 5, 12b, 13; 2 Cor 1:17; 5:16; 10:2, 3b.

154. See the section "*Sōma* and Its Significance" on p. 48.

155. Spiritual dimension means, "The non-material, psychological faculty which is potentially sensitive and responsive to God; Louw and Nida, *Greek-English Lexicon of the New Testament*, s.v "πνεῦμα."

156. Matthew 26:41; Mark 14:38. Luke 24:39; John 6:63; 1 Pet 3:18; 4:6 (literal, the human body of this earth); John 3:6 (who was born in physical sense); 2 Cor 7:1; Rom 7:14, 25 (as the physical component of the human being, see v. 23); and Rom 8:12, 13; Gal 3:3, Col 2:5

157. Rom 8:10, 13, 23; 1 Cor 6:19; 12:13; Eph 4:4.

158. 1 Cor 5:3; 7:34; 1 Thess 5:23; James 2:26.

159. Robinson. *The body*, 19–25.

160. Ibid., 26–28.

LITERARY BACKGROUND

Although, for A. Robinson, flesh is relative to world, but for Malcolm Peel[161] there is a possibility to have a different kind of flesh, a spiritual one.

When both *sōma* and *sarx* are used in the same clause,[162] their distinction is made clear.[163] These terms refer to different aspects of the person as was shown. Thus, *sarx* refers to a physical, earthly person, and *sōma*, to the totality of the individual (Rom 8:13, Col 2:23) or the church (Col 1:24). Flesh also represents a specific part of the body (flesh of the body, Col 2:11) or a specific kind of body (body of flesh, Col 1:22).

In conclusion, *sarx* is the physical earthly composition or state of the human being, and *sōma* is the unity of the shape of the human being that could include the flesh and its inclinations. If *sōma* is separated from life (breath) it dies.[164] Its nature can be fleshly (*sōmati tēs sarkos*, Col 1:22; 2:11), natural (*sōma psychikon*, 1 Cor 15:44), mortal (*thnēta sōmata*, Rom 6:12; 8:11), earthly (*sōmata epigeia*, 1 Cor 15:40), of sin (*sōma tēs hamartias*, Rom 6:6), or vile (*sōma tēs papeinōseōs*, Phil 3:21); or it can be heavenly (*sōmata epourania*, 1 Cor 15:40), or glorious (*tōi sōmati tēs doxēs*, Phil 3:21).

Paul uses both *sarx* and *sōma* in 1 Cor 15:35–55. The discussion begins with a question about *sōma* (15:35), goes on to explain the existence of different kinds of *sōma* (15:37, 38), and then compares them with the different kinds of *sarx*. Does Paul intend a spiritual discussion contrasting sinful nature with the life led by the Spirit of God? The plain answer is, no. The comparison between the *sarx* of humans and animals discourages such an interpretation. Paul discusses the differences between things beyond this earth such as the moon, sun, and stars, and then returns to *sōma* (15:40 cf. 15:41). Moreover, Paul is talking about the physical composition of things; for plants he uses *sōma*, for men and animals he uses *sarx*, and with the celestial objects he uses again *sōma*, comparing their existence with the earthly existence of *sōma*. Then he mentions glory as if it is the flesh of those celestial objects (15:41). Finally, Paul goes back to the initial point, resurrection. He says, "So also is the resurrection of the dead" (15:42). In that context he uses the phrase "spiritual bodies" (*sōma pneumatikon*, 1 Cor 15:44).

---

161. Peel. *The Epistle to Rheginos*, 146.

162. Six times in NT: Rom 8:13; 1 Cor 6:16; Col 1:22, 24; Col 2:11, 23.

163 The exception is 1 Cor 6:16, which was already discussed. There both terms are synonymous.

164. *To soma chōriz pneumatos nekron estin* (the body without breath is dead) Jam 2:26, cf. *soma nekron* (dead body) in Rom 8:10.

The application of the comments of this section, regarding the significance of the anthropological terms in 1 Cor 15:35–55, allows the reader to see a clear reference to human nature that is in line with a monist approach. *Sōma* represents the unity of an organism or the whole object referred to, and *sarx* represents the nature of that body. The expression *sōma pneumatikon* is not a part of an individual, but another kind of individual, a whole person (*sōma*) with that special nature (*pneumatikon*), in contrast to the earthly nature. Neither *psychikon* nor *pneumatikon* refer in this pericope to a dimension of the human being or to a dimension in a human relation with the Holy Spirit in ethic contrast to sin, but to the anthropological composition of the body.

This anthropological setting of the discussion leads the Corinthians and modern readers to take the discussion of 2 Cor 5:1–10 in the same way, anthropologically. Paul refers to this background by the word *oidamen*. Paul is therefore speaking about the nature of human existence rather than about soteriology. His preconception is that the body represents the existence of an individual and there cannot be life apart from the body. The following section considers how a change of nature can be experienced in a monist conception of human existence.

The Change of Nature

The main argument in Paul's exposition of the irrelevance of the physical difficulties in view of the future realities in 2 Cor 5:1 is the change of existence from an earthy to a heavenly one.[165] It is in this aspect, as it was shown in the previous section, that 1 Cor 15:35–55 stands as the basis for that hope. This anthropological change of nature has implications regarding human nature, death, and resurrection. These aspects are more developed in 1 Cor 15:35–55 than in 2 Cor 5:1–10. Therefore, the consideration of this issue on the first passage illuminates the meaning of the issues on

---

165. Paul uses the verb *allassō* to refer to that change. Most English translations in 1 Cor 15:51, 52 use the word *change*. The term occurs only six times in the NT. In Acts 6:14, false witnesses accuse Jesus of attempting to "alter" the customs. In Rom 1:23 men "exchanged" the glory of the incorruptible God for images. In Gal 4:20 Paul wants to be with the Galatians and "change" the tone of his voice. In Heb 1:12, the writer speaks about the "changes" on the earth and heaven in contrast to the immutability of God. The other two instances appear in 1 Cor 15:51 and 52. In all instances the word seems to refer to a switch from one state to another. Nowhere (including OT, where it occurs twenty five times) it refers to a spiritual transformation in a soteriological sense.

Literary Background

the second. This section will reveal what the nature of the body is in the context of resurrection. In this matter, a consideration of the language and comparisons Paul makes in 1 Cor 15:35–55 will reveal that the body represents the personal existence after resurrection, as it does before death, in a monist perception of the human being.

The question of "how are the dead raised" (1 Cor 15:35) is made in the context of physical resurrection. This section will show that Paul introduces two different natures, one before death and the other after resurrection. These bodies represent two different kinds of existences, the earthly one and the heavenly one. A comparison of the terms[166] that Paul uses to contrast the earthly from the heavenly existence will show that both of them are physical, although of a different nature. It also shows that the human existence is represented as an indivisible unity.

Another aspect to be considered in this section is the nature of the resurrection itself. The implication is that if the body represents human existence, and resurrection will bring a change to the nature of the body, then resurrection means re-creation rather than resuscitation of the body.[167] Finally, the way Paul introduces a change made without experiencing death equals this phenomenon with the change produced through resurrection at the Parousia.

Building the case of two different kinds of bodies in 15:37, Paul uses the example of a grain. The mere grain, naked or without cover (*gymnon kokkon*), is the first body, and a plant is the second—the body that will be (*to soma to genēsomenon*). Paul is clear in saying that that "which you sow *is not* the *body* which will be" (emphasis mine). The implication is that the nature of the second state of the grain is not (Greek οὐ) the first, but (Greek ἀλλὰ) different. Here Paul uses the term *sōma* to refer to the product that will be, rather than *phyteia*, "plant," which will be the logical term, to emphasize the change of body nature which will answer the initial question in 15:35.

In this example of the grain, the grain does not possess a new body after it grows, but it is a new body. God transforms the grain into a new form

---

166. The term itself gets its meaning from the image it represents in the context. For example, the Greek noun *kokkon* (grain) here does not represent any literal grain, but it is used as an image to explain the concept of the nature of the body. It is supposed that some specific characteristics are taken to speak of something else, but not every detail. For this reason, to speak of images here I speak of terms and expressions.

167. On the view of resurrection as re-creation see also Hick, *Death*, 279; Reichenbach, *Phoenix*, 176; MacKay, *Brains*, 100–102; and Kaiser and Lohse, *Death and Life*, 139.

of existence—a plant. However, the resulting existence is not unrelated to the first one; it is the same grain that was sown. The image presents God as giving a new body to the grain (15:38). Here the verb *didōsin*, "to give," expresses the origin of the resulting existence, but also it represents the fact that God gives something new to the grain,[168] something different. This introduction marks the issue: kinds of existence. These two existences are expressed as kinds of bodies.

Paul then presents two series of contrasts between existences using the image of bodies.[169] The first series refers to present coexistent bodies, and the second refers to the contrast between chronologically subsequent bodies—one before the change and the other after it. The audience must not be surprised that another kind of body exists after the process of change if there are different kinds of bodies in the present life.

The first series (15:39–41) compares the fleshes of fish, birds, beasts, and humans; and then, the glory of celestial objects. The terms compared in this series are *sarx* and *doxa*, "glory." What is *sarx* for the living organisms is *doxa* for objects (15:40). At the end of the series (15:42) Paul uses the expression "so also [*houtōs kai*] is the resurrection of the dead" to point to the second series, related to resurrection, as an application of the first series. Thus, the examples presented in 15:38–41 can be also applied in some sense to the human natures before and after the change.

Sarx expresses the difference of the natures of living organisms (15:39). The difference of flesh in the present nature anticipates the difference between the natures of the existences before and after the resurrection. This mention of *sarx* emphasizes the existence of physical elements as the structure of the nature of the body after resurrection, rather than the spiritual or moral aspects. The bodies are different after resurrection because they are of a different kind of material, which is different in its lastingness[170]

---

168. There is incongruence, perhaps intentional, between the tenses of *didōsin* (to give in present tense) and ēthelēsen (desire in aorist). The reception of the "body" happens every time that the grain germinates, but the kind of "body" everyone has, is already determined.

169. This contrast can be seen by the use of the Greek particle *men* (on the one hand) and *allē*, "another," in 15:39. Bauer, BDAG, s.v. "μὲν." See the same use of this formula in Matt 13:5–8; Mark 6:15, 8:28; Luke 9:19; 1 Cor 12:10. In verse 40 Paul changes the conjunction δὲ, of contrast, to καὶ, in addition (*kai sōmata epourania*, "there are also celestial bodies") as adding a new kind of things in the same series. Also it justifies the use of an implied verb (to be) in this new clause. See Wallace, *Grammar*, 38 for the use of implied equative verbs.

170 The terms, perishable and imperishable (*phthorai* and *aphtharsiai* in 15:42)

Literary Background

from the one before. This is clarified when Paul says that the earthly flesh and blood cannot inherit the kingdom of God (15:50). A conclusion is that the existence after resurrection is physical, as it was before death, but of a different nature.

The other element mentioned in the first series, as characteristic of *sōma*, is its *doxa* (15:40, 41). The kind of *doxa* is different depending on the kind of *sōma*, earthly or heavenly (15:40). In the same way, while the human *sōma* is earthly in the first state, it is heavenly in the second state after resurrection (15:47, 48). The *sōma* from heaven will come with a kind of *doxa* that contrasts with the earthly one, which was without honor (15:43).[171]

The term *doxa* in this text is explained by comparing celestial *sōma* with terrestrial ones.[172] Following the flow of the context, this glory or brightness could be comparable to the different kinds of *sarx* (15:39), as if the glory were the flesh of the celestial bodies. A good translation for *doxa* in 15:40, 41, and 43 could be "shining," "splendor," or "brilliance."[173] It fits with the context that refers to the sun, moon, and stars that are different in nature, and thus in *doxa*. This difference seems to express the difference on the nature of human existence.

Doxa does not contradict bodily resurrection. Moses may be a good example of how this glory works in corporal resurrection. He appeared together with Elijah coming to meet Jesus and three of his disciples. Peter, who saw them, understood that they have a body since he offered Jesus, "Let us make here three tabernacles: one for You, one for Moses, and one for Elijah" (Matt 17:4). This attempt to offer tabernacles would have been nonsensical if physical appearance was not in sight. They had *doxa*,[174]

---

introducing the second series highlight lastingness as the characteristic of the nature of the body.

171. According to Low-Nidia, *Lexicon*, s.v. "ἀτιμία," the meaning of *atimia* (dishonor) is an antonym of *timē* (honor). But it also can be opposite to *doxa* when used with this connection as is the case in verse 43. See 1 Cor 10:4, and Thayer. *A Greek-English Lexicon of the New Testament*, s.v. "ἄτιμος."

172. The Greek editors used here the colon to introduce an explanation, as English does. See Morris, *Hellenika*, 22.

173. Bauer, BDAG, s.v. "δόξα." In this context of physical nature the reference to glory could be linked to the kind of splendor Moses had after being with God (*dedoxastai*, Exo 34:29), or to the splendour Jesus, Moses and Elijah had in the transfiguration (Matt 17:2, Mark 9:3).

174. Although the word *doxa* does not appear in the experience of the transfiguration, the light in their faces recalls the same light Moses had after he spoke with God on

brightness or shining, like Jesus also had, yet they were physical (bodily) persons.

Paul ends his first series of comparison of nature by using *doxa*. Figure 2 shows these kinds of bodies. It shows that, when Paul introduces the issue of glories, he is comparing the heavenly bodies with the flesh of the earthly ones in 15:39. Thus, the earthly and the heavenly beings have bodies and glory, but, as the flesh is different, the glory is also different.

These bodies exist at the same time in different objects or organisms. Paul is using the differences to call the attention of the readers to the existence of different natures in the present world. The application to the resurrection phenomenon begins in 15:42: "So also is the resurrection of the dead." There are differences in the nature of the resurrected ones. Unlike the first series, the differences now happen in the same body. The body changes from one nature to another. The comparison between the images that Paul uses to speak about the characteristics of the natures before death, and after resurrection, highlights their lastingness. Paul also calls them, *chiokos*, "earthly," and *epouranois*, "heavenly," bodies (15:48). The body in the first state, *chiokos*, is perishable while the body in the second state, *epouranois*, is imperishable.

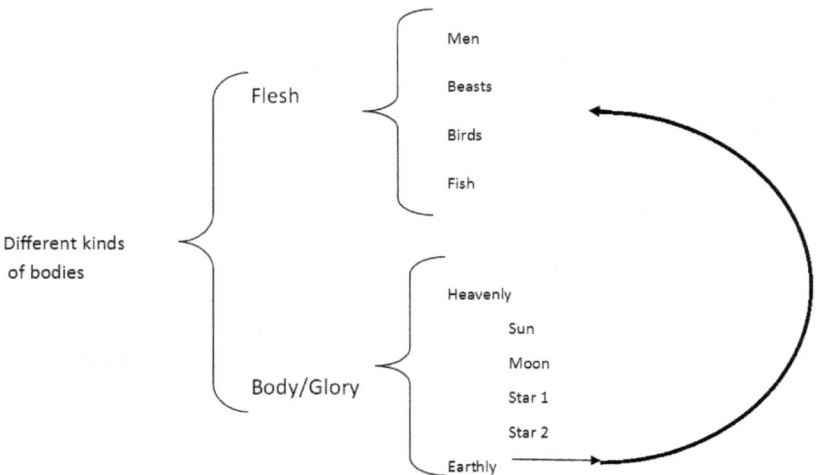

Figure 2. Kinds of bodies in 1 Corinthians 15:35–55.

Sinai. Referring to that occasion Paul does use the word *doxa* (2 Cor 3:7).

As it happens with the naked grain (15:37), the human body with the characteristics of corruption, lack of glory, and weakness (15:42–46), is sown or put into earth through death in order to be risen in incorruption, glory, power, and a spiritual nature (15:41–44). In this contrast, the terms *psychikon* and *pneumatikon* (15:46) come from *psychē* and *pneuma* respectively. They are adjectives qualifying the term "body," that basically can be translated as 'natural' and "spiritual" respectively.

This implies that one kind of body is sowed and another kind of body is raised. Paul says, "There is a natural body, and there is a spiritual body." The difference has to be with the origin of the matter that the bodies are composed of. The natural bodies are from the earth while the spiritual are from heaven (15:47).[175] The first is brought to existence inheriting the nature of Adam (15:45), but the second as a result of the life-giving power of Jesus (*pneuma zōopoioun*).

The body after resurrection is qualified as spiritual. Brunt says that, by using this adjective, Paul is talking against some early type of Gnostic heresy that had influenced at "least a group of Corinthians."[176] Brunt applies the term *pneuma* to the origin of the motivation after resurrection. He says that, by *pneuma*, Paul "does not emphasize the immaterial, or nonphysical. Instead it points to human life empowered by God," and adds, "it is life under the power of God rather than the power of sin and death."[177]

Following this idea, this text infers a resurrection without the effects of sin (15:56) and even without sinful inclinations. The introduction of law (*nomos*) as the power (*dynamis*) of sin in 15:56 turns the discussion to the reason of the entrance of sin, and consequently death. It leads the discussion to ethical applications, the victory in Jesus, and the value of working for the Lord.

However, based on the literary context, the word *pneumatikon* in 15:44 refers to a kind of body. This is an imperishable or supernatural body[178] created by God with another kind of substance. In Figure 3, which

---

175. Another view applies this term relating to the manner that the body is animated; "The present body is animated by soul and is therefore mortal; the resurrection body is animated entirely by immortal and life-giving spirit, and is therefore called a spiritual body." Bruce, *1 and 2 Corinthians*, 152. This view, however, is dualistic, and is hardly sustained by the context, if Bruce was right, Paul would not have used inanimate examples like the sun, moon, or stars.

176. Brunt, "Resurrection," 350.

177. Ibid., 352.

178. Geisler uses the word supernatural as a suggestion for πνευματικός and relates it

is a fragment of Figure 1 in page 81, the comparison of the images of the earthly body contrasting the characteristics of the heavenly body highlights the anthropological sense of these images. It is important to note that the term *sōma*, qualified by this adjective, in 1 Cor 15, "always means body, a real entity, visible to our eyesight. It is not an abstract concept. It is an organism."[179]

"With what kind of body do they come?" (1Co 15:35)

Earthly body			Heavenly body		
v.	Translation	Greek	Greek	Translation	v.
44	natural body	σῶμα ψυχικόν	σῶμα ψυχικόν	spiritual body	44
45	living soul	ψυχὴν ζῶσαν	ψυχὴν ζῶσαν	life-giving spirit	45
46	natural	ψυχικόν	ψυχικόν	spiritual	46

Figure 3. Psychikon and pneumatikon contrasted.

The Adam-Jesus comparison of Paul brings more clarity to this point. Adam stands for the nature before death as Jesus stands for the nature after resurrection. Although Adam was created in a non-perishable world in intimacy with God, and with a nature capable to be in the presence of God, the result of his fall in his nature shows that there was no natural, unconditional immortality in his nature.[180] Paul refers to him as *psychēn zōsan* (living being, 1 Cor 15:45),[181] as it was done at creation, inferring its earthly nature. In contrast, he uses *pneuma zōiopoioun* (life-giving Spirit) to refer to Jesus after his resurrection. The difference in nature is the contrast between natural and spiritual. In this sense, Paul says that the resurrected ones will bear this spiritual nature of Jesus after resurrection.

---

with 1 Cor 10:4. See Geisler, *BECA*, 109.

179. Richards.*1 Corinthians*, 268.

180. The new nature after resurrection exceeds the nature of Adam before sin, since in that state he represents the first state of the human nature in contrast with the second Adam, Jesus. The first Adam had conditional immortality; he had to eat of the tree of life (Gen 3:22) in order to live forever. The resurrected ones will have immortality in an imperishable existence (body) given to them from heaven. The total victory over death has occurred. The immortality, through the power of Jesus (*pneuma zōiopoioun*), is no longer conditional (1 Cor 15:54–56); although not inherent.

181. See the explanation of *psychē zōsan* on p. 61 under the section *Psychē* in First Corinthians.

Literary Background

In this context of resurrection (15:42, 43), and qualifying *sōma*, there is no possibility that *psychē* or *pneuma* refers to a separated independent entity apart from the body as in a spiritual resurrection (without a body). On this point, Brunt says that the spiritual body, in the sense of a nonmaterial body, "is not part of Paul's thinking."[182] The anthropological context is also clear enough to avoid the allusion to spiritual experience after conversion, or a simple luminous vision, as Gerald O'Collins mentions.[183] Therefore Paul is speaking about some kind of body after resurrection that represents the monist existence of the person.

In relation to the nature of Jesus after resurrection, he may not be the example in all aspects, as humans cannot have his eternal existence. He is God-man and his condition is different from human condition. In relation to death and resurrection, Jesus said about himself, "No one takes it [life] from Me, but I lay it down of Myself. I have power to lay it down, and I have power to take it again. This command I have received from My Father" (John 10:18). No human could say this.

However, Paul uses the comparison between Adam and Jesus, the second Adam, as an example of bodily resurrection (1 Cor 15:45), so we can extract some facts from this comparison. In the first part of the comparison (15:21, 22) Paul is talking about the physical effects for humanity of the fall of Adam and the resurrection of Jesus. This argument is in the section that argues in favor of resurrection, but it does not deal with the nature of his body.

The second part (15:45–47) of the discussion concerns the nature of the body started in 15:35. Adam, representing the present condition of humanity, is natural, and made of dust, earthly. On the contrary, Jesus, representing the resurrected ones, is spirit, from heaven, which means heavenly. In this comparison, the word spiritual in verse 46 contrasts with natural and earthly. Figure 4 clarifies this point by showing the terms used to compare Christ and Adam; it highlights the difference in nature between the present bodies and the bodies after resurrection. By this contrast, the word "spiritual" can be paraphrased as "unknown nature" or with an "imperishable

---

182. Brunt, "Resurrection," *HSDAT*, 362.

183. O'Collins refers the Fuller's view about Jesus' resurrection as a luminous vision, not a real corporal resurrection. Also he mentions Perkins's view of the resurrection as a spiritual experience, like conversion. O'Collins, *Interpreting the Resurrection*, 6–16.

nature."[184] Maurice Carrez uses the word "imperishable" as a translation for "spiritual" in this text following the flow of the context.[185]

	Verse	Adam	Christ
Effects	21	by man came death (δι' ἀνθρώπου θάνατος)	by Man also came the resurrection of the dead (δι' ἀνθρώπου ἀνάστασις νεκρῶν)
	22	for as in Adam all die (πάντες ἀποθνήσκουσιν)	in Christ all shall be made alive (πάντες ζωοποιηθήσονται)
Nature	45	living being (ψυχὴν ζῶσαν a person)	life-giving spirit (πνεῦμα ζωοποιοῦν)
	46	natural (ψυχικόν) (die for or die willing)	spiritual (πνευματικόν)
	47	made of dust (ἐκ γῆς χοϊκός)	from heaven (ἐξ οὐρανοῦ)
	48, 49	earthly (χοϊκός)	Heavenly (ἐπουράνιος)

Figure 4. Comparison between Adam and Christ.

Calvin wrote, "The new body is of the same substance as the former, but of a different quality."[186] So the quality of the substance could be different in order to show different characteristics, as shining or majesty, but, even so, it is a corporal substance. Although from heaven, heavenly or spiritual do not specify the nature of the substance the new body is made of, it suggests something that does not belong to earth.

Regarding the physical body of Jesus after his resurrection, the Bible says that the disciples did see and touch Jesus, and he ate fish and bread with them.[187] When Jesus came to his disciples,[188] he said, "See My hands

184. Richards explains this concept and concludes that the body of Jesus after resurrection was the same like the one God's people will receive. Richards, *Essentials*, 269. This interpretation of spirit agrees with the previous discussion about *pneuma* in this book.

185. Carrez, "With What Body Do the Dead Rise Again?" 95.

186. Brunt, "Resurrection," 368.

187. For O'Collins Jesus eating fish means he experienced bodily resurrection, O'Collins, *Interpreting*, 45. Stephen Davis writes that "Paul's notion about the spiritual body reconciles the physical evidences in gospel stories and ethereal parts of the same stories, as appearing in a room despite locked doors, etc." Davis et al, *The Resurrection*, 139.

188. Geisler relates the fact that Jesus appeared and disappeared instantaneously in the room with the experience of Philip with the Ethiopian. He also disappeared, even

LITERARY BACKGROUND

and My feet, that it is I Myself; touch Me and see, for a spirit does not have flesh and bones as you see that I have" (Luke 24:39). The disciples who were walking to Emmaus first thought that he was a common man (Luke 24:15–31). For that reason it is easy to conclude, in agreement with Stephen Davis, that the "resurrection is essentially and entirely material objects."[189]

The difference, however, is that Paul uses *zōiopoioun*, "life-giving," for Jesus instead of *zōsan*, "living," used for Adam. This participle gives Jesus the power to give life.[190] This characteristic goes beyond the boundaries of the human being and places Jesus as the author of the new life, in contrast to Adam, who brings corruption. It refers to the effects produced by Jesus and Adam mentioned in 15:21, 22, as Figure 4 shows. On the other hand, *zōiopoioun*, meaning a "life giver" and applied to the creative work of Jesus over the resurrected ones, infers that the existence after resurrection is a living experience. And, because this living experience is contrary to death and corruption that affects the body, the new experience also is necessarily a bodily experience.

Then, resurrection is not the reconstruction of the old body, but the re-creation of the old individual body in a brand new existence. Reichenbach believes that the body is not the one to be resurrected, but the whole person—the individual. He explains accurately that there is no such thing in the NT as resurrection of the body, but a re-creation.[191] Then, there is no disembodied entity surviving death, nor a body reserved for resurrection, but the power of God giving life back to the same individual, but with a different nature—one not made with "flesh and blood," because this nature "cannot inherit the kingdom of God" (1 Cor 15:50).[192]

---

though he was an earthly human being, so this phenomenon does not mean that they had an immaterial body. Geisler, *BECA*, 119, 120.

189. S. Davis dedicates an entire chapter (6) in defending this point. Davis, *Risen Indeed*, 110.

190. Based on the context of 15:2, 17, 21, 22, 34, and 56, that speak of soteriological issues, this life that is to be received at resurrection corresponds also to the soteriological life received when Jesus is accepted anytime. This link between soteriological issues and anthropological ones (as have been defined in this book) makes some exegetes see the primary issue of the passage as soteriological, not anthropological. I see the soteriological as a secondary reading of the anthropological explanation. This anthropological explanation does not demerit the main focus of Paul regarding the gospel of salvation. The Pauline style of alternating between practical-moral issues and theological ones has not to be mistaken and every part has to be differentiated.

191. Reichenbach, "Resurrection," 34.

192. See the section of Continuity of Identity on p. 152 on how two different

The hope of resurrection, as a new creative act of God,[193] appears already in Job 14:7–15, where Job compares the living man to a tree. He says, "If it is cut down, that it will sprout again" (14:7). Job declares that after receiving water, it will flourish like a plant. In the Hebrew expression *kkĕmô-nāta'*, "like a plant," in 14:9, the conjunction *kkĕmô* could have the meaning of "as when." Thus it could be translated as "new plant," or "like it was." The implication is that, although a tree that sprouts again does not have the same particles as the first tree, it is still considered the same tree, even though the shape will be different.

Speaking about the man at death, Job asks, "Where is he?" (Job 14:10), and he answers, "As water evaporates from the sea, And a river becomes parched and dried up, So man lies down and does not rise"(14:11, 12). Job compares this state of nonexistence to sleep. I will elaborate this concept in the next chapter. At this moment, the unique hope after death is that God could "remember" the man (14:13). He says, "You shall call, and I will answer You" (14:15), and he adds, "The work of Your hands," referring to the man after resurrection. The comparison of the resurrection of man with the image of a tree that sprouts again speaks of "new" material that represents the same individual. It is reinforced by the comparison of a dry river. Therefore it is an act of re-creation.

Like Job, Paul also uses the same image of a plant in 1 Cor 15:36. In verse 35 he answers the question of resurrection and the kind of body that the resurrected will have: "What you sow is not made alive unless it dies" (15:36). In this comparison the result of the growth process is a new plant with a different composition than the seed that was put in the earth. In the case of the seed, this process is natural though still amazing. But in the case of the human being after death, the process is contrary to the law of degradation, and it needs a miraculous work of God. Hence, the same divine power of creation is needed.

In addition, Paul clearly alludes to the creation process in 1 Cor 15:47, 48, where he refers to the creation of Adam from (Greek ἐκ) dust. The preposition ἐκ is followed by a genitive of material.[194] The first man is made from *gēs*, "earth," while the second is from *ouranou*, "heaven." Although it

---

existences, the one before death and the other after resurrection can be related to each other in a continuity if nothing survives death.

193. Andreasen uses the expression "new creative act by God" for what I call here re-creation. See Andreasen, "Death," 332. Tertullian also used the expression "mere re-creation." Setzer, *Resurrection*, 1.

194. Wallace, *Grammar*, 91.

can (primarily) refer to origin, making Adam representative of the earth and Jesus representative of heaven, the adjective *choikos*[195] (from earth) reminds the material Adam was made of (Gen 2:7). Thus he is comparing the creation of Adam with the creation of the new body upon resurrection. In the same way, the adjective *epouranioi* in 15:48, applied to the resurrected ones, can be seen also as refereeing to a different nature, not from earth.

The comparison describes two acts of creation. The first one is at the beginning, when God made Adam from earth, and the second one is the creation of new individuals, but now from heaven. If this is true, the implications are that, because the individual existed before, this act is an act of re-creation of the individual, and that the heavenly characteristic refers to a body composition. In 15:40, Paul says that, "there are also heavenly bodies" referring to the stars, sun, and moon. It does not mean that the objects are made of a matter called "heaven," but rather that their nature is not from what is known on earth. In Phil 2:10 Paul uses the adjective without noun to refer to those who belong to heaven, in contrast to those who belong to earth.[196]

Another consideration is that the term *zōiopoieitai*, "come to life," used in 1 Cor 15:36, implies re-creation. At the moment of creation, God "breathed into his [Adam] nostrils the breath of life [*zōē*]" (Gen 2:7). The inert body received life, or came to life. The noun *zōē* is related to *zōiopoieitai*. Paul was clearly aiming to bring back this experience of creation to the mind of his readers.

Zōiopoieitai is part of a conditional sentence.[197] There, "to die" (*apothanēi*) is the condition that needs to occur if "to come into life" is expected. Because, in order to die, the grain must have been alive; here Paul is speaking about a transition from one kind of life to another. The creation of the "new" life is indeed not a creation of a new person. The person existed before but with another nature. Therefore it is a re-creation rather than a creation.

Paul confirms again this concept when he introduces the expression "image" in 15:49, where Adam received the image of God when he was created. In the same way the resurrected ones will bear *tēn eikona*

---

195. *Choikos* has the sense of material and it is used only here in the biblical text.

196. *Epouraniōn kai epigeiōn kai katachthoniōn* (ἐπουρανίων καὶ ἐπιγείων καὶ καταχθονίων, "[those who are] in heaven, and on earth, and under the earth").

197. This is a 3rd class conditional in a logical connection. It means that the condition leads to the fulfillment in the form of "if A, then B." See Wallace, *Grammar*, 696.

tou epouraniou, "the image of the heavenly." He recalls the experience of creation, but now referring to the resurrection. It is clearly an allusion to re-creation.

This concept of re-creation in the eschatological resurrection is different from the restoration that happened in the experience of Lazarus, who was resurrected. He was not resurrected in the same form that the righteous will be resurrected at the last day. He was in the tomb for four days, and his body was corrupted (John 11:39). This is the natural result of death and the reversal of the process of biological decomposition is naturally impossible. So, by the power of Jesus, the particles of his body were restored, to the same form, composition, and nature that Lazarus had before death, but without sickness.[198] There was a restoration in the same way that the body of the leper, or the legs of the invalid, were also restored by the same power. The result was a healthy but perishable body, which still was evidence of the creative power of God. But in the case of the eschatological resurrection, the result is an imperishable nature.

Carrez sees the power needed to give life at the beginning (as a creator) as the same power needed to give life to the new body of the plant and of the resurrected ones at resurrection. Therefore, the same creative power is still present each day, according to the Hebrew concept, and it will be there at the moment of the resurrection.[199]

The experience on the resurrection day will be a re-creation in the sense that not all individuals will be new, as it happened in the creation of Adam. He became a living being that had not existed before. For Adam all experiences were new. But, in resurrection, Paul and Job speak about some kind of continuity of the identity of the living being. The body will be new, but the identity has already existed before, so, the person will have the same character that he had before; he will recall all experiences and knowledge he had before, but now with a new and different body. As such, it is the "same" creation that was before death in terms of identity, but now

---

198. Geisler calls this act a resuscitation differentiating it from resurrection. Geisler, *BECA*, 123.

199. Carrez makes a good exposition of resurrection as a creative act of God. See Carrez, "What Body," 94. He presents three initiatives of God. First God created man, but man fell, so there is need for a second act of creation, which takes place at the moment of the conversion. But man is still imperfect, so at the end, the resurrection represents God's third creative act through which man is made perfect and is capable of living eternally, Ibid., 96, 97.

re-created in a non-perishable way. Hence, the expression re-creation is more appropriate than simply creation.²⁰⁰

On the other hand, if creation gives God the authority to claim worship, then re-creation has the same effect (1 Cor 15:57). The question of resurrection in Jewish thinking stands in the context of the question of theodicy.²⁰¹ According to James Ian Hamilton MacDonald, "If Yahweh has the power of creation and re-creation; he also exercises the royal prerogative of Judgment within history."²⁰²

There is another consideration regarding the change required to enter into the kingdom of God. Paul presents this change through either resurrection, or a kind of change, without experiencing death. He says that those who will not die will still experience the same change that the resurrected will have (15:51–52). This change will take place at the same moment, at the second coming of Jesus (15:52). For clarity and brevity I will use the word "transformation" in this study to refer to the experience of change the living ones will experience at the Parousia.²⁰³ Both resurrection and transformation have the same results: death being swallowed up in victory (15:55), and the perishable nature changed into an imperishable one (15:52, 53).²⁰⁴

Figure 5 displays the images of change in three sections, those that show the process of resurrection, those that show the process of transformation, and those that, though addressing primarily resurrection, are used also for transformation. The images associated with the first and second processes in 15:52–54 can actually be applied to either process. This means

200. This issue of continuity of identity will be considered in Chapter 4.

201. Wilckens, *Resurrection*, 86.

202. McDonald. *The Resurrection*, 8.

203. Although *transformation* and *change* are synonymous, I will use the word *change* for the experience of change itself; while I will use *transformation* to refer specifically to the transformation of the body nature in a flash, without experiencing death, at the Parousia, distinguishing it from the change made through resurrection. In my view there is no intrinsic difference between these phenomena, but only the way they occur, through resurrection or without it. The distinction here is just to avoid long explanations every time a change is referred to. Theologically the word *glorification* has been used to refer to the bodily change at the Parousia, but this term embraces both resurrection and transformation (as it is defined here). It also entails the idea of soteriological process, from justification to sanctification, to glorification. To avoid misunderstanding I will use just *change* for the eschatological experience in general, *resurrection* for that experience if it includes death, and *transformation* if it does not include death.

204. For Paul, death is not only a phenomenological absence of life, but also a state of the human nature before transformation; he calls it a nature "subject to death" (*thnēto*, 1 Cor 15:53).

that the characteristics of the body after the change will be the same no matter if it is attained through resurrection or transformation.

Before the last trumpet (*eschatēi salpingi*) the body is perishable and mortal (15:53, 54), represented by the word "death" (15:54). After the final trumpet, the body is imperishable and immortal (15:53, 54), as indicated by the word "victory" (15:54). The very nature of the heavenly body stands as victory over death. Thus, the influence of death is taken away, either by resurrection or transformation, since even those who did not fall asleep were also under the influence of death in the earthly body (15:42, 53–54).

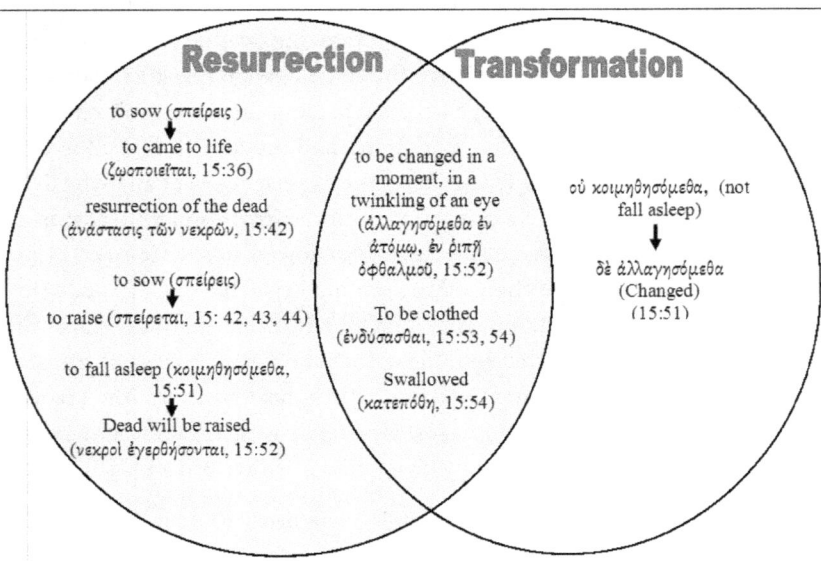

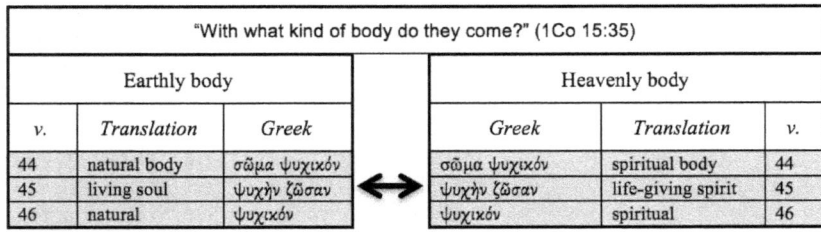

Figure 5. Two processes of change in 1 Corainthians 15.

There are some terms that differentiate two phases of being dead. The first phase is the punctual action or process of entering into death; the second state refers to the time spent between the first one and the second one.

The verb *apothnēiskō*, "to die" (15:36), clarifies what I mean. It is the instant in which a living person is no longer considered "alive." Paul uses *speireis*, "to sow," in parallel to *apothnēiskō*, to refer to that "entering" instant. These terms contrast directly the words *zōiopoieitai* and *egeiretai*, which clearly refer to resurrection. The other terms describe the state of death. The combination of these terms gives the idea of what death is. Here I will only mention them, but their consideration will come in comparison with *gymnos* in the next chapter. Paul uses *gymnon*, referring to the condition of the grain (15:37); *nekrōn*, "dead" (15:42, 52); and (c) *koimēthēsometha*, "fall asleep" (15:51). These terms, in association with the characteristics of the earthly body, are strong arguments in favor of the anthropological sense of the passage, without negating a secondary spiritual application.

Summary and Conclusion of chapter

The conjunction *gar* in 2 Cor 5:1 links the passage with the context of 2 Cor 4:7–18, and to the theme and flow of the whole letter. This background enlightens the meaning of *gymnos*. The discussion about the holder of the ministry (the earthen vessel), sufferings, the hope of resurrection and the irrelevance of bodily decay, places the theme on anthropological settings. The pericope is a unit from 4:7 to 5:10 that is seen through the fluency of the letter. This pericope explains how this process of change from the decaying nature to a new one, the eternal one, happens.

The verb *oidamen* also in 5:1 links the pericope with a broader background. Though Paul uses the Greek language, his theology is clearly detached from Greek, the philosophical context. Rather, the concepts and terms fit more with the OT. Moreover, 1 Cor 15:35–55 stands as the best background for 2 Cor 4:7–5:10. The way Paul uses anthropological terms in his first letter, in comparison with their use in the LXX and the Hebrew words they translate, shows an anthropological setting and an OT mindset. The issue in both pericopes is a change of existence from earthly to heavenly. According to Paul this existence is intrinsically linked to the body, so the nature of the body represents the nature of the person and the life itself. This changing experience in the Parousia constitutes a re-creation of the individual with the same identity.

This fundamental teaching, which the readers of Paul's letter had already as background (*Oidamen gar*, 2 Cor 5:1), provides the hope they need in the midst of physical tribulations. The new existence "we have" through the resurrection of Christ (2 Cor 4:14 cf. 1 Cor 15:42, 49) puts the earthly existence that "is torn down" as irrelevant for Christian experience and as evidence of Paul's apostleship and authority as an earthen vessel. Paul says to the Corinthians in his second canonical letter, "For we know," which paraphrasing the verse could say, "According to what I wrote to you in my previous letter and according to the teachings of the OT, that if physical destruction comes to our present earthly existence, we have the assurance of the change into a new immortal and heavenly existence."

Chapter 3

Gymnos in 2 Corinthians 5:3

THE PREVIOUS CHAPTER SHOWED the close parallel between 2 Cor 4:7–5:10 and 1 Cor 15:35–55, and the dependence of both pericopes on the OT. It made clear the monist anthropologic theme of resurrection and transformation as the background of 1 Cor 5:3. Now the focus goes to the state of the individual between death and resurrection and the issue of nakedness. The study in this chapter embraces three tasks: (a) A literary and textual analysis shows that the issue discussed in the pericope (4:7–5:10) is the nature of the physical existences, referred to as houses—the earthly temporal for the present nature, and the heavenly eternal for the future nature. The pericope has a pattern similar to that in 1 Cor 15:35–55, showing how the change of nature takes place either through resurrection or transformation. (b) A study of the term *gymnos*, outside the pericope and in its literary context, shows that the image of nakedness represents death, as the absence of existence since no house is inferred. And finally, (c) a comparison with other images that speak about death shows that *gymnos* is used to imply continuity of identity.

The concept of bodily resurrection considered in the last chapter, that emphasizes monism, does not necessarily solve the issue of monism during the first death. If the body, which is the person, is real and physical in resurrection, but different in nature from the one before death, it appears as if someone is receiving this body. Some writers do see the resurrection as a "reuniting" of the body and soul. Seltzer suggests that at the time of Judaism and early Christianity, they believed that the resurrection would be with a glorious body (spiritual), and she refers to 1 Cor 15; however, she says that the resurrection body would be possessed by an immortal soul.[1] Adam Clarke, quoting Rab Levi, explained his belief that souls in heaven are clothed with celestial light, which will remain with them when they return "to the body." Then, "the body shall shine like the splendour of the firmament of heaven."[2]

However, it seems that Paul argued against Greek mentality and dualism.[3] Writing to Greek people, the Corinthians, who had been introduced to the Gospel based on the OT teachings, the image of *gymnos* arises as a very appropriate term to refer to death. This chapter shows what the meaning of naked is in the context of 2 Cor 5:3 is, its relation with the earthly and heavenly realms, and its significance regarding the hope of new life and the continuity of identity.

Literary Analysis

This literary analysis is focused on the study of the language and syntactical relations that reflect, on one hand, the two different dwelling places and the natures they represent, and on the other, the process that produces these two existences. The first section shows that nakedness is not a dwelling place, but being a state of no dwelling place it means emptiness. The second section shows the process of transformation without experiencing death, and Paul's desire to avoid nakedness, to avoid death.

The Earthly Tent and the Building from God

In this section we will see how the peculiar use of terms and images, such as *endyō*, "put on" (2 Cor 5:3) in distinction of *ependyō*, "put on in addition"[4] (2 Cor 5:2, 4), and references to different habitations, shows that the issue refers to two physical natures, one before *ependyō* and the other after. A comparison of expressions related to these houses with the expressions used in 1 Cor 15:35–55 will confirm this reality. The syntactical relations in this periscope, which form a parallel within it, are also important. This

---

1. Setzer, *Resurrection*, 17.
2. Clarke, *Clarke's Commentary*, s.v. "1 Cor 15:44."
3. Sevenster, "Some Remarks," 210.
4. Lexicons agree that the addition of Greek preposition ἐπ to ther verb ἐνδύω adds the idea of "over" or "in addition." See the explanation on p. 136.

parallel reveals that a process divides these two existences. There, nakedness stands apart from the two existences as an undesirable condition.

Use of terms.

The image of *gymnos* in 2 Cor 5:3 is necessary in order to contrast the verb *endyō*. The specific section related to what is to be worn and what not (*gymnos*) is 5:1–4. Here it is important to highlight the difference between the verb *ependysasthai* (ἐπενδύσασθαι from ἐπενδύω), and *endysamenoi* (ἐνδυσάμενοι from ἐνδύω); however, before considering the differences, there is a textual variance that needs to be discussed.

The Critical Text (CT), which is the most authoritative Greek text of the NT in academia, uses the verb *ekdysamenoi*, "put off" or "unclothed," in 2 Cor 5:3.[5] The text reads, εἴ γε καὶ ἐκδυσάμενοι οὐ γυμνοὶ εὑρεθησόμεθα, "and even though we are unclothed, we shall be found naked." The *criticus apparatus* of the CT, however, notes an important variant. "The two chief witnesses to the Alexandrian text,"[6] codex Sinaiticus (א) and codex Vaticanus (B) use *endysamenoi* instead of *ekdysamenoi* as follows:

א ΕΙ ΓΕ ΚΑΙ ΕΝΔΥΣΑΜΕΝΟΙ ΟΥ ΓΥΜΝΟΙ ΕΥΡΕΘΗΣΟΜΕΘΑ[7]

B ΕΙΠΕΡ ΚΑΙ ΕΝΔΥΣΑΜΕΝΟΙ ΟΥ ΓΥΜΝΟΙ ΕΥΡΕΘΗΣΟΜΕΘΑ[8]

What of the readings is preferable, the CT (*ekdysamenoi*) or the א/B (*endysamenoi*)? Bruce M. Metzger explains:

> It is difficult to decide between ἐνδυσάμενοι and ἐκδυσάμενοι. On the one hand, from the standpoint of external attestation the former reading is to be preferred. On the other hand, internal considerations, in the opinion of a majority of the Committee, decisively favor the latter reading, for with ἐνδυσάμενοι the apostle's statement is banal and even tautologous, whereas with ἐκδυσάμενοι it is

---

5. Aland et al., *Nestle-Aland Novum Testamentum Graece*, 479.
6. Metzger, *A Textual Commentary on the Greek New Testament*, 5*.
7. Tischendorf, ed., *Bibliorum Codex Sinaiticus Petropolitanus* s.v. "2 Cor 5:3." Emphasis mine.
8. Tischendorf, ed., *Novum Testamentum Vaticanum*, s.v. "2 Cor 5:3." Emphasis mine.

The Naked State of Human Being

characteristically vivid and paradoxical ("inasmuch as we, though unclothed, shall not be found naked").[9]

The argument seems to be interpretative rather than textual. Perhaps this is the reason Metzger adds to the edited commentary his personal notation: "In view of its superior external support the reading ἐνδυσάμενοι should be adopted."[10] The Greek texts based on the "Majority Text" or "Byzantine" have opted for *endysamenoi* (ἐνδυσάμενοι). Figure 6 displays some samples.

BYZ (Byzantine Text Form) εἴγε καὶ ἐνδυσάμενοι οὐ γυμνοὶ εὑρεθησόμεθα.
GOC (Greek NT of the Ortodox Church) εἴ γε καὶ ἐνδυσάμενοι οὐ γυμνοὶ εὑρεθησόμεθα
MGK (Greek Vamvas Bible 180. Modern Greek) ἄν καὶ ἐνδυθέντες αὐτὸ δὲν θέλωμεν εὑρεθῇ γυμνο
TextusReceptus ειγε και ενδυσαμενοι ου γυμνοι ευρεθησομεθα
MajorityText Εἴ γε καὶ ἐνδυσάμενοι οὐ γυμνοὶ εὑρεθησόμεθα.
MET (Metaglottisis) Και βέβαια, αν γδυθούμε το σώμα μας,ᵃ— δε θα βρεθούμε γυμνοί.
SCR (Scriveber) εἴ γε καὶ ἐνδυσάμενοι οὐ γυμνοὶ
STE (Stephanus) εἴγε καὶ ἐνδυσάμενοι οὐ γυμνοὶ εὑρεθησόμεθα
TBT (TrinitarianBibleSociety) εἴ γε καὶ ἐνδυσάμενοι οὐ γυμνοὶ
TIS (Tischendorf 8th) εἴγε καὶ ἐνδυσάμενοι οὐ γυμνοὶ εὑρεθησόμεθα.
TRG1 (Tregellestextnocorrected) εἴ περ καὶ ἐνδυσάμενοι οὐ γυμνοὶ εὑρεθησόμεθα.
TRG2 (Tregellestextcorrected) εἴ περ καὶ ἐνδυσάμενοι οὐ γυμνοὶ εὑρεθησόμεθα.
WHT (WestcottandHort) ⌜εἴ γε⌝ καὶ ἐνδυσάμενοι οὐ γυμνοὶ εὑρεθησόμεθα.

Figure 6. Textual evidences for *endysamenoi*.

What makes this case one of the most interesting in the CT is that, besides the argumentation of the variants and the decision of the committee to maintain *ekdysamenoi*, English Bible translations use "put it on," "putting it on," or "clothed." Figure 7 is a sample of it.

American Standard Version if so be that being clothed we shall not be found naked.
English Standard Version if indeed by putting it on we may not be found naked.
King James Version If so be that being clothed we shall not be found naked.
New American Standard Bible inasmuch as we, having put it on, shall not be found naked.
The NET Bible if indeed, after we have put on our heavenly house, we will not be found naked.
New International Version because when we are clothed, we will not be found naked.
New King James if indeed, having been clothed, we shall not be found naked.
New Living Translation For we will put on heavenly bodies; we will not be spirits without bodies.
Young's Literal Translation if so be that, having clothed ourselves, we shall not be found naked.

Figure 7. Biblical translations of *endysamenoi*.

---

9. Metzger, *A Textual Commentary*, 511.
10. Ibid.

In my opinion, the variant *endysamenoi* fits better than *ekdysamenoi* in the syntactical and logical flow of the argument. The section "Gymnos in Its Literary Context" will demonstrate this. Here I would like to suggest that the clause is linked to *ependysasthai*, "to put on in addition" in 5:2. The negative adverb οὐ in *gymnoi* therefore provides a contrast. Thus, the best option is one that is opposite to *gymnoi* but would be in agreement with *ependysasthai* in 5:2. The parallelism with 5:4 also demands this contrast. In 5:4 Paul says, "We do not want to be unclothed, but to be clothed." The syntactical relation with 5:3 demands the same contrast there.[11] The dualistic interpretations of the text have taken *endysamenoi* to see some kind of dualism. For the sake of argumentation I also will take this variant so the discussion may proceed to the exegesis rather than get bogged down in textual criticism. Even if *ekdysamenoi* were chosen, dualistic or monistic arguments could still be made.

In relation to the verb *endyō*, Paul applies it to habitations rather than to cloths, as would be logical. In this way one can "wear" an "earthly house of tent" (*hē epigeios hēmōn oikia tou skēnous*, 5:1), a "building from God" (*oikodomēn ek theou*, 5:1), a "building from heaven" (*to oikētērion hēmōn to ex ouranou*, 5:2), or just a "tent" (*skēnei*, 5:4). This unusual use of *endyō* gives an alternative significance to other terms in the passage. Moreover, the use of *ependyō* when *gymnos* could logically require *endyō* and the comparison with 1 Cor 15:35–55 suggest a different process for the change of houses.

The term *endyō* comes from the root *dyō* (δύω), which is not used in its basic form in the NT. It can be translated as "get into" or "put on."[12] It is used thirty-seven times in the NT in five compound forms: *en-dyō*, "to dress," or "to put on," *ek-dyō*, "to undress," or "strip," *epi-dyō*, "to set," "to go down" (used only in Eph 4:26), *pareis-dyō*, "slip in stealthily," or "to creep in unnoticed," (used only in Jude 1:4), and *ep-en-dyō*, "to put on over" (or in addition). This variety of uses suggests that the core of the meaning has to do with entering into (or going out to) a condition that represents what can be seen of a person or thing.

As in 2 Cor 5:1–4, there are some instances in the NT where *endyō* is not applied to clothes and instead refers to a process of change from one stage to another. In Luke 24:49 the disciples have to wait until they are clothed (*endysēsthe*) with "power from high." This promised power would

---

11. See Figure 10 on p. 120 and related comments.
12. Bauer, BDAG, s.v. "ἐνδύσω."

act in the whole life of the disciples. It would modify the way they would act, testify, and live. It is not something to live in, but to be changed by. They do not enter into that power, but they are changed by it.

The same is the case with Col 3:12. There believers are invited to integrate, "to wear" (*endysasthe*), their life characteristics like "a heart of compassion, kindness, humility, gentleness, and patience." This change of life that reproduces the life of Christ in their character is presented as if Christians have "to wear" (*enedysēsthe*) him. Galatians 3:27 says that those who were baptized "*into* Christ" (*eis Christon ebaptisthēte*, emphasis mine)[13] have clothed themselves "with Christ."

This experience of change of self is clearer when one is wearing a new experience, or life, as Eph 4:24 and Col 3:10 suggest. There, one is called to wear the new self.[14] In this experience there is no entity coming out from the old self to enter into the new one, but it refers to a change of nature—spiritual nature in this case. The change is real and produces visible changes in the life of the individual.

The context of 2 Cor 5:1–4 suggests this same sense of the use of *endyō* and its related words. Here, the use of the image of wearing a new body nature seems to be an echo of the image Paul started in 1 Cor 15:53, 54: "For this perishable must put on [*endysasthay*] the imperishable, and this mortal must put on [*endysasthai*] immortality. But when this perishable will have put on [*endysētai*] the imperishable, and this mortal will have put on [*endysētai*] immortality, then will come about the saying that is written, 'Death is swallowed [*katepothē*] up in victory.'" Paul says that this wearing experience means that "death is swallowed up in victory," a case of change of nature, where death disappears to give place to life.[15]

In 2 Cor 5:1–4 the initial nature or state is the earthly house. The second, after the change, is the heavenly house. This interest in body nature was already anticipated in 2 Cor 4, especially verse 10 (cf. 14, 16). In the sentence of 5:1, in the expression *oikia tou skēnous*, "house of tent," *tou skēnous* is a genitive of apposition that defines or explains the nature of *oikia*. It gives to tent a temporal meaning.[16] It could be paraphrased as "a

---

13. In the same context of putting on Jesus Paul includes anthropological terms, but with a spiritual sense. See Rom 13:14.

14. *Endysathai* and *endysamenoi* respectively.

15. Regarding the use of *ependyō* instead of *endyō* in 2 Cor 5:2–4, see The Process of Change on p. 128.

16. Philip Hughes, points out the transitory character of *tent*. Hughes, *Paul's Second Epistle to the Corinthians*, 162. Also J. Osei-Bonsu makes a good short argument to show

temporal house."[17] Most of the lexicons give *skēnos* a metaphorical meaning in this passage. It refers to the human body.[18] Paul does not use any other element of the human being such as soul or spirit; in which case *oikia tou skēnous* refers to the totality of the human being.

A comparison of the expressions referring to the state before and after the change in the pericope helps build up this argument. The expression *oikodomēn ek theou*, "building from God," contrasts *oikia tou skēnous*, "house of tent," or "temporal house" (5:1a). They show two kinds of buildings. This shift contrasts the lastingness of a building with the temporariness of a tent. The temporal sense is reinforced by adding the word *aiōnion*, "eternal," to building (5:1b). This is similar to 1 Cor 15:35–55 where Paul also presents a contrast of terms illustrating the natures before and after the change. Figure 8 displays the expressions used in the pericope to speak of the earthly existence in contrast to the expressions that speak of the heavenly existence.

The image of the earthen vessel opens the discussion related to the nature of the holder of the ministry. Paul then adds a series of images that, on one hand, reveal the temporariness of the earthly existence and, on the other, reveal the lastingness of the heavenly existence. Thus, the temporal house is to be "given over to death" (4:11) which is compared to "carry the death of Jesus in the body" (4:10). The building from God, by contrast, which is eternal, not made with hands, and from heaven (5:1), is the "life of Jesus manifested in the flesh" (4:11) or "in the body" (4:10). Notice that the nature after the change is still manifested in the body and flesh, as it is still οἰκία, as it was before the change (5:1). It seems that the change is made from the subjection to death to the subjection to life. Paul represents the two natures by the contrasts of "mortal"↔"eternal," and "from earth"↔"from God."

---

that the expression *earthly house* refers to the present, earthly body (though he presents no arguments for his view of the naked state with the preconception of duality of the human being), Osei-Bonsu, "Resurrection Body," 82. BDAG refers to the meaning of *skēnos* as a temporal as opposed to a permanent structure. Bauer, BDAG, s.v. "σκῆνος."

17. See the section *Tent* on p. 50.

18. Nevertheless they use the preconception of the duality of the human being to explain it. See for instance Friberg, *ANLEX*, s.v. "σκῆνος," Liddell, LSJ, s.v. "σκῆνος," and Thayer, s.v. "σκῆνος." Although there is no other allusion to the body using this noun, Peter (2 Pet 1:13, 14) uses the related noun *skēnōma* to refer to his body (The King James Version translates *skēnōma* as tabernacle and NAS as earthly dwelling), which clearly is the contrast with *oikodomēn* in its temporal character.

The Naked State of Human Being

	Earthly existence		Heavenly existence	
v.	Translation	Greek	Greek	Translation
4:7	earthen vessels	ὀστρακίνοις σκεύεσιν		
4:10	dying of Jesus in the body	νέκρωσιν τοῦ Ἰησοῦ ἐν τῷ σώματι	ἡ ζωὴ τοῦ Ἰησοῦ ἐν τῷ σώματι	Jesus' life in the body
4:11	given over to death, mortal	εἰς θάνατον παραδιδόμεθα	ἡ ζωὴ τοῦ Ἰησοῦ φανερωθῇ ἐν τῇ θνητῇ σαρκὶ	Jesus' life manifested in the flesh
5:1a	temporal house	οἰκία τοῦ σκήνους	οἰκοδομὴν ἐκ θεοῦ	building from God
5:1b			οἰκίαν ἀχειροποίητον αἰώνιον ἐν τοῖς οὐρανοῖς	a house not made with hands, eternal in heaven
5:2			τὸ οἰκητήριον ἡμῶν τὸ ἐξ οὐρανου	dwelling from heaven
5:3	being clothed	ἐνδυσάμενοι		
5:4a 5:4b	tabernacle	τῷ σκήνει		
5:4c	subject to death	θνητὸν	τῆς ζωῆς	the life
5:6a	at home in the body absent from the Lord	ἐνδημοῦντες ἐν τῷ σώματι ἐκδημοῦμεν ἀπὸ τοῦ κυρίου	ἐκδημῆσαι ἐκ τοῦ σώματος (5:8) ἐνδημῆσαι πρὸς τὸν κύριον (5:8)	absent from the body at home with the Lord
5:9	at home	ἐνδημοῦντες	ἐνδημοῦντες	at home

Figure 8. Earthly and heavenly existences in 2 Corinthians 4:7–5:10.

A note is needed here in relation to the images in 4:10, 11. In 4:10 Paul says that he and those like him "carry about" (*peripherontes*) the dying of Jesus in the body (4:10). In 4:11 he adds that they are "given over to death." These two expressions should be seen in the context of 4:8, 9 that speaks of the physical difficulties[19] they suffer in the name of Jesus. In these expressions there is still hope in the future, so that the difficulties do not mean the end of their physical experience. The hope is "in the future," because in 4:12 Paul is clear that in the present experience death is working in him and those like him, while those who do not have the same physical conflicts

---

19. "We are afflicted in every way, but not crushed; perplexed, but not despairing; persecuted, but not forsaken; struck down, but not destroyed" (2 Cor 4:8, 9).

are under the effect of life. The possibility of physical death due to physical difficulties is a strong possibility for him.

On the other hand, in 4:10 he says that the purpose (ἵνα) of endurance is that the life of Jesus may be manifested (*phanerōthēi*) in his body. He uses the subjunctive to emphasize something that is not present but possible. In 4:11 he adds that that life may be manifested in his flesh. How could this be possible? Is he speaking of a Christian experience through the power (or life) of Jesus? If the life of Jesus means a positive soteriological experience, then death means a negative experience. Death and flesh are equivalent to sin. But Paul argues that "given over to death" is something done for "Jesus' sake" (4:11), which contradicts this soteriological interpretation.

The life of Jesus may be manifested in the body (4:10), which means "in the flesh" (4:11) like the dying experience of Jesus was (4:10). This "death," does not refer to sinful inclinations or a negative Christian experience. If the death of Jesus is manifested through physical difficulties, then the death of Jesus, in this context, is the human perishable physical nature. His mortal nature ended through his resurrection (4:14) that gave him life. In the same way, God will raise (*egeirei*) believers (4:14) to enjoy that life of Jesus in the flesh, which means to be physically alive.[20] Therefore, the life of Jesus in the body means the new nature after the change.

Jesus also used the image of a building to refer to his body.[21] He said, "Destroy this temple, and in three days I will raise it up" (John 2:19). Jews interpreted his words as referring to an actual building. John explains that Jesus was speaking of his body in the context of death (2:21). John uses in this passage the word *lysate*, "destroy," from the root *lyō*, which is the same root for *katalyō* used in 2 Cor 5:1. After his resurrection the disciples "remembered that He said this; and they believed the Scripture and the word

---

20. Although ἐγερεῖ is used in both the OT and the NT to refer to any kind of rising, including rising from sleep or rising to a specific function, in this passage, since it is related with *pisteuomen* (we believe), and *laloumen* (we speak) it is recognized as a kerygmatic statement about the resurrection of Christ; see Gillman, "Thematic Comparison," 446. This term also has been used many times to refer to resurrection. See as examples referring specifically to the resurrection of Jesus using this verb without specific reference to death, Matt 27:52, 63; 28:6; Mark 16:6, 14; and Luke 24:6, 34. See also Matt 27:64; and 28:7 where the verb is directly followed by *apo tōn nekrōn* (from the dead) and John 21:14 where is followed by *ek nekrōn* (from the dead).

21. Lowery relates the reference to the eternal house in heaven not built by human hands to this image of the body of Jesus in Mark 14:58. See Lowery, "2 Corinthians," 2:565. Although the gospels were written later Paul may have had access to this knowledge of Jesus' sayings.

The Naked State of Human Being

which Jesus had spoken" (22). For John, the resurrection is a way to change the nature from a building made with hands to a building made without hands (Mark 14:58); likewise Paul presents this change in 2 Cor 5:1. This example links the images in 2 Cor 4 with those used in 2 Cor 5. The life that believers will receive from Jesus in the body (4:10), or manifested in the flesh (4:11), in order to be present with the living ones (4:14) will occur after the resurrection.

The passage shows a change from the process of resurrection to the process of transformation. This change is marked by the use of the expression *kai gar en toutōi*, "for *also* in this," in 2 Cor 5:2, and the inclusion of some new images that speak of the change. To be "clothed over" appears as a process that infers that previously the person was unclothed (5:4). If being clothed by any house means to have a nature and therefore to exist, then, to be naked (5:3) is the opposite. Furthermore, to put clothes over a previous set of clothes without being unclothed has to imply a change without experiencing cessation of existence. This signifies a new process of change not considered before in the pericope. As I argued, and in consonance with the comparisons showed in figure 8, that we saw already, the characteristics in 2 Cor 4:7–5:1 correspond to those in 2 Cor 5:1–9, the earthly and heavenly existences. What is different is the process of change, which is associated with the desire of Paul expressed by "a groan" in 5:2. The consideration of the introductory expression in 5:2 will show this shift in the process of change.

The expression *kai en toutōi* is used to add something more to what has already been said in a discourse.[22] Usually *toutōi* points to something that follows in the argument. But the addition of *gar* to the expression, which occurs only in 2 Cor 5:2, seems to add the idea of "cause, clarification, or inference,"[23] and goes back to something already said. Thus, the use of both *kai* and *gar* together, introduces an expression that clarifies something already said, and at the same time, adding something else. The other element of the expression is the neuter demonstrative pronoun *toutōi*, "this." What is *toutōi* referring to? Some translations suggest it refers to the tent mentioned in 5:1.[24] For the NAS it points back to the "house"; others leave the inference indeterminate by translating the word, "in this."[25]

---

22. See Phil 1:18; Heb 4:5; 1 John 2:3, 4; 3:19, 24 where the phrase occurs.
23. Bauer, BDAG, s.v. "γάρ."
24. See the New English Translation and New Living Translation, as examples.
25. See for instance, King James Version and the English Youth Literal Translation.

The demonstrative pronoun *toutōi* in this passage is neuter while *oikia* and *oikodomēn*, "house" and "building," are feminine. The only possibility that agrees in gender is *skēnos*, which is also neuter. As such, Paul is saying, "in this tent we groan." The implication is that, while being in this earthly, temporal condition, Paul desires to be "clothed over" rather than just "clothed." If he desired to be "clothed" it would imply that he would first need to be unclothed. But he does not desire to be unclothed, but only to put the new clothes over the ones he currently has: his temporal existence.

In 2 Cor 5:2 *skēnos* probably works as a genitive of apposition. This means that *oikia* is synonymous to *skēnous*. There are two *oikia* in 5:1, one linked to *skēnous* and the other to *aiōnion*, "eternal." The reference to the former, by the use of neuter, which agrees with *skēnous*, specifies which of the two οικία is referred to by the use of *toutōi*: the temporal.

Another possibility is that *skēnous*, as a genitive noun, modifies *oikia*, giving the idea of temporality to the house. In such case, *toutōi* will not refer only to the genitive *skēnous*. Rather, it could refer to the process of change. The clarification in 5:2 seems to focus in a new process of being "clothed over" rather than receiving a new building if the house of tent is destroyed. Paul changes the image of house for the image of habitation (*oikētērion*) to emphasize the process instead of the structure. As such, a possibility that agrees with the focus of Paul's groan and the gender of τούτῳ is that it refers to the change in general.

This change is expressed by the verbs *katalyō*, "to destroy," in 5:1 and *ependuomai*, "clothed-over," in 5:2.[26] *Kataluthēi* entails a process, since two kinds of structures are mentioned, *oikia*, which is being destroyed and disappears, and *oikodomēn*, which replaces it. The focus of the change of structure is expressed first through the verb *katalythēi* in 5:1. But it is also represented by the verb "to be clothed over," *ependysasthai*, in 5:2. This second verb infers that the first dress, which is *oikia skēnous*, is not destroyed, since the new heavenly habitation is put on *over*, and not only put on. The inference is that there is no *katalythēi* of the *oikia skēnous* necessary in order to experience the *ependysasthai* of the heavenly habitation.

In other words, *toutōi* could refer to the issue that the present existence is being destroyed (2Cor 5:1). Since a verb has no gender, it is proper to use *toutōi* in neuter to refer to the antecedent. The verb *katalyō* speaks

---

26. The pronoun *toutōi* is also used to refer to the subject that is discussed without specifying a noun, but referring to the verb. See for instance John 4:37; Phil 1:18, 1 John 2:3 Rom 4:18, etc. See the discussion on *ependyō* in p. 86.

The Naked State of Human Being

about the destruction of the existence, which can be compared to becoming naked. That is what Paul wants to avoid. Then, the images of transformation in 5:2–4 entail another possibility that does not include the destruction of the house of tent, and the resulting emptiness of existence or nakedness. The object of Paul's desire is to avoid that state of nakedness.[27]

Paul had already begun to experience the destruction of his life (4:16). He is living the process of being destroyed, and in that condition he longs to be rather clothed over, without being stripped. In this sense, the reference to verbs with the use of *toutōi* includes also the image of *skēnous*, which speaks of a temporal house; but the emphasis is in the process of change. The expression *kai en toutōi*, "for *also* in this," can refer then, at the same time, to the "destruction" (*katalyō*) mentioned in 5:1 and the "clothing over" (*ependuomai*) that follows. This shift from the experience of resurrection to the experience of transformation is the groaning desire of Paul. At the same time, if *toutōi* refers to the earthly human condition, *skēnous*, the sense does not change. In this condition he groans, desiring to avoid nakedness and preferring instead to be clothed over.

A comparison between 1 Cor 15:35–55 and 2 Cor 4:7–5:10 will show the contrast between temporal and eternal natures, and the context of physical natures and eschatological change.[28] Figure 9 puts together the images of the natures of the human body before and after the change in both passages. The similarities in language and sense anticipate similarities in anthropological conclusions; the natures before and after the change can be compared through the two passages.

The passage of 1 Corinthians 15:35 introduces clearly the issue of the discussion: "What kind of body" will the resurrected believers have? 2 Cor 4:7 shares the same concern—the nature of the earthly vessel. Resurrection is mentioned in 2 Cor 4:14 with the emphasis on παραστήσει, "cause to be present." The term conveys the sense of putting someone, or something, at someone's disposal. The idea of physical presence is intrinsic in the term.

---

27. Figure 11 on p. 114 summarizes graphically how this new process avoids nakedness by the use of the terms that express states and processes. I prefer to put it there because it is more relevant after the consideration of *gymnos*.

28. Gillman points out the images used in this passage as clues to compare it with 2 Cor 5. Gillman, "Thematic Comparison," 439–54.

Gymnos in 2 Corinthians 5:3

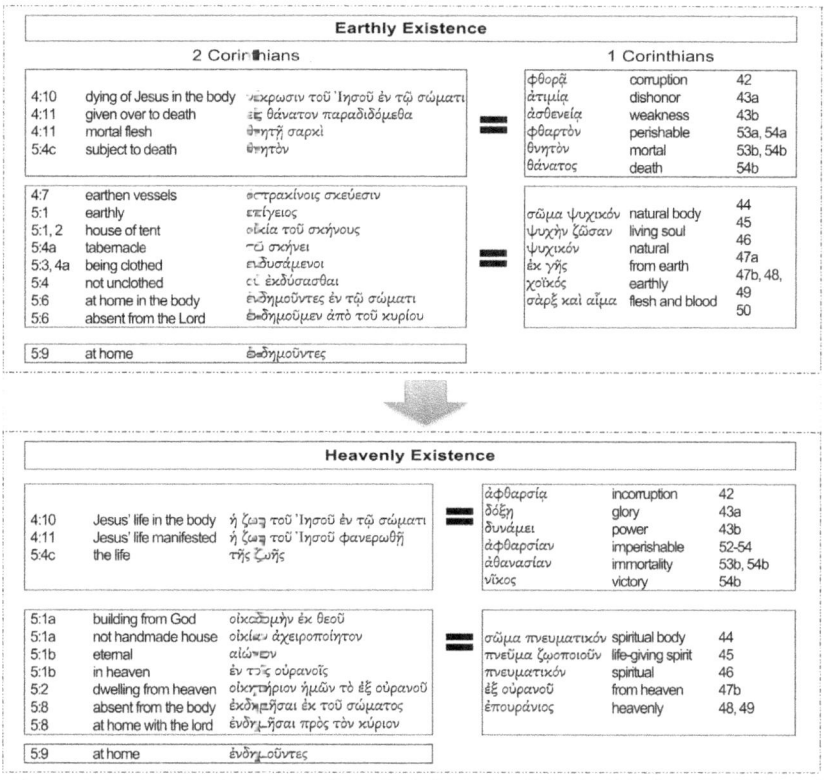

Figure 9. Comparison of existences in 1 Corinthians 15 and 2 Corinthians 4–5.

In addition to resurrection, Paul also introduces the process of transformation in 1 Cor 15:51–54. He focuses also on that process in 2 Cor 5:2–4. Therefore, the images in both passages, 1 Cor 15:35–55 and 2 Cor 4:7–5:10 show strong similarities.

In Figure 9, on the side of 2 Corinthians, a number of terms are used to describe earthly, temporal existence as well as death. The word *thnēton*, "mortal" in 5:4c, also used in 1 Cor 15:53, 54, is semantically related to *phthorai* and *phtharton* (1 Cor 15:53, 54). *Thanatos* (1 Cor 15:54, 55, 56) marks the end of earthly existence and emphasizes the anthropological sense of other terms used. *Thanatos* is also used in 2 Cor 4:11, 12 and is semantically related with *nekrōsin* in 2 Cor 4:12, which is here used in relation to Jesus. This last use, the semantic relationship of the different terms, and the inclusion of Jesus in the list, makes it impossible to relate these terms to sinful nature and see them purely soteriologically. They refer

The Naked State of Human Being

instead to the physical mortal body. The second list of terms in Figure 9, under Earthly Existence, refers to the natural realm of this earth.

The expression *ek gēs* in 1 Cor 15:47 shares a similar meaning with *epigeios* in 2 Cor 5:1,[29] and semantically also with *choikos* in 1 Cor 15:47, 48, 49. They are also related with *psychikon* and *psychēn zōsan* (in the same part of Figure 9) reminding of the context of Adam, who came from the earth. In the creation account he is referred to as *psychēn zōsan*. 2 Corinthians uses the image of a house to speak of these characteristics. To be "clothed" with that house is to have an earthly existence, and hence, be "at home in the body" (2 Cor 5:6). The word *sōma* is also used in both passages (2 Cor 4:10 c.f 1 Cor 15:44). The last image in this series summarizes the meaning of these images; to have an earthly existence is to be *endēmountes*, "present," or "at home," to exist (2 Cor 5:9).

The second part of Figure 9 notes the images related to the heavenly existence. On the side of 2 Corinthians, the expression *oikodomēn ek theou*, and *oikian acheiropoiēton aiōnion en tois ouranois* speak clearly about the heavenly realm. The first list in each passage is related to each other through the concept of life. The second list in each passage refers to the heavenly existence. As was the case with the earthly existence, the summary of the characteristics of the heavenly existence is also represented by the same term *endēmountes*, "at home" (at the bottom of Figure 9). Although I will consider this term in more detail later, here I can propose that for Paul to have a body, either earthly or heavenly, means to exist. A lack of body means to be absent, which is the opposite of life.

This comparison shows that in this specific context, the earthly tent is referring to the present, literal, and earthly human body. The eternal building from God in heaven refers to the eternal body of the changed saints. The strong link between the earthly and heavenly existences with the body and its characteristics is evidence that a change of existence has to be made through a change of body.

---

29. The term *epigeios* comes from ἐπί (from) + γῆς (earth), which literally means: *On, from* or *of the earth*. See Liddell, LSJ, s.v. "ἐπίγειος," and Zodhiates, s.v. "ἐπίγειος," as examples. Perhaps Paul uses ἐκ γῆς in 1 Cor 15 47 to emphasize its origin (see Acts 7:4, 40, Heb 8:9 and Jude1:5 as examples of the use of this construction).

Syntactical relations.

Elements of 2 Cor 5:1–4 allow taking this portion of the pericope as a literary unit.[30] This unit uses parallelism to show two different natures or states divided by the process of being clothed-over. In the parallelism the image of nakedness stands as an undesirable condition that does not represent any nature or existence.

The literary unity of 2 Cor 5:1–4 can be seen by the use of the Greek conjunction δὲ at the beginning of 5:5 and the language of the unit. The conjunction *de* breaks the flow and language started in 5:1. Then, 5:5, though following the thematic of the pericope and being part of it, starts another unit emphasizing the implications of living by faith. Logically and thematically speaking, the flow of Paul's thought is not affected if the reader skips 5:1–4.

The statement in 2 Cor 5:1 works as an introduction statement for the topic of verses 2–4, while at the same time explains the previous context in 4:6, 17. It presents another aspect of the holder of the message (4:7), the relation of the earthly vessel to the heavenly one to be received according to what "we know" (5:1). Thus, the language and use of the conjunction *gar* at the beginning of 5:1 and again at 5:5 makes 5:1–4 a literary unit in itself[31] within the larger unit of the pericope. Figure 10 shows the three syntactical constructions (sentences) that constitute this small literary unit.

The first construction (I) introduces the issue to be tackled. Paul uses a parallelism marked by both the repetition of the leading verb *stenazomen*, "we groan," in the following two syntactical constructions (II and III), and the verb *ependysasthai* also in II and III. The introductory statement construction I puts the temporal house (*oikia tou skēnous*) as the initial condition before the eternal building (*oikodomēn aiōnion*). There, the expression *ean hē epigeios hēmōn oikia tou skēnous katalythēi*, "if our temporal earthly house is destroyed"[32] works as a protasis or condition, and the rest of the

---

30. Some commentators see the same limits of this unit. See Johnson, *The People's New Testament*, 143; and Patterson, *The Woman's Study Bible*, s.v. "2 Cor5:1." Some other commentators include verse 5 in the unit, such as Kistemaker, *Second Corinthians*, NTC, 176; Plummer, *Exegetical Commentary*, 140; and Belleville, *2 Corinthians*, s.v. "2 Cor 5:1"; among others; however these commentators give no specific reasons for the division.

31. I use *literary unit* in order to differentiate it from the whole pericope (4:7–5:10) but recognizing the independent nature of this small pericope in terms of thought and syntax.

32. This is my translation. The genitive τοῦ σκήνους seems to work as a description of the house which is the nominative, and the implication is temporariness in contrast

verse as the apodosis or result, which is explained in constructions I–II in Figure 10. Thus, the elements of the conditional sentence are (a) if the earthly tent is torn down, (b) then, we have an eternal house in heaven.

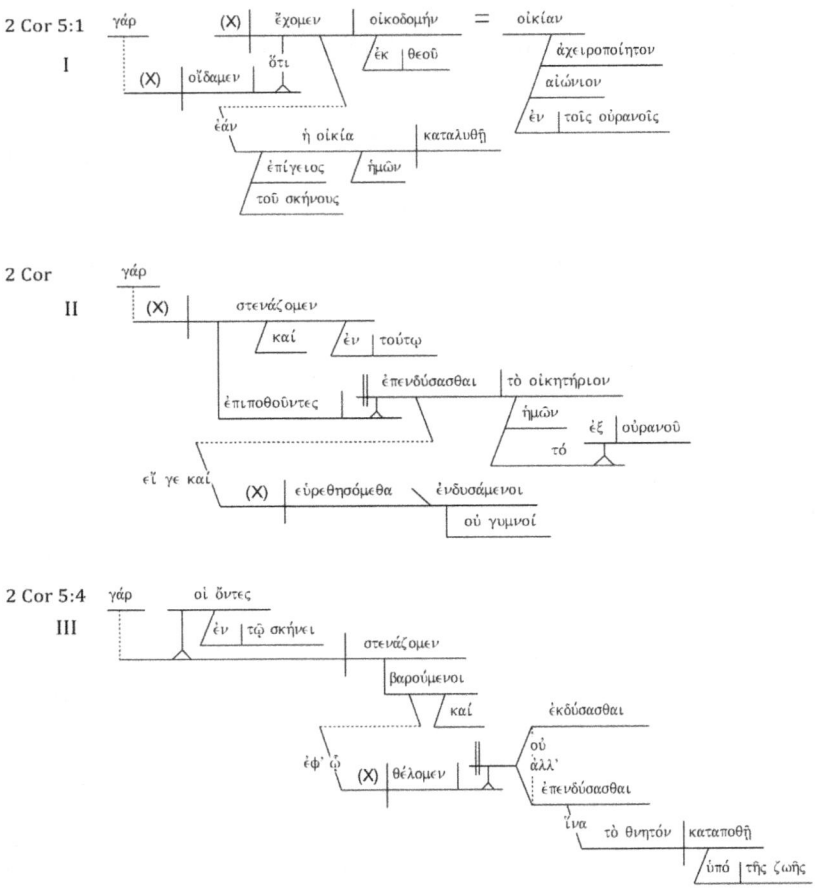

Figure 10. Syntactical diagram of 2 Corinthians 5:1–4.[33]

This conditional result comes after the previous state and not at the same time. The tense of the verb *echomen*, "we have," in the syntax responds not only to the parallelism, but also to the conditional. If it so happens that

with αἰώνιον, which modifies the house not made with hands (οἰκίαν ἀχειροποίητον) in heaven (ἐν τοῖς οὐρανοῖς) in the same verse.

33. This diagram is adapted from Leedy, *BibleWorks New Testament Greek Sentence Diagrams*.

this tent is destroyed, then, *echomen* a building. This is a futuristic present that puts the stress of the verb in a future time, when the conditions are fulfilled. The intention, however, is not to set a chronological immediateness between the two states, but to emphasize the certainty of that building.[34] In this regard, H. A. Kennedy says that, "There is no reference here to the detail of time . . . the *echomen* ('we have') is simply equivalent to 'there awaits us as a sure possession,'"[35] after the first is destroyed.

The two conditions can be seen also in constructions II and III, and there they are separated by *ependysasthai*. The verb *stenazomen* is modified by the participles *epipothountes*, "to long for," in II and *baroumenoi*, "to burden," in III. In III, the verb *thelomen*, "to desire," parallels also *epipothountes*. It shows that the reason of this groaning in both sentences (II and III) is the desire to be clothed-over with a building from heaven (*to oikētērion hēmōn to ex ouranou*) in the first case (II) and from life (*tēs zōēs*) in the second case (III). This construction parallels the "building from heaven" with "the life." They become synonymous here as the object of the *ependysasthai*. At the same time, the diagram (Figure 10) shows what the result of *ependysasthai* is.

The condition or state before *ependysasthai* in III is to be in the temporal house (*en tōi skēnei*). The temporal habitation parallels mortal life (*to thnēton*), since the word *skēnous* in I is linked with *skēnei* in III. In construction II a conditional sentence points to the previous state or condition as well. This condition is to be clothed (*endysamenoi*), not naked (*ou gymnoi*). Then, to be clothed on or in addition (*ependysasthai*, "clothed-over") can take place. The expression being clothed parallels not naked as synonymous.

In construction III, the explanation of purpose (*ina*) for *ependysasthai* is that the mortal may be absorbed (swallowed up) by life. Comparing this statement with II, where the habitation from heaven uses *ependysasthai* as the process through which to substitute the temporal habitation, the conclusion is that mortal and life are also two physical experiences or existences, one before *ependysasthai* and the other after. Therefore, the habitations mentioned in this text are not literal houses, but physical existences. They refer to the condition of the earthly vessel and the eschatological hope of better existence.

---

34. Wallace, *Grammar*, 535, 536. See also Kistemaker, *Second Corinthians*, NTC, 168, where the futuristic present is the explanation of *echomen* in 2 Cor 5:1.

35. Kennedy, *St Paul's Conceptions of the Last Things*, 265.

The Naked State of Human Being

Paul also introduces in construction III two contrasting options by the use of οὐ, "not," and *alla*, "but." These two options have the same previous state, that of being in the temporal house. While in their earthly nature, Paul and the believers can be unclothed (*ekdysasthai*) or clothed-over (*ependysasthai*). Both verbs are in infinitive middle form. If the second is a process, the first is a process as well. Of these two, Paul groans desiring not to experience the first, but the second. The implication is that Paul wants to avoid the process of being unclothed (*ekdysasthai*).

This desire corresponds to what is expressed in the parallel construction II. There, in order to experience *ependysasthai* Paul has to be found clothed (*endysamenoi*), which is synonymous of *ou gymnoi* and corresponds to *ou ekdysasthay* in III. What Paul wants to avoid is nakedness. Therefore, the process of being clothed-over produces buildings from heaven, eternal and not made with hands. By contrast, the process of unclothing produces no buildings or tents, but a void, nakedness. This nakedness cannot be another state or existence since it lacks any tent or building.

The Process of Change

As shown in chapter 2, 2 Cor 4:7—5:10 explains that what happens to the earthly vessel[36] through tribulations and the possibility of being destroyed is irrelevant to the message it carries. Moreover, the change of the earthly body into a heavenly one points to the believers's hope beyond this earth and the present existence. It could happen after the body is totally destroyed, through resurrection, or before the destruction of the body, by being clothed over the present nature without being unclothed. This hope surpasses the physical present mortality and makes it irrelevant.

These two possibilities are introduced by a conditional sentence in 2 Cor 5:1 and presented through two devices. The first is the structure of the pericope, which compared to 1 Cor 15:35—55 shows the same pattern and presents the same possibilities. The second is the use of the verb *egeirō* for resurrection, the first possibility, and the verb *ependuomai*, which is used only here in the Bible. It is a compound of the verb *endyō* (used in 1 Cor 15:53, 54) for transformation, and the preposition επι. The word *ependuomai* represents well the possibility of transformation in case the present body is not destroyed, as will be shown here.

---

36. Bruce emphasizes the appropriateness of the image comparing it to the lamps the Corinthians could buy at the market. Bruce, *1 and 2 Corinthians*, 197.

The conditional sentence in 2 Cor 5:1 marked with *ean* in construction I in Figure 10 shows two processes. The protasis, "if the earthly tent which is our house is torn down," is not necessarily the only condition since it has the sense of contingency.[37] In other words, the destruction of the house or tent (5:1) is a possibility, but not the only one; the other possibility is that the house of tent is not destroyed. The verb *katalythēi* seems to be the culmination of the previous issue, the decaying of the body represented by the verb *diaphtheiretai*, "to destroy," in 2 Cor 4:16. The solution to the problem of the destruction of the body in the previous section (4:8–16) is the resurrection (4:14). Now in 5:1–4 he alludes to the same argument in the protasis of the conditional sentence but infers another possibility, namely, that the body may not be destroyed.

Paul uses the argument of faith for the presentation of these possibilities, the change after the destruction of the body and the change without any destruction. Unlike Paul and others,[38] the Corinthian readers were not eyewitnesses of the resurrection of Jesus; that is why the hope of resurrection is based on faith. Thus an expression of faith works as a link between the sections in Paul's presentation, forming a structure as follows:

Presentation of the argument	4:7–12
<u>Expression of faith</u>	4:13
Possibility 1, resurrection	4:14
<u>Expression of Faith</u>	4:15–18[39]

---

37. Regarding this sense of contingence in conditional sentences of 3rd class see Wallace, *Grammar*, 313.

38. 1 Cor 15:8; Acts 20:24; 1 Cor 11:23; Gal 1:12; 2 Cor 12:1–4; cf. 1 Cor 15:5–7. These texts show the experience of meeting the Lord personally after his transformation through resurrection.

39. As a clarifying note, the expression *our outer man* (ὁ ἔξω ἡμῶν ἄνθρωπος) in 4:16 contrasts with *our inner (man)* (ὁ ἔσω ἡμῶν). These expressions are related with the immediate context related to *do not lose heart* (οὐκ ἐγκακοῦμεν) and *day by day* (ἡμέρᾳ καὶ ἡμέρᾳ). They are syntactically related with *momentary troubles* (τὸ παραυτίκα ἐλαφρὸν τῆς θλίψεως ἡμῶν) in 17 and also with *temporal* and *eternal* (πρόσκαιρα/αἰώνια) in 18. This focus of the argument is an emotional appeal explaining ἐγκακοῦμεν. Therefore these images of inner and outer man are not considered as images of the nature of the body but as part of the expression of faith, and they do not appear in figure 8 we saw already. On the other hand, linked to the expressions of faith, they represent the basis for a secondary reading of the text, a soteriological one, where the life of Christ works for good before the eschatological Parousia. This secondary focus does not explain all the implications of the argument and the context, and remains a secondary emphasis.

Possibility 2, transformation	5:1–4
Expression of faith	5:5–8
Conclusion of the argument	5:9, 10

There is a similar pattern in 1 Cor 15:35–58; however, the link phrases between possibilities are different due to the difference of the argument in the broad context, which was the defense of the truth of the resurrection. The transitional thought there is that a change from one existence to another is necessary to enter into the heavenly realm (36 and 45–50).[40] That change could be either by resurrection (37–44) or by transformation (51–54).

Presentation of the argument	15:35
Transitional thought	15:36–41
Possibility 1, resurrection	15:42–44
Transitional thought	15:45–50
Possibility 2, transformation	15:51–54
Transitional thought	15:55–57
Conclusion of the argument	15:58

Therefore, both 1 Cor 15:35–58 and 2 Cor 4:7–5:10 speak about the change from the earthly and physical body and existence into a heavenly and spiritual body and existence. A change is necessary to enter into the realm of God in heaven. Also both passages present the same two possibilities for such a change: resurrection or transformation.

In 2 Cor 4:7–5:10 the first possibility is presented in 4:7–18. It argues that even though this present physical condition is not good (4:8–11), that situation is irrelevant because believers will be resurrected as Jesus was (4:14). Tribulations suffered by love (4:15) produce a renewed interior man (4:16) and an eternal weight of glory (4:17) because of that hope and not because of the tribulation itself. Paul contrasts death with life (4:10, 11) before introducing resurrection.

---

40. The transitional thoughts also have practical implications. A Pauline distinctive characteristic is to alternate practical issues with theological ones. In 2 Cor 4:7–5:10 he alternates between anthropological and soteriological issues related to faith and judgment, and their practical implications. Note for example the similitude of the conclusions, both 1 Cor 15:58 and 2 Cor 5:9, 10 regarding practical Christian life. This secondary (and parallel) focus does not demerit the first one, the nature of existences, but complements it.

The point is that resurrection takes place from death, as *egeirō* suggests. Paul uses the term *egeirō* thirty-five times in his writings, of which thirty-two clearly refer to resurrection from death and only three may refer to something else.[41] In the near context, 2 Cor 1:9 uses the expression *tōi egeironti tous nekrous* (raises the dead), clearly referring to resurrection from death in the same sense as it is used in 5:15 and is contrasted with *apothanonti*. Moreover, in the parallel passage of 1 Cor 15:13, *egeirō* parallels *anastasis nekrōn*, which clearly means resurrection from death; and in 15:20, 35 *egeirō* is directly linked with *nekrōn*. The conclusion is that *egeirō* here means a literal resurrection from death. This is a process to change the earthly body into a heavenly one in order to be present with the living ones and with the Lord (1 Cor 4:14) since perishable nature, flesh and blood, cannot inherit the kingdom of God (15:50).

In the second section (5:1–4) Paul introduces another possibility of the process to change the earthly existence to one besides resurrection. He uses the image of being clothed-over (*ependuomai* 5:2, 4) and parallels this image with death being swallowed up (*katapothēi* 5:4). In this sense, to be clothed-over is a process that "swallows" the first cloth. The first cloth is no longer there after being clothed over. Paul includes this image represented by *katapothēi* (5:4) in order to avoid the idea of having both natures at the same time, as this could be inferred if only *ependuomai* was used. According to 5:6, 8, to be at home in the body means to be absent from the Lord and vice versa. This is a change from one state to another.

The structure of the passages shows that Paul uses the same logic in both 1 Cor 15:35–55 and 2 Cor 4:7–5:10. In his first letter he starts from a common belief, which is resurrection, and continues with the exposition of the one that is a mystery (15:51): transformation without sleeping. If Paul follows in 2 Corinthians the same logic, it is easy to assume that in 2 Cor 5:1–10 Paul will continue with the transformation possibility after speaking about resurrection. Notice that, after the mention of the first possibility, the body is destroyed in the introductory statement in 5:1—there is no more mention of resurrection or death from 5:2–10—and yet there is a shift of nature between the earthly, temporal state into the heavenly, eternal one.

---

41. Rom 13:11 refers to spiritual sleep and there is no clue to link it to resurrection. Eph 5:14 also may refer to a spiritual lethargy and, although it parallels death in the same verse, this death also seems to be a spiritual rather than a physical one. The last is 1 Cor 6:14 which may be relevant, since καταργήσει in 6:13 referring to stomach and food may point to resurrection in light of the use of ἐγείρω in 14.

Paul then introduces the term *ependysasthai*, which appears only twice in the whole Bible, both in this passage (5:2, 4). The question is why does Paul use *ependyō* rather than *endyō* which he used already in 1 Cor 15:53, 54 on the same topic?[42]

The particle *ep* (ἐπ) is the contraction of the preposition *epi* (ἐπὶ), which means "over" or "upon." The morphological meaning would be clothed over or to put on in addition.[43] Bauer defines this word as "to put a garment on over an existing garment, put on (in addition)."[44] Gingrich also adds, to put on the note "in addition."[45] Thayer defines it as "to put on over."[46] And Liddell and Scott define it as "to put on one garment over another."[47] This understanding of the term agrees with secular writers who use this term with the same meaning.[48]

The fact that Paul desires to be clothed without being unclothed or naked (5:2, 4) emphasizes the meaning of putting on a cloth without taking off the previous one. The syntactical structure in 5:4[49] also shows that *ependysasthai* does not include *ekdysasthai* (being unclothed). Thus, it is possible to understand the term as the process of being clothed by putting on something over a previous cloth and without being unclothed.

The concept of being over-clothed includes (or brings to result) the expression "that which is mortal being swallowed by life" in 5:4. The first use of *ependysasthai* in 5:2 is linked with the condition after the process: the house from heaven (*to oikētērion hēmōn to ex ouranou*). The second use (5:4) mentions the condition before the process: this tent (*tōi skēnei*). The expression *hina katapothēi* (in order that may be swallowed, 5:4) then summarizes the purpose of the process by using both the condition before

---

42. According to Harris, it has become almost traditional to hold that ενδύω is used in 1 Cor 15 for resurrection whereas *ependyō* in 2 Cor 5 for transformation, though he is not in agreement with that view. See Harris, "Watershed," 43.

43. This additional weight of the meaning of ἐπὶ joined to a word could be seen in many other words. For instance, ἔρχομαι means "to come" but ἐπέρχομαι "to come upon"; αὔριον means "tomorrow" and ἐπαύριον "on tomorrow or on the next day."

44. Bauer, BDAG, s.v. "ἐπενδύομαι."

45. Gingrich, *Lexicon*, s.v. "ἐπενδύομαι."

46. Thayer, s.v. "ἐπενδύω."

47. Liddell, LSJ, s.v. "ἐπενδύω."

48 "καὶ ἐπὶ τοῦτον ἄλλον εἰρίνεον κιθῶνα ἐπενδύνει," Herodotus, *The Histories* 1.195.1; "καὶ σάκκους ἐπενδύντες ταῖς στολαῖς," Josephus, *Antiquitates Judaicae* 5.1.12; and "ἐπενδυσάμενος δ' ἐξ ὑακίνθου πεποιημένον χιτῶνα," Josephus, *Antiquitates* 3.7.4.

49. See syntactical construction III in Figure 10 on p. 128.

the change, "subject to death" (*to thnēton*), and the condition after, "life" (*tēs zōēs*). The conjunction *hina* embraces both (a) the process of unclothing in order to be changed and (b) the process of clothing-over in order to be changed (2:4).

The condition before the change and the condition after the change can be compared to those used in 1 Cor 15:54: "death" (*thanatos*) and "victory" (*nikos*). The context in 1 Cor 15 emphasizes the existential shift as a flash process without the state of death (1 Cor 15:52). *Katepothē*, "swallowed up," in 1 Cor 15:54 embraces both processes, including *endyō* in 1 Cor 15:53, 54.

In comparison to 2 Cor 5:4, the new word *ependyō* represents better this concept of transformation without becoming naked, and distinguishes it from resurrection. If to be clothed means either an earthly or heavenly existence, this process of *ependyō*, through which one existence takes over the other, comes without experiencing nakedness—the emptiness of existence—which death is.[50] The groan (*stenazō*) of Paul is to avoid death (5:2, 4) by being alive at the Parousia in order to experience the transformation. Paul groans for that because, by that time, the possibility of being alive at the Parousia was becoming blurry. In 2 Cor 1:8, 9 he says that "he despaired even of life" due to a sentence of death, and he put his trust in the resurrection. Then in 4:14 he places himself among the resurrected ones, contrary to 1 Thess 4:15 where he places himself among the living ones.

Naked State

The image of *gymnos* deserves special treatment. Why does Paul use this image even when he uses houses instead of clothes in his metaphor? Here a brief study of the image of *gymnos* helps to understand what the meaning of naked is in this passage, and to define if Paul has a specific background in mind when he uses this term in relation to the strong desire to avoid it. Then, a review of the literary context reveals that nakedness is, contrary to what a dualist reading expects, a very appropriate term to speak of monism and to infer a continuity of identity.

---

50. I elaborate this concept in the next section.

Uses of the Term

The clear physical and literal meaning of *gymnos* is "naked," meaning to be uncovered and without clothes.[51] Nevertheless, there are some facts to be considered here in order to move towards a specific meaning in this specific context. The way the OT presents the image of nakedness could explain its use in 2 Cor 5:3 in contrast with the sense in the extra biblical references which denotes a desirable state. In this section I will consider some of these OT uses of the image.

Before going to the OT, it is valuable to look at some extra biblical texts which many commentators use to interpret 2 Cor 5:3. Plato in his dialogue between Socrates and Hermogenes speaks about the naked soul going to the god of the underworld, where souls were believed to go and be judged.[52] Likewise, Philo describes the death of Moses saying that he felt "a separation of the different parts of which he was composed, namely of his body, which was now removed from him like a shell from a fish, from his soul which was thus laid bare and naked."[53] Here nakedness is a conscious state of the soul without the body. For Plato, this state is not terrifying, but a desirable state of virtue and purity.[54] This is a common thought in Greco-Roman thinking. In this context the naked state of the soul is desirable,[55] being freed of the evil body at the moment of death.

It seems that even in daily life, speaking about literal nakedness, this state was not avoidable, but highlighted. In some forums, like athletics, nakedness was acceptable.[56] Representations of naked bodies can be found in Greco-Roman archaeology and art. John Mouratidis even suggests that, "This type of nudity in Greek art shows that the early Greeks believed that there was in nudity something heroic and sacred."[57] Michael Wilson says that, "To the Greco-Roman mind, nakedness was an indication of nobility and intellectual superiority. Nakedness also indicated spiritual refinement."[58]

---

51. Bauer, BDAG, s.v. " γυμνός."

52. Plato, *Cratylus*, 403B; Plato, *Gorgias*, 523E–24D.

53. Philo, *Virtues*, 1.76. There are many other examples from Philo with this sense of nakedness. See also for instance Philo, *Legum Allegoriarum*, 2.22, 57, 59.

54. Plato, *Cratylus*, 403B–404A.

55. Plato, *Phaedo*, 67 DE.

56. Satlow, "Jewish Constructions of Nakedness in Late Antiquity," 451–53.

57. Mouratidis, "The Origin of Nudity in Greek Athletics," 221.

58. Wilson, "Nakedness, Bodylines and the New Creation," 44. He refers even to

On the contrary, for Jews in general, and especially in the OT, nakedness has an undesirable connotation.[59] Paul, contrary to the Greek outlook, groans to avoid it. Nonetheless, although in Jewish and gentile culture perceptions of death were different, the use of *gymnos* to allude to death was common. There was perceived to be some kind of relation between death and nakedness. Moving on, below we will look at some OT references to nakedness that can serve as an alternative background for the use of Paul in 2 Cor 5:3.

Exposedness.

In a Hebrew setting, nakedness can denote clearness, openness, or exposedness. That is the sense of Job 26:6: "Naked is Sheol before Him and Abaddon has no covering." It could be argued that 2 Cor 5:3 could be understood in a similar way since people's deeds will be exposed at the moment the judgment referred to in verse 10. Indeed, Paul uses naked also in Heb 4:13 to refer to the exposedness of these deeds.

Nevertheless the specific context of 2 Cor 5:3, its syntactical relation to 5:2, 4, and the strong anthropological language, do not fit with this sense for the word. There is no syntactical relationship between the nakedness in verse 3 and the judgment in verse 10 to link them. Moreover, while Paul desired to avoid nakedness, there was no question of avoiding the judgment, since for Paul everyone (*pantas*) will appear "before the judgment seat of Christ" (5:10)—a phrase which implies judgment. Furthermore, Paul was not afraid of being exposed in the judgment. The exposition of his life would help his case. Therefore, if the meaning of nakedness was exposure, he would not groan, desiring to avoid it.

Shame.

One of the most important inferences with the sense of shame in the OT is the experience of Adam and Eve in Eden. Initially they were not ashamed, despite the fact that they were naked (Gen 2:25). Shame was the result of their disobedience (Gen 3:7; 3:10, 11) and the entrance of sin. Nakedness

---

mixed baths in the first century.

59. Bonfante, "Nudity as a Costume in Classical Art," 543–70, esp. 563 (cf. 562) and Smith, "The Garments of Shame," 217–38, esp. 220. Also compare them with Plato, *Cratyl*, 403B.

caused them to hide in order to avoid being found naked in the presence of the Lord. Nakedness became a shame state and a symbol of an undesirable condition.[60] God then clothed them with permanent clothes instead of the temporal ones of fig leaves that they put together. Nakedness in this example brings shame because it is related to sin. It reveals disobedience.

Shame has to do more with the kind of robes they had than with the lack of them. Adam and Eve were not naked when they were hidden. But the robes were not adequate. Unlike what Paul expects in 2 Cor 5:4, Adam and Eve were not clothed over the fig leaves, but they had to take them off to put on the clothes provided by God. Moreover, as has been shown already, the anthropological context of 2 Cor 5:3 makes it hard to take the sense of shame as the reason for Paul's desire to avoid nakedness.

Death.

Another option to consider is the sense of death that nakedness has. In the case of Adam and Eve, God indicated that eating the forbidden fruit would produce death, but the immediate consequence after eating was nakedness. Nakedness then could be understood as a symbol of death that was eventually to come. But there are no other OT references that support this connection between death and nakedness; the concept is more prominent in a secular context; however, this link with death depends not only on a direct connection, but also on nakedness as emptiness or lack of something. When related to life, the emptiness of nakedness could relate to the loss of life, as I will endeavor to demonstrate in the following paragraphs.

Emptiness.

The term *gymnos* can allude to the literal condition of nakedness at the moment of death. In Job 1:21 and Eccl 5:14 (5:15 in English translations) nakedness refers to emptiness and lack of clothes, pointing out the condition at the moment of birth and comparing it to the moment of death. Everyone goes naked to death. Perhaps the reference here is not only to lack of clothes, but also possessions.[61]

60. See Ezek 16:7, 22; 16:39; 23:29 or Isa 20:2–4. The LXX sometimes uses αἰσχύνη, "shame," (eg 1 Sam 20:3; Isa 20:4) or ἀσχημοσύνη, "shameless deed," (eg Lam 1:8; Ezek 16:8) as translations of the Hebrew ʿerwāh that literally means "nakedness."

61. C.f. Job 22:6–10; 31:19–20; Eccl 5:15; Hos 2:5 (2:3 in English translations);

The term can also be used to express a state of lack of protection,[62] covering,[63] pride or dignity,[64] or even with the sense of being unarmed.[65] As such, the sense of *gymnos* signifies the lack of something. Following this idea, the specific meaning of *gymnos* in each context depends on what is lacking in that specific context.

When the context is a specific kind of existence, like in 2 Cor 4:7–5:10, *gymnos* signifies a lack of that existence. Thus, in 5:3 it means a lack of house that has to be worn either earthly or heavenly. The concern about the body and earthly existence in the pericope, the sufferings of the body and the mention of mortality (5:4), invites us to take *gymnos* as lack of life, which means death. This seems to be a better option than any of the others that have been suggested. Moreover, we have shown in chapter 2 that for Paul, existence (life) is necessarily linked to a body. A lack of a body would then mean a lack of life and thus, death.

This meaning of *gymnos* in relation to physical bodies and existence, points to the interpretation of death as the complete cessation of life, the dissolution of the whole person in a monist-mortalistic point of view. This cessation of life is common to all forms of living beings, human or animal,[66] and is valid regardless of whether a person was righteous or wicked. Paul explains in 1 Cor 15:16–18 that the condition at death is the same for those who sleep in Christ as it is for others. The difference is not their condition at death, but the faith in Jesus they had while still in this life, which in turn will give eternal life to those who believe. Even resurrection is the same for all humans according to 2 Cor 5:10. Everyone will rise and will receive the reward according to what they did while in life, either good or evil. For Paul, what makes the difference between those who believe and those who do not is what happens at resurrection, the change from mortal or perishable into immortal or heavenly, not what happens at death. Thus, *gymnos* fits with the monist-mortalist view of death.[67]

Amos 4:3 (absent in the MT); Mic 1:8; Isa 58:7; Ezek 18:7, 16. Compare with Matt 25:36, 38, 43, 44 and James 2:5.

62. Job 24:7 cf Rev 7:16.

63. Job 26:6; and 31:19–20, compare with Heb 4:13.

64. 1 Sam 9:24; Isa 20:2–5; 32:11; Ezek 16:7, 22, 39.

65. Amos 2:16 cf. Josephus, *Ant* 6:286, and 2 Macc 4:12, 13.

66. See Ps 104:29, 30 regarding death in animal existence and compare with Ps 146:4 and Eccl 12:7 regarding human existence. See also Eccl 3:19–21 showing the equivalence in human and animal death.

67. This is true especially when *gymnos* is compared to *koimaō*, as sleep is comparable

Even though the hope in the resurrection changes the final fate of those who sleep in Christ, the possibility of being transformed without experiencing a temporal cessation of existence is preferable over resurrection. Nakedness has then the intrinsic Hebrew sense of an undesirable condition. This use of *gymnos* agrees with the highlighted groan of Paul not to be found naked. We will gain further clarity if we look at this image of nakedness in the specific context it appears in the Corinthian correspondence.

Gymnos in Its Literary Context

A close view of *gymnos* in its own literary context helps to confirm its meaning. Three main arguments will show that *gymnos* means a lack of tent or building, meaning lack of life, and therefore nonexistence. These arguments are (a) the use of the conditional sentence in the syntax flow; (b) a literary comparison with 1 Cor 15:37; and (3) the present-absent argument of Paul.

The use of the conditional sentence.

Second Corinthians 5:2–4 could be divided into three syntactical constructions or sentences, as can be seen in the syntactical diagram in Figure 10 on page 128.[68] There, construction II follows (*kai gar*) the argument from construction I (5:1) about two houses. The verb στενάζομεν is linked with ἐπενδύσασθαι by the verb ἐπιποθοῦντες. The two instances of στενάζομεν, in construction III and construction II, are parallels. Construction III retakes the argument from construction II. Thus, the conditional clause (5:3) in construction II works as an explanatory parenthesis regarding ἐπενδύσασθαι in clause II and, by extension, in clause III. In other words, 2 Cor 5:3 is a parenthetical explanation of what it means to be clothed-over.

The marks of the conditional sentence, which are the particles εἴ γε καὶ, show a first class conditionional sentence[69] that assumes truth for the sake of the argument. The same particles are used by Paul in Gal 3:4, Eph

---

with the cessation of life or emptiness of existence. See the section "*Gymnos* and *Koimaō*" on p. 153.

68. I will not transliterate the Greek Words here so the reader can compare them with the words in Figure 10.

69. First class conditionals use the particle εἴ with the indicative in any tense (Wallace, *Grammar*, 309), which is the case here, linking εἴ with the verb εὑρεθησόμεθα.

3:2, 4:21 and Col 1:23, always with the same intention. In each case the expression works as a parenthesis meaning, "if really it is true that . . ." arguing by making a contrast to the previous point. The complete formula εἴ γε καὶ is used in Gal 3:4 as a parenthetical expression recognizing two possibilities: having suffered things (a) in vain, or (b) not in vain.

In each case using this combination of particles, the protasis (conditional element) comes after the apodosis (result or consequence). In this specific case, the apodosis is to be clothed-over (ἐπενδύσασθαι) but without being unclothed (ἐκδύσασθα), as he adds in clause III. The condition (protasis), then, is to be found clothed, which means not naked. Despite the desire of Paul, the fact is that he shows here the two possibilities: (a) to be found naked, after being unclothed, and (b) to be found clothed, with the temporal house, which is the apodosis in the conditional. Then, if naked, he will be just clothed with the heavenly dwelling; but if clothed he can be clothed-over, which he rather prefers.

The explanation is in clause III. Paul, repeating the *groan-desire* element, says that if the clothing-over experience comes and he is not unclothed (death), death will be swallowed up by life (ὑπὸ followed by genitive case). Therefore, if to be clothed-over means to be clothed without being unclothed (naked), and if clothed-over means transformation, then nakedness refers to death. This conclusion agrees with the context and the background as was shown. To be clothed means to be alive and to be unclothed or naked means to be dead.

The idea of resurrection, which was the consolation of Paul in 4:14, is presented again in 5:1. God is the one who will raise the dead, but he has to find them dead in order to resurrect them. If they are not dead, then resurrection is not needed, only transformation. *Gymnos* entails the idea of resurrection. Figure 11 summarizes graphically the relationship between clothed, clothed over, and the possibility to be found naked.

A literary comparison with 1 Cor 15:37.

Paul also uses the image of *gymnos* to refer to death in 1 Cor 15:37. It speaks about the state of the grain at the moment it is being sowed. Paul says "You fool! That which you sow does not come to life unless it dies, and that which you sow, you do not sow the body which is to be, but a bare (*gymnon,*) grain, perhaps of wheat or of something else" (15:36, 37).

The Naked State of Human Being

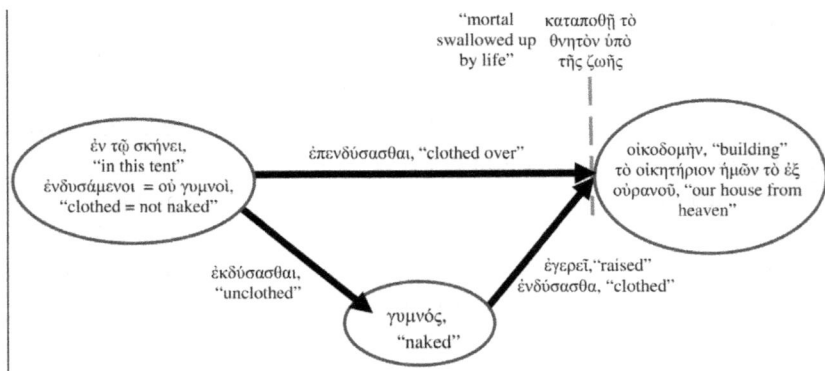

Figure 11. The place of *gymnos* in the process of change.

Paul explains the process of germination of the new plant paralleling *apothanēi*, "to die," with *gymnon*, as he parallels *zōiopoieitai*, "to come to life," with *sōma tò genēsomenon*, "the body which is to be." Figure 12 shows this comparison clearly.

It is easy to notice that the meaning of *gymnos* in this context of 1 Cor 15:37 is also death. Considering the language of Paul, the previous state (before the sowing) could be the same of the state after, at least in the example of grain. So in order to avoid confusion, he adds immediately other examples to express the difference in nature of the body after resurrection. 2 Cor 5:3 has the same context; Paul contrasts the present earthly body under afflictions with the heavenly body after the resurrection. There is another stage between these two stages in case of the first possibility, nakedness, which is introduced in the parenthesis of 5:3 and explained in 5:4. In contrast to resurrection, to be clothed-over skips the state of death (nakedness), if the condition of to be found clothed, but no naked is given (5:3).

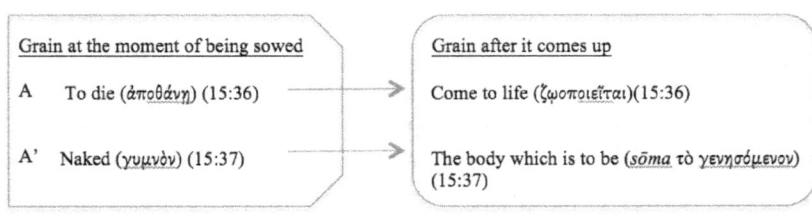

Figure 12. Plant germination image.

114

Gymnos in 2 Corinthians 5:3

The present-absent argument.

Paul reinforces his argument by using the image of being present with the Lord[70] and absent from the body, or present in the body but absent from the Lord. Figure 8 on p. 92 shows how these images are related with others in the same pericope (compare with Figure 9 on p. 97). Being in the earthly tent means to be present in the body but absent from the Lord (5:6); this is the earthly temporal existence.

Here Paul explains that this absence is not spiritual but physical, since Christians do not see the Lord in this present condition and we have to walk by faith and not by sight (5:7). If this allusion referred to the spiritual realm, then we are present with the Lord even if we are in the earthly tent. But the expression infers that the existence after the change means to be physically present with the Lord and absent to the earthly existence.

The words used for being present or absent are verbs etymologically related to the noun *dēmos*, which literally means a "country-district," "country," or "land."[71] It is "related to people of the same homeland."[72] The addition of the prepositions ἐν or ἐκ to form ἔν-δημος or ἐκ-δημος gives the idea of dwelling or staying in one's native place, or being absent from it respectively. These expressions are only used here in the whole Bible. The context is earthly and heavenly habitations. The home-dwelling-place then changes from one to another giving the impossibility to be at the same time in both earthly and heavenly ones. The sense of these terms is nearer to the English word home than to the word house. It represents the idea of belonging to some place.

Here Paul introduces for the first time in the discussion about houses the word *sōma* (2 Cor 5:6). The previous time he uses it is in 4:10 speaking about the physical earthly body and its difficulties, and contrasting it with the life of Christ. Also the contrast between to dwell at home in (*en*) the body in 5:6 and to dwell at home with (*pros*) the Lord in 2 Cor 5:8, identifies the word body as the earthly one. To have an earthly existence is to dwell at home in the body. Body then is the house. On the other hand, to have a heavenly existence is to dwell at home with the Lord.

---

70. The expression Ἐνδημῆσαι πρὸς τὸν κύριον in 5:8 clearly implies spatial proximity to the Lord. See Harris, "Watershed," 46–48.

71. See Liddell, LSJ, s.v. "δῆμος."

72. Bauer, BDAG, s.v. "δῆμος."

The Naked State of Human Being

The expression at home with the Lord does not include any mention of house or body. It only alludes to the heavenly existence. Thus, when in 5:8 Paul prefers to be "absent" (out of the native house) from the body but present with the Lord, he does not mean to be dead, but to be in the heavenly existence, since he would still be "dwelling at home" with the Lord.[73] The expression in 5:6 and 7 is clear, to be at home in the body means at the same time to be absent from the Lord, as to be absent from the body means to be at home with the Lord. To be absent and not at home in the body or not at home with the Lord, means plainly to be absent altogether.

Paul avoids the mention of any kind of house in 5:9 and the reference is only to be either present or absent (*eite endēmountes eite ekdēmountes*). The issue now is not the nature of the house, but if the individual is "at" or "out" of any house either earthly (body) or heavenly (with the Lord). The meaning is none other than being alive in an earthly or heavenly existence or being dead—to be or not to be, to exist or not to exist. Not having a house then, has the same meaning as *gymnos*. This understanding gives death, represented by *gymnos*, the sense of total cessation of existence or life.

The conjunction διό in 5:9 suggests the beginning of the conclusion of the pericope. This fact, plus the lack of a specific nature of presence (earthly or heavenly), could also have some theological implications. They are discussed in Chapter 4.[74]

This present-absent argument suggests also that to be naked means to be not with an earthly body nor with a heavenly body, not in the "earthly tent which is our house," nor in the "house not made with hands, eternal in the heavens" (5:1). Naked is the stage of being completely absent, both to the earthly body and to the Lord. This is the core of the concept of nakedness in its use as emptiness: the meaning of lacking of something—in this case, a lack of existence.

Then, *gymnos* is nonexistence.[75] Following the logic, and in consonance with the context, *gymnos* cannot signify to be in some way at the presence of the Lord, either consciously or unconsciously, because to be at the presence of the Lord is something desirable (5:8), but nakedness is un-

---

73. Paul recognizes (5:9) that even being absent (dead) one can be εὐάρεστοι (acceptable) to the Lord, not because one can do something at death, but because of what one did while alive (5:10).

74. See p. 186.

75. Kistemaker holds that the metaphor of taking down a tent points to the "end of not only our physical body but also our entire earthly existence." See Kistemaker, *Second Corinthians*, NTC, 167.

desirable (5:4). This kind of sense of nakedness agrees more with a Hebrew setting than a Greek setting.

The main point in this literary unit (5:1–4) of the pericope, in contrast to the previous one (4:14–17), is to present the change of the earthly vessel without experiencing death (transformation). In that context the explanation of 5:3 is important in order to link the hope with Paul's desire to skip death, which has been mentioned since 1:10. The complete argument is that due to the hope of the resurrection, death is not the end; it is not something which should cause believers to lose heart (4:16) or which discredits Paul's ministry. Nevertheless, to skip death means to be transformed in a flash, as Paul desires since the previous letter, and this is preferred over resurrection from the dead. It implies that Paul considers the possibility of being alive at the Parousia,[76] although at the moment of writing this letter this possibility seemed not to have been very strong. This is the reason for his groan.

Another implication of this present-absent argument, when the necessity of a body or house either earthly or heavenly is considered, is that a body is needed in order for a person to be alive. To live means to be present either in an earthly or heavenly form. The lack of a body then means also a lack of existence, a state of emptiness. This is precisely what death is in a monist view. Scholars agree that for Paul, resurrection presupposes a body. Christ had a body, a body of glory (*sōma tēs doxēs*, Phil 3:21) in his resurrected state, which implies that to be present to the Lord, resurrected or transformed ones need also to have a body.[77]

The significance of *gymnos* then includes an existence with a body before death and after resurrection, and nonexistence in between; however, the additional input the image has in relation to the reward at the presence of the Lord is its implication on identity. If a person ceases to exist at death, how is identity carried over to the resurrection? Fernando Vidal notes as much when he says that, "Beyond eschatology and anxiety, however, the central problem of the Christian discourse about the resurrection is personal identity and particularly the relationship between self and body."[78] This is an important question. It will be addressed here in relation to the

---

76. See for instance 1 Cor 15:51 and 1 Thess 4:15–17 which place those events (resurrection and transformation) at the presence of the Lord, the Parousia. At that moment no one will precede another but the resurrected ones and the transformed living ones will be taken together to the presence of the Lord.

77. Harris, "Watershed," 50.

78. Vidal, "Brains, Bodies, Selves, and Science," 934.

Corinthian context, and in a separate chapter from a broader theological perspective.

Continuity of Identity

Despite the sense of emptiness or lack of existence, there is also, in the use of *gymnos,* an idea of continuity. The essence of something does not change just because there was a change of cover or clothes (1 Cor 15:37); if a cover means existence, and nakedness means nonexistence, then nakedness should refer to something besides existence that can be kept without signifying that some component of the person survives death. This is the intrinsic idea of nakedness. I propose that this something is the human identity that is not an entity as part of the individual, but as a record of his life. Here a literary comparison builds the argument, since Paul does not develop it as modern theologians do.

The first task is to justify the use of relevant images in order to do a comparison. It is done by a consideration of the term *gymnos* in 1 Cor 15:37. Second, two other images, namely *koimaō*, "to sleep" and *en rhipēi ophthalmou*, "in the twinkling of an eye," are compared to *gymnos* looking for common ground in their meaning. Each image will be treated in separated sections.

The syntactical diagram on page 128 shows a clear relation between *gymnos* and *endysamenoi* (2 Cor 5:3). In the context of dressing (*endyō*), the logical term to be used as a contrast should be undressed (*ekdysamenoi*) but Paul uses *gymnos* instead. The purpose could be (a) to link the images of buildings with the significance of nakedness, alluding to the sense of emptiness. Thus, it is clear that what is taken of is the habitation or nature, which is the issue discussed in the periscope; however, another purpose could be (b) to link the discussion with 1 Cor 15:37, the only other passage where *gymnos* is used by Paul in the same context of change of nature; and so, it would infer a link with the issue of continuity of identity. This seems to be the first intention in 1 Cor 15:37 and to link the discussion on 2 Cor 5:3 to it will bring the same significance to the term in this new discussion of buildings.

In 1 Cor 15:37 Ralph Martin sees this continuity of identity (although he does not call it so) by the use of the image of the sowed grain, even if "what is *sown* is not identical with what is *grown*."[79] He recognizes a relation

---

79. Martin, *The Spirit and the Congregation*, 133–34 (italics are his).

between the two stages of the grain. It is indeed the same grain, whether "wheat or . . . something else." It has the same identity, but surprisingly it has another nature, and according to Paul's argument, another body. The identity then does not correspond to the nature of the body since the body can change, but the identity remains. Then, the other two images used for death (*koimaō* and *en rhipēi ophthalmou*) in that context add significance to the discussion of nakedness as referring to death in the view of identity.

Gymnos and *Koimaō*

The euphemism of sleep (*koimaō*) is, perhaps, the most used image in the Bible to refer to the phenomenon of death. The comparison of this image with *gymnos* permits us to extract inferences regarding the continuity of identity despite the change of nature and unconsciousness. The term appears eighteen times in the NT and nine of them are Pauline.[80] Out of eighteen, there is only three times that it is used to refer to the natural and literal sleep,[81] and the rest of the instances refer to death. The reference to death is clear, but the implications of this imagery to the state of the dead are not.

Murray J. Harris, a dualist, believes that the term per se does not describe what he calls the intermediate state, but the manner through which one enters death and, perhaps, the manner one exits from it.[82] He says that it does not compromise Paul's basic anthropological monism, nor does it imply any psychopannychism. For him, *koimaomai* portrays "Christian resurrection as a restoration of the person to full self-conscious activity and development."[83]

The use of the Greek *koimaomai* agrees with such a statement.[84] As a metaphor for death it refers mainly to the act of entering into death (the process of dying). Based on this use, *koimaomai* speaks not of the state of those who are dead, but of the rupture of the relationship with them, as one

---

80. The instances are restricted to 1Thess and 1 Cor (1 Thess 4:13, 14, 15; 1 Cor 7:39; 11:30; 15:6, 18, 20, 51).

81. Matthew 28:13; Luke 22:45; Acts 12:6.

82. Harris, "Watershed," 49.

83. Ibid. Harris's analysis of sleep reveals some inconsistency with the dualism he presents later in the same paper.

84. Of the nine instances Paul uses the term, with the exception of 1Thess 4:13, all speak clearly of the process of falling asleep as a punctual event. Other instances such as Matt 27:52; John 11:11, 12; Acts 7:60; 13:36; and 2 Pet 3:4 have the same sense.

loses the contact with those who go to sleep even if one can see the body lying there.

Perhaps the only use of *koimaomai* as referring to the state of being dead or perhaps to the span between death and resurrection is 1 Thess 4:13. There, the participle present middle form is used. The same form is used in Matt 28:13, Luke 22:45, and Acts 12:6 to speak of the time spent sleeping in a natural sense. Paul wants believers not to be ignorant about "those who are asleep." A simple comparison of the metaphor with the other two uses in the immediate context (4:14, 15) seems to refer mostly to the unconsciousness of the one sleeping, rather than to some kind of sleeping experience.

The other two uses of the term in the context speak of a punctual event of falling asleep, which gives some clue on the use of the word. Moreover, the context of resurrection, and the comfort the living ones need in relation to them (4:18), requires the use of this image that gives the assurance of resurrection as Jesus did in the resurrection of Lazarus and the daughter of Jairus.[85] Paul uses this image to refer especially to those dead who believed in the eschatological resurrection.[86] The image then, seems to be an echo of the oral tradition of Jesus' use of it eventually recorded in the Gospels and perhaps of the OT view of death.[87]

The concern of Christians was about those who had died. The answer of Paul emphasizes the expected reunion with them. This means that those who will be resurrected will have the same identity that they had before they died. Beyond other references to death, which include cessation, dissolution, or destruction of the self,[88] the euphemism of *koimaomai* points

---

85. It seems that the only two instances where Jesus applied the image of sleep to death was the resurrections of Lazarus and of Jairus's daughter (Luke 8:41). Regarding Lazarus, John uses *koimaomai* (John 11:11 cf. 11:12, 13); regarding Jairus's daughter the synoptic gospels use *katheudō* (Matt 9:24; Mark 5:39; and Luke 8:52). In both instances bystanders were confused by Jesus' reference to sleep, for they did not recognize he was referring to death. Both events ended in resurrection, in agreement with the line of my argument.

86. Martin Völkel says that the term *koimaomai* has been "in all instances, including 1 Cor 7:39, used consistently of Church members, David (Acts 13:36), or the *hagioi* (Matt 27:52)." He sees "an affirmation of both the fact of death and the Christian hope." He considers that like *oi nekroi en Christōi*, "the dead in Christ," *koimaomai* is a "term directly relevant to death and the associated Christian hope." The parallel of the expression with *oi koimēthentes en Christōi*, "those who sleep in Christ"(1 Thess 4:13b; 1 Cor 15:19; cf. 1 Cor 15:18) supports the assertion. Völkel, "κοιμάομαι," 2:302.

87. E.g. Deut 31:16; 1 Kgs 2:10; Job 14:12; Dan 12:2.

88. See Matt 2:18 where death means "to be no more." See also the term ἀπόλλυμι (to destroy or kill) as referring to death (Matt 2:13, 8:25; 10:39; 12:14; 27:20; John 10:28;

to the reality of having the same individual after resurrection as before death. Despite the death of believers there is a hope of seeing them again and joining them at Parousia. Paul uses the image of *koimaomai* in order to differentiate believers from "the rest who have no hope," and to avoid the discouragement that stemmed from a common view of death, whereby it lead to the loss of beloved ones forever. Therefore, in that context, *koimaomai* implies continuity of identity.

Another use of the term in the context of the Pauline discussion of bodily resurrection is found in 1 Cor 15:18. Paul says that if there is no resurrection then those who have slept in Christ have indeed perished. It means that the condition of one who sleeps is the same of one who perishes, except for the hope of resurrection. If resurrection is a divine act of re-creation, then resurrection is not a product of the nature of the one who is dead. It is a divine act, not an intrinsic power of the one who is dead. In the natural sleep, when the strength is recovered, the natural process is to wake up. By contrast, the only way to wake up from death is by the power of God. Paul highlights this aspect of sleep by putting the source of the resurrection power in God alone even when it applies to Jesus (1 Cor 15:15), and especially when it applies to others (15:22).

"Those who sleep in Christ" are different from those who sleep without him only because they are sleeping "in Christ," not because they are "sleeping." They will rise first. The expression itself infers that there are others who sleep, but not in Christ; otherwise, in this context, the only use of the term *koimaomai,* without the addition of "in Christ," would make a difference between the death of believers and the death of unbelievers. But Paul says, "in Christ" so he differentiates between the two groups. If "all who sleep" have to appear before God to account for their acts, then all will resurrect. This means that the evil, like the righteous, are also asleep as Dan 12:2 and John 8:28, 29 show.[89]

The meaning of the term is important in that it implies that the same self who died will appear after resurrection to be called to account of deeds

---

Acts 27:34; 1 Cor 10:9; 15:18; Jude 1:5; among others), and the verb τελευτάω, "come to an end,"(Bauer, BDAG, s.v. "τελευτάω") that is used also for death (Matt 2:19; 9:18; 22:25; Luke 7:2; John 11:39; Acts 7:15; and Heb 11:22 among others). The basic meaning of ἀποθνῄσκω, translated as "to die'" means the cessation of vital functions, Bauer, BDAG, s.v. "ἀποθνῄσκω," cf. ibid. s.v "θνητός." Some examples of this use are, Matt 8:32 (speaking about animals); 9:24; 22:24; Mark 5:39; Luke 20:36; John 8:53 (speaking about Jacob); 11:14 (Lazarus); 8:32 (Jesus).

89. Compare with Acts 24:15; Matt 25:46; and Rev 20:12.

performed while alive, regardless of the nature of the body. The person who rises from the dead is not a new person. The same person who closed the eyes to sleep will open them with a new existence at the resurrection.

That is the essence of the use of *gymnos* when Paul uses it in 1 Cor 15:37.[90] The same grain "perhaps of wheat or of something else" which is sowed is the same that comes up after, though "the body which is to be" is of a different shape or even nature form the one which was sowed. Verse 38 adds that each seed receives from God a "body of its own." By the power of God there is no duplicity or confusion of identity. Identity remains from the body that is sown to the body, which is to be.

The expectation of Paul in 2 Cor 4:14 is to be reunited after resurrection with those who survive until the Parousia. It is expected then that the language he uses to speak of the change of the earthly vessel into the heavenly one, either by resurrection or transformation, reflects that assurance. Another element involved is the reward to be received at the judgment for the things done during the time life lasted. Although the issue is not identity, it is implied in the fact that body change, regardless of the process, does not affect the continuity of the identity of those who will receive the reward. Paul recognizes the possibility of death before the Parousia and hopes to be there after resurrection with those who survive and to be presented by Jesus—he himself and no other.

Therefore, by the same use of the image of *gymnos*, and the image of *koimaomai* we can conclude that they are required to link the identity at death with the identity at the resurrection. The context, the theme of the parallel pericopes, and the view of eschatological judgment suggest it.

The implication of sleep on the perception of those who are asleep means that there is no perceptible lapse of time between the moment they face death and the moment they arise through resurrection, since *koimaomai* implies unconsciousness. It is true even if centuries have lapsed for those still alive. In that sense, *koimaomai* also shares the meaning with *gymnos* in its meaning of cessation of life. Paul presents the lapse on the consciousness between bodies due to death as something insignificant. It happens in the twinkling of an eye.

---

90. The comparison between *gymnos* in 2 Cor 5:3 and 1 Cor 15:37 on p. 146 allows us to see *gymnos* as reference to death there and as such, a parallel of *koimaomai*.

In the Twinkling of an Eye

The expression *en rhipēi ophthalmou*, "in the twinkling of an eye," is the second image *gymnos* could be compared to in the same context is. This comparison unveils the issue of time consciousness on the side of the dead. At the same time it puts the experience of change in the same level for both resurrection and transformation.

Paul refers to the moment of the eschatological Parousia by the use of the last trumpet sound motif (1Cor 15:52). It places the events of resurrection and transformation at the second coming of Jesus. In that moment, both those who have died and those who will still be alive (15:51) will receive the incorruptible and eternal body. It does not require too much to see in the Greek term *atomos*, "moment," the meaning of an indivisible unit of time, although this adjective is not always used for time. Here, due to the time context, it "refers to the smallest conceivable instant."[91] There is no gradual change either for the righteous who are alive or the righteous who have died.

The sense of quickness is further emphasized by the use of the expression *en rhipēi ophthalmou* (15:52). Paul does not do a poetic parallel here, but he is implying something else by the comparison of these two expressions. The common meaning of both *atomos* and *en rhipēi ophthalmou* has to do with the insignificant lapse of time the change requires to take place. The twinkle of an eye takes no more than an instant. "The phrase 'in the twinkling of an eye' is appositional; it represents a momentary wink of the eyelid. (Our [sic] equivalent is 'in a split second,' which commonly signifies the shortest possible moment)."[92]

In the expression "we shall not all sleep" (1Cor15:51), the double use of the Greek *pantes* includes the ones to be transformed without experiencing death and those who will indeed sleep. Both will experience a change of nature. This makes clear that the expression *en rhipēi ophthalmou* includes both groups.[93] It means, for both the survivors and the resurrected ones, the change will take the same amount of time in their perception. It is something that happens in a flash and something the individuals experience in a flash. As somebody closes and opens the eyes without changing his or her

---

91. Garland, *1 Corinthians*, 743.

92. Kistemaker and Hendriksen, *Exposition of the First Epistle to the Corinthians*, 582. The emphasis is his.

93. Gillman also agrees in this point. Gillman, "Thematic Comparison," 443.

self-consciousness, so too those who have died will experience resurrection, which means change, in a flash, and with no sense of the lapse of time between events. The expression *en rhipēi ophthalmou* seems to add the idea of continuity to *atomos*, which is beyond a simple poetic parallelism.

The implication is that during the time death lasts, the dead are unconscious. Another implication is that their identity is linked from one stage to the other. The self-perception and the memory of their past is linked to the resurrected condition, just as it happens with those who did not die but survived until the Parousia. At the end, both groups have a transformed nature received in a flash, in a twinkling of an eye. In the dead's perception there is a jump between the very moment of death and the moment of resurrection regardless of the lapse of time.[94] Conciousness of oneself is not affected. The one who died will be the same person after resurrection just like a person who literally twinkles an eye is the same person after that simple act.

Summarizing, the study on the term *gymnos* in its literary context and in comparison with its uses outside of the pericope, as well as the consideration of the images related to it, and the parallel images in the same thematic background, suggests interpreting *gymnos* as death. In that context death includes the lack of body, either earthly or heavenly. It is totally void of the person. Nevertheless, it also aims to suggest continuity of the identity of the person, linking the dead with the resurrected ones despite the fact that nothing survives death. As nakedness has no cover, death has no existence and thus, no sense of time, just as *koimaomai* or *en rhipēi ophthalmou*. And yet, it remains the same as if no death would occur from the earthly existence to the heavenly.

---

94. I am aware of the discussion of Near Death Experiences where those supposed to be dead perceive a paradise where they see light or other sights according to their background, but I'm also aware of the arguments against such phenomena. What rules the discussion in this study is not a phenomenological or paranormal discussion of death, but what the Bible says.

Chapter 4
Theological Implications

SOME SCHOLARS SEE INCONGRUENCE between identity and the monist view of the human being, since the total cessation or interruption of the life of an individual would mean the interruption of his or her identity. The solution for them is to have something that survives death to be linked with the new body after the resurrection, even if this something, often called the soul, would be unconscious.

Nevertheless the problem of dualism against monism in the context of the continuity of identity was not the issue for Paul. Berecz says that Paul was monist in his view of man following what he calls "Hebrew tradition."[1] Paul's use of the anthropologic terms to speak of the individual as a whole and the terms he uses to speak about the dead unveils the issue of continuity of identity from a monist-mortalistic perspective, as something taken for granted and non-contradictory in itself, as was shown in this study.

This chapter will show how the monist-mortalist significance of *gymnos* fits with the concept of death and the continuity of identity. A brief study of identity in theological and biblical teaching confirms also the appropriateness of its use. The final section touches the theological

---

1. Berecz, "Monistic," 287. Despite the variety of Jewish views on man, death, and resurrection in the time of Jesus, Berecz sustains that, "Hebrew thought was not dualistic in any Platonic sense." Ibid., 280. In this regard David Stacey says that, "the Hebrew did not see man as a combination of contrasted elements, but as a unity that might be seen under a number of different aspects. Behind each aspect was the whole personality. Platonism, Orphism, and the Greek view generally, provide the opposite point of view. In this matter, Paul was in the Hebrew tradition. Every word in Paul refers to the whole man." Stacey, *View of Man*, 222.

implications of the concept of death and identity in relation to judgment, which is the concern in the conclusion of the pericope.

The Concept of Death

The very core of the concept of death derived from the use of *gymnos* in 2 Cor 5:3, as shown in chapter 3, and the inclusion of those who did good and evil in 2 Cor 5:10, presupposes no difference between the first and second death in their nature but only in the hope of resurrection, which is absent from the latter. *Gymnos* as representing death means nonexistence and presupposes an impossibility to interact with the dead. This concept of death agrees with the concept of death in the Scriptures.

Scripture sustains the Hebrew monist view of the human being.[2] This truth is "becoming increasingly clearer to theologians in various Christian denominations."[3] On the other hand, in recent times, monism appears to be more in agreement with modern neuroscience. Alan J. Gijsbers shows that the so-called "higher functions" of the mind are directly related to the brain, rather than to an immaterial soul.[4] Cooper says also that science demonstrates the "dependence of mental and psychological states on the brain, thereby undermining the basis for considering the soul a separate substance."[5]

Death is final. In consistence with monism and the Pauline use of *gymnos* in 2 Cor 5:3 and 1 Cor 15:37, the OT (like the NT) also teaches that death is the end of life, a cessation of existence and thus, "the opposite of life."[6] If a resurrection, which means a return to life, is not considered, death is final. But if resurrection comes, death ends. In this sense the old expression of Epicurus summarizes the concept: "When I am, death is not, and when death is, I am not."[7] 1 Cor 15:16–18 uses the word perished

---

2. See Katz, *Jewish Ideas and Concepts*, 100–102; Buttrick, *The Interpreter's Dictionary of the Bible*, 243; Milne, *Know the Truth*, 120–22; Barton, *1 & 2 Corinthians*, 341. Marvin E. Tate says that, "The Hebrew conceived man as animated body and not as an incarnate soul." See Tate, "The Comprehensive Nature of Salvation in Biblical Perspective," 477.

3. Cairus, "Man," *HSDAT*, 212.

4. Gijsbers, "The Dialogue Between Neuroscience and Theology," 1.

5 Cooper, *Body*, 34.

6. "Even in traditions where concepts of life after death are prominent." Richards, "Death," 2:109.

7. Rorty, *Contincengy, Irony, and Solidarity*, 23.

Theological Implications

(*apōlonto* 15:18) and 2 Cor 5:1 the word destroy (*katalyō*) as references to this sense of the state of death.

The difference between naturalistic annihilation and biblical death (monist-mortalism) is not the nature of death. Biblical death, in its nature, has the same characteristics as naturalistic death, with the exception that the total cessation of existence in biblical death is not the end if resurrection is in view. The Scriptures teach that both believers and unbelievers will be resurrected[8] (although not all at the same time), and they will be the first ones to die no more, and the second ones to die without hope of future resurrection.[9] The difference between the first death, interrupted by resurrection, and the second death, which is eternal, lies not in the nature of death itself, but in the temporariness of its nature. The condition and nature of the being during death is the same for both believers and unbelievers.[10] Thus the OT sometimes mixes this concept of first death and second death without differentiating between them.

Both believers and unbelievers have to live again in order to receive the reward for their faith, or lack of. Nevertheless, resurrection does not affect the ontological nature of death in itself, but defeats it to bring people to life. During the lapse of death and until the bodily resurrection, death is total nonexistence in the same sense that total nonexistence is the final fate of unbelievers at the second death.[11]

The argument of Paul being absent from God and also from the earthly body in the nakedness state in 2 Cor 5:3–9 agrees with the nonexistence state at death.[12] If a person is absent from the Lord (heavenly existence) and absent from the earthly body (earthy existence), where is he? In order to be "present" the human being needs a body (cf. Job 13:14). Thus, at death a person no longer exists. Paul compares this to nakedness where it is related to the lack of houses (2 Cor 5:3, 4).[13]

---

8. Daniel 12:2; John 5:28, 29; Acts 24:15. See also Rev 20:4, 5. See also Sevenster, "Some Remarks," 205.

9. This is called annihilation. This is the second death. See Froom, *Conditonalist Faith*, 69–82.

10. Froom, *Conditoncalist Faith*, 79. See also Eccl 3:19–21 where human death is compared to the death of an animal in terms of its nature.

11. The difference is that after the second death, there is no more memory of them.

12. See Job 7:2; 10:19. These verses present the grave or death as nonexistence.

13. In 2 Cor 5:3 "naked" contrasts "unclothed." See also the section Present-Absent Argument on p. 147.

But not all will die—some will be transformed without experiencing death. About this transformation, Paul speaks clearly only in his letters to Corinthians (1st and 2nd) and in Phil 3:21. In the OT the imminence of the Parousia was not an issue, so transformation was not the common view as the way to enter into the new life, but resurrection from death.[14] Nevertheless, the experience of Elijah implies some kind of transformation in order for the human body to enter into heaven (cf. 1 Cor 15:50). He and Moses shared the same nature at the transfiguration (Matt 17:2–4; Mark 9:3,4; Luke 9:29–32). Moses received it by resurrection while Elijah received it by transformation (cf. Dan 12:3, 13 and Matt 13:43). Immortality, then, does not require death to be granted. Death is not a prerequisite for the reward since everyone, according to Paul, has to be alive to receive it. Death is an accident that can be overcome through resurrection, or a final and eternal cessation of life if resurrection is not granted.

On the other hand, death paralleling the image of nakedness in 1 Cor 15:37 is compared by Paul to sleep. Jesus used the same image in John 11:1–37. Sleep is a common euphemism used for death in the rest of the Bible,[15] as well as in Pauline writings.[16] Through this image and in consonance with nakedness, it is possible to draw some conclusions: (a) at death there is no consciousness (Eccl 9:5); thus, no thinking (Ps 146:4), no communication with the living (Eccl 9:6), no emotions (Eccl 9:6) are expected; (b) at death there is no body of any kind,[17] neither physical activities (Eccl 9:10); (c) death shall end when Jesus wakes up the dead through resurrection at his Parousia (1 John 5:28, 29); (d) the same individual who falls asleep is the same who will rise again, no other (Job 19:27); and, (e) there is no sense of time from the moment of death until the moment of resurrection (Phil 1:21–23).

Therefore, the theological implication of *gymnos* is that there is no disembodied existence in death, but *gymnos*[18] designates a state of nonexistence. Only the remembrance of the dead is kept in the Lord's mind for resurrection.[19]

---

14. Davies, *Rabbinic Judaism*, 300.

15. E.g. 1 Kings 2:10; 11:43; Ps 13:3; Jer 51:39; Matt 9:24: John 11:11–14.

16. 1 Cor 7:39; 11:30; 15:6, 18, 20, 51; 1 Thess 4:13, 14, 15.

17. 2 Cor 5:3 cf. Job 34:15; Ps 104:29; Eccl 3:20; 12:7.

18. There is not even an interval of reduced or suspended consciousness or latent existence as is the idea of Harris, among others; see Harris, "Watershed," 49, 50.

19. Rev 14:13, Exod 32:32 cf. Rev 20:12.

Identity

The connection *gymnos* in 2 Cor 5:3 has with the present-absent image in 5:6–9, and the conclusion of the pericope in 5:10 regarding judgment and deeds while in the body, imply continuation of identity as was shown in the relevant section.[20] The meaning of *gymnos* contrasts the allusion to nonexistence with the allusion to a link between the existence before death and the existence after resurrection. This section explains how these two meanings of the term are not contradictory, but complementary, and in agreement with the concept of continuity of identity derived from the Scriptures. It explains how the same identity is maintained after the resurrection if nothing of the individual survives death.

Identity is neither the individual (person) nor the soul (a supposed separated entity), but a record of the life and intrinsic characteristics of an individual. It is referred to in the Bible as a name written in a book. Thus, the memory of the living ones, in the acquaintances, and especially in the mind of God, provides the connection between this life and the life after resurrection.[21]

Andreasen maintains that the "biblical formula of life and death rejects all possibilities that anything except the survivor's memory of a person survives death."[22] Although the word survives could imply something that remains alive after death, this is not the case of real life in an anthropological or biblical sense; what survives is only an ideological presence.[23]

---

20 See the section Continuity of Identity on p. 135.

21. Andreasen, "Death," 318.

22. Ibid., 317.

23. I see a difference between things that really exist and those that are present only in the mind and that need some external manifestation to be physical, or in order to have a real existence. I do not negate the existence of ideas, but they do not exist in a physical sense. In order to explain this difference without going into philosophical argumentation on the use of the terms I will use an illustration. If a potter has some fine ceramics designed in his mind but it never comes to the worktable, this is only an idea. It is real in the sense that he can produce it, it exists in some sense, but the ceramic doesn't have a real existence. At the moment it is produced by his hands the ceramic has a real existence and can be used and interacts with other things such as water or whatever comes in, on, under or beside it. Let us suppose that someone sees the ceramic and gives a down payment to purchase it. But before the delivery time comes the ceramic is broken and completely destroyed. The buyer calls the potter to ask if he has it. The potter answers, "yes." He does not have the real ceramic in his hands. No one can use it to hold anything. No one can see it. But the ceramic has an ideological presence in the mind of the potter, and due to his ability to recreate it at any moment; it is taken as having a real existence

This so-called memory of someone is neither a material nor an independent entity, but only information regarding the real life and character of somebody in the past (before death), especially in the mind of God. Since God is beyond our temporality I can say also that this memory in the mind of God includes the real life of a person after resurrection. In the Scriptures this "memory" of a person represents his identity, which transcends death. Here two issues are considered: the concept of identity as memory and its implications, and the support of this concept in the Bible and the image of being alive in the mind of God while a person is indeed nonexistent at death.

Memory

The identity includes the consciousness someone has of himself and his past, the recognition his acquaintances have of him, and the relationships with the exterior. This section does a very brief exposition of the relation between memory and identity. It will show that memory can define identity in a general sense, even in biblical settings.

Psychologically, it is possible to say that human identity can be summed up in one word: memory. For Tipler, life is "a form of information processing."[24] Memory can be defined as a complex function of the mind having at least four distinct phases:[25] (a) memorizing or learning through formal teaching, empirical or experimental processes,[26] (b) retention of the information learned, (c) recall of the information (e.g.,words, experiences, images, sounds), and (d) recognition, or the mental mechanism of association of the present perception with the information recorded in the mind. In medicine, memory is a cognitive reconstruction that links the present with the past.

---

even though it has not. At this moment this presence in the mind of the potter, what I call *ideological presence*, has a correspondence with a past reality and a future one, since he can recreate it. At the very moment the potter recreates the ceramic in order to deliver it, the ideological presence comes to real existence, and then the ceramic can be used.

24. Tipler, *The Physics of Immortality*, 124.

25 *Biology Online Dictionary*, s.v. "Memory."

26. A dictionary defines it as "The store of things learned and retained from an organism's activity or experience as evidenced by modification of structure or behaviour or by recall and recognition." *Merriam-Webster's Collegiate Dictionary*, 11th ed. (2003), s.v. "Memory."

Theological Implications

Philosophically, according to Baker, this kind of memory is linked with what she calls the first-person-perspective.[27] For her, identity has two components, this first-person-perspective (the fact that I know that I am I) and a body.[28] One is a physiological (organic) process of the mind, based on memory, which is the organization of the brain in a very specific way, built up through experiences and learning.[29] The other is the physical cells that perform that process, or that are organized in that way. A way to see it is as a line of people waiting for a bus. The people are the body, and the line, straight or curved, short or long, is the memory. There is no line without people. In the same way, the people have to stand in some way to wait there.

I recognize that the concept of memory is complex; however, it could be categorized in two phases: (a) the conscious one that includes what could be recalled voluntarily, and (b) the unconscious one—information that makes a person act with a particular and distinctive way, a person's character and individuality.[30] This second phase is in charge of involuntary reactions when interacting with the surroundings.

Memory is intimately related with identity as a prerequisite of moral responsibility.[31] Harold Noonan includes other psychological facts when he defines identity. So, it is not only the concept of oneself as an identifiable individual, but other types of psychological continuities.[32] The encyclopedia Britannica shows the philosophical personal identity as a summary of the past experiences and real past life. It is related to memory. "Someone existing now is the same as someone existing yesterday because he remembers the thoughts, experiences, or actions of the earlier person."[33]

Thomas Reid says that it is hard to define identity without the risk of confounding it with diversity or leaving out some relations that include

---

27 Baker, "Death," 385. I used the same term in a wider sense. That self-recognition has to be with the memory one has of oneself, the character and the ability to recall the past. She seems to use it just as the consciousness that one is an individual separated or distinguishable from others.

28. Baker names this theory of identity the constituency view, and she presents it as a monist view of the human being, which can solve many problems regarding resurrection with a philosophical basis. Baker, "Death," 385.

29. Smith, *Here and Hereafter*, 229.

30 Harold Noonan also sees different parts in the memory, which he calls memory and knowledge. Noonan, *Personal Identity*, 48–49.

31. Ibid., 48.

32. Ibid., 10.

33. Shoemaker, "Personal Identity."

it. Nevertheless he says that identity "supposes an interrupted continuity of existence."[34] He sees death as the end of identity, as well as the end of the continuity of existence and its relation with the past. This concept can agree with Derek Parfit's view that relates personal identity with memory,[35] since it is linked with the past. He sees memory as a link for the necessary continuity of the same identity.

Therefore, although the concept is complex, I can simply say that, if after resurrection one can be conscious that she is herself, recall her own past experiences memories and hopes, and reacts to the surroundings as would be expected (according to her personality), then we have the same person that was there before death. This is true even if the bodily characteristics are different.

The capacity to recall the past links the hope in God's promises that the person had before death with the fulfillment of those promises after resurrection. In other words, in order to receive the fulfillment of a promise, it is necessary that the person who was waiting for it is the same person who will receive it; and that person must be able to recall it. Uriah Smith said that the source of "consciousness and the power of memory" has to remain after resurrection.[36]

On the other hand, there is another sphere were identity works. It works not only in the mind of the person itself, but also in the mind of his acquaintances. Identity in the sphere of others's minds implies that, in some sense, the identity of a person remains despite the loss of the person's own consciousness of identity (identity in the mind of the person himself). Some mental disorders damage the cognitive systems that control memory. Memories may become jumbled, leading to mistakes in recognizing people or places that should be familiar.[37] In this sense, a problem in the memory affects the personality and identity if the person lost the first-person-per-

---

34. Reid, "Of Identity," 108, 109.

35. Parfit, "Personal Identity," 210.

36. Smith, *Here and Hereafter*, 226, 227. Although he recognizes the power of God to recreate the same person after resurrection without having the same body particles he sees the need, at least, of keeping safe that small portion of the brain (matter) that keeps the memory of the person with the purpose to link the identity with the past. Although he recognizes that the memory is not physical or material, he says there is a portion of matter of the body where God keeps the identity and which has to enter into the new body in order to link identity. Ibid 229.

37. This concept is developed from the "Definition of Memory," *MedicineNet*, under "Definition of Memory," para. 1.

Theological Implications

spective. Nevertheless the identity of that specific person has links with his past in the memory of his acquaintances; however, the remembrance of his past life has to be reorganized in their minds to conciliate it with the present condition of that person.

Such was the case of Nebuchadnezzar during his mental illness (Dan 4:33–36). He was the king of Babylon even though he was not in a position to carry out that role. He lived with the beasts and he was not able to recall his memory and all it implies; however, when he recovered his memory (called reason in 4:36) all the implications of his past were restored to him. His acquaintances kept a memory of him and conciliated to his condition while he was lost, and again when he was recovered.

This memory of the identity of someone is also seen in the story of Jesus' resurrection. What would have happened after the resurrection of Jesus if none of those who were alive at that moment could link him with his identity before death? Even if he were resurrected, his present state and his previous state would have no interconnection in the minds of his acquaintances. But the Bible records that people recognized him even if he himself did not reveal his identity clearly. They used the memory they had of his voice (Matt 28:9; John 20:16), and his manners and words (Luke 24:30–32; John 21:6, 7) as linking tools.

In the OT the memory (remembrance) in the minds of others had a very important significance. In order to utterly blot out a nation it was necessary to erase the memory of that nation.[38] That was Absalom's concern when he built up a column to conserve his memory (2 Sam 18:18); he did it not for his own mind but for that of his acquaintances. Thus, the memory in the mind of others, and especially in the mind of God, provides a connection between this life and the life after the resurrection.[39]

In a similar way, if a person knows who he is, and has the ability to recall his past and link it with the present, he is he even if no one else recognizes him. He has the same identity. In such a case, the owner of the identity uses the memory of his acquaintances to link the present with the past in order that they can link him with the identity he had before death. Luke records an occasion when, due to fear and confusion (Luke 24:37), the disciples failed to recognize Jesus. He uses the crucifixion marks as

---

38. In Exod 17:14 God promises "I will utterly blot out the remembrance of Amalek from under heaven." Deut 32:26 is another example of this.

39. Andreasen, "Death," 318.

evidences to link him with the image they had of him (Luke 24:39–43, cf. John 20:27, 28).

Therefore, identity links not only the person with his past, or the memory others have with the past, but also the person with his acquaintances in the same relation they had before. It seems that this is the function of identity in resurrection. Once his disciples recognized Jesus he could interact with them with the same authority and expect the same response of faith and commitment (John 21:12–19, cf. Matt 28:17–20).

God keeps the memory of the dead, and because he is the only one who can re-create the same person, that identity in his mind represents the continuity of the identity of a person. At resurrection, God re-creates the same person such as that person was. The same identity is given to him. Thus the person has the same first-person-perspective and a body in a real existence, regardless of whether the physical composition is the same or not. When the person opens his eyes, the link between the moment he closed them and the moment when he opens them is in place. He recognizes himself, and so do his acquaintances. And he receives the same fulfillment of the promises he was expecting before death.[40]

---

40. Dualists such as Cooper see that the problem of monism based in the memory theory for the continuity of identity is the lack of historical continuity of existence. This thought is followed by the argument of multiple replications that hypothetically presents God as creating many persons with the same identity. For dualists this "logical" possibility denies monism. See on this Cooper, *Body*, 185–195, especially 191; however, this is not a problem of continuity of identity, since the same power God has to do a hypothetical multiple replication at resurrection is the same power God has to replicate a living being without the necessity of death-resurrection. It means that the same challenge to identity through death-resurrection could affect the identity before death. It is a matter of God's respect for identity rather than the continuity of it, or his power. The same reason God has for not doing it now is the same reason he will have after resurrection. On the other hand, Cooper argues on continuity besides the first-person or third person perspective. It means that identity remains despite the recognition of oneself or a third person, or, even if one thinks of being someone and the others recognize him in that way, it is possible that he will be only a copy and not the real original person. He defines the real person based in historical continuity without taking into account the changes the same individual undergoes in time. The base is put only in a theoretic reality beyond the first and third-person perspective. The logical conclusion in such a case is that God, in his absolute existence, is the only one who can recognize this continuity. Now if we have put in God that responsibility we can accept his prerogative to avoid multiple replications now or after resurrection.

Biblically speaking, the identity of a person is sealed when the person dies. While someone is alive, the identity changes day by day. Nonexistence (or at least unconsciousness) is necessary at death for a person to be resurrected with the same identity. If the person "exists" during death the identity would continue changing, and, at the resurrection

Theological Implications

Biblical Continuity of Identity

As has been mentioned earlier, the Scriptures do not contain a developed teaching regarding identity; however, there are some allusions to it.

Perhaps one of the clearest passages addressing this issue is the question of the Sadducees about the continuity of the covenant of marriage after the resurrection (Luke 20:27–40). The core of the question was not marriage per se, but identity, after resurrection. A brief analysis of this passage therefore is useful to see its continuity in this section. I will do a brief scriptural exposition of biblical identity using other examples, such as names written in the book of life and the mention of the dead as coming from the tombs, dust, or sea at resurrection. A point to highlight is the concept of ideological presence[41] inferred in Luke 20:38, which links this passage with 2 Cor 5:10.

The Sadducees did not believe in resurrection but questioned Jesus regarding this in order to highlight the incoherence that existed in their view between belief in resurrection and continuity of identity. The question was placed using the continuity of the marriage covenant after resurrection: "In the resurrection therefore, which one's wife will she be? For all seven had her as wife" (Luke 20:33). Regardless of their intentions, Jesus took advantage of the question to teach that death indeed ends the marriage covenant,[42] but not the covenant of God with his followers. He says, "Those who are considered worthy to attain to that age and the resurrection from the dead, neither marry, nor are given in marriage" (Luke 20:35). Resurrection links the promises of God with people who die with the same people after resurrection. Then Jesus answers the question of continuity of the covenant despite death and its unconsciousness implication.

In the background of Exod 3:6, Jesus says, "But that the dead are raised, even Moses showed, in the passage about the burning bush, where he calls the Lord the God of Abraham, and the God of Isaac, and the God of Jacob.

---

would not be the same as at the moment of death. If the person ceases to exist, the record of who he was is kept in a perfect state in the mind of God until resurrection. God can re-create the person in the same "identifiable" state; although with different nature (the anthropological nature is not a resource of identification).

On the other hand, the continuity of identity has to be in the relationship between God and the individual. It benefits them more than it does acquaintances. Practically, only if both sides of the relation are "identifiable," to each other is continuity possible.

41. See footnote 23 on p. 129 regarding the meaning of the expression "ideological presence" in this book.

42 See also in this regard Rom 7:2 and 1 Cor 7:39.

The Naked State of Human Being

Now, He is not the God of the dead but of the living; for all live to Him" (Luke 20:37, 38).[43] The expression "for all live to Him" includes the patriarchs who were dead when Jesus was speaking. Jesus linked the covenant[44] made with the patriarchs before their death with its fulfillment after the resurrection. Jesus introduces the continuity of God's covenant after solving the problem of marriage and the resurrection. In that context there is some kind of ideological presence in the *sight of God*. The remembrance (Exod 2:24) of the covenant, and the recognition of the identity of his children (Exod 2:25) connects the promises with patriarchs with the Israelites 450 years after. According to Jesus, the mention of God's relation with the patriarchs also teaches about resurrection, although they were dead.

The sentence "for all live to Him" in Luke 20:38 is a translation of the Greek sentence *pantes gar autōi zōsin* (πάντες γὰρ αὐτῷ ζῶσιν). The pronoun *autōi* (to him) appears in the dative form. It could be understood as an instrumental dative in which case the phrase could be translated, "because all [people] live *by* him."[45] Then the meaning of the expression is that, God is the means for all to get life; however, the instrumental sense implies three persons, the source of the action, the receptor, and the instrument. It seems that God, being the ultimate source of life, does not need to also be the instrument. Another possibility with a closely related meaning is the dative of cause,[46] in which case the sentence could be translated as "all live because of Him." In such a case, the meaning would be that the fact that life comes from God makes the state of death irrelevant for the covenant, since God can give life whenever he wants and to whomever he wants.

Nevertheless, the most common usage for this construction is the dative of sphere.[47] The meaning would then be, "For all live in the sphere

---

43. Luke 20:38

44. That is the issue of Exod 3; God "remembered" the covenant with them and decided to release the Israelites from Egypt. See Exod 2:24, 25 cf. 3:7–10.

45. Wallace says that an instrumental dative has four keys of identification. One of them is that the verb the instrumental is related to should be in passive (Wallace, *Grammar*, 163, 164), which is not the case here. In my opinion the intransitive nature of the verb ζάω (to live) supplies the need for a passive verb.

46. Ibid., 167.

47. Ibid., 153, 154. Dative of sphere seems to be a derivation of the locative (ibid., 139, 140) but with non-physical implications. Someone could argue for the locative use of the pronoun, since the form is the same. Then the translation would be "all live *with* God," answering the question Where? However, the very mention of resurrection, which implies a coming to life, makes it impossible that Jesus speaks of "dead" living *with* God before receiving *life* through resurrection. On the other hand it seems that πάντες in Luke

of God." *God's Words to the Nations* translates the passage in this way: "In God's sight all people are living." The instrumental and causative forces of the relation between the life of people and God are appropriated; God is indeed the beginner and sustainer of life; however, in the context of Luke 20:38 the issue of the discussion with the Sadducees is resurrection and the possibility of the resumption of life at the resurrection, rather than the source or instrument of life. Thus, in my opinion the more appropriate use for this pronoun in this context is the dative of sphere.

To live in the sphere of God or "in the sight of God" represents a kind of ideological presence, which agrees with the monist-mortalist concept of death as the Scriptures holds, rather than a physical or ethereal existence with God. At the same time it links the life before death with the life after the resurrection in order to provide a continuity of the covenant with God

According to Jesus, by introducing himself as the God of Abraham, Isaac, and Jacob in Exod 3, God wants us to see them as alive in his sight or sphere, even though they had died and were buried already long before. This ideological presence (or existence) can be comparable with the use of a name in the OT.[48] In Exod 3 God uses his name as his identity to be remembered for all ages (3:15). It was his past relation with the patriarchs, and the record of that issue in the mind of the elders of Israel that provided identity to God in the minds of the Israelites. For many years after Joseph died, God appeared to be physically absent from the midst of the people of

---

20:38 includes νεκρῶν and ζώντων. Then, to argue that the dead are *with* God implies that people who are alive are also there, in heaven with God, which is obviously not the case. The best option that applies to be the dead and the living is the dative of sphere.

48. "In the ancient world generally, a name was not merely a convenient collocation of sounds by which a person, place, or thing could be identified; rather, a name expressed something of the very essence of that which was being named. Hence, to know the name was to know something of the fundamental traits, nature, or destiny of that to which the name belonged." Freedman et al, *Eerdmans Dictionary of the Bible*, 94c. "The name in the Bible is more than a means of identification: it is part of the bearer's personality, often expressing his role or character." Jeffrey, *A Dictionary of Biblical Tradition in English Literature*, s.v. "Name." Allis show also the importance of the names in the Pentateuch. Allis, *The Five Books of Moses*, 299–304. Introducing a person's name in the Bible "show[s] the importance of personal identity and preservation in cultural memory, an idea also attested by the inclusion in the canon of many long lists of names." Ryken et al, eds., *Dictionary of Biblical Imagery*, 582. The interest to know someone's name reveals also the interest to know the character or past history (Gen 32:27); a change of the name in the Bible follows a change of the character (see the cases of Abraham, Jacob, Caleb, Esther, Peter, etc.). Alec Motyer says that, "The new name may indicate a new character and status with God." See Motyer, "Significance of Names," 2:1524.

Israel. But for those who kept his identity in their minds, he was present all that time.[49] In the same way, the names (identity) of the patriarchs were kept in God's mind.

For Jesus, given the lack of a sense of time for patriarchs during death and the assurance of their resurrection, time cannot be taken into account in the covenantal relationship while they are dead. There is a void of time in the dead's perception for that covenant. God can consider them as being alive in his sight (mind) during the lapse of time that death lasts[50] because he sees the end from the beginning and because he has the power to re-create them. Thus, the identity (name or record) in the mind of God provides the connection between this life and the life after resurrection.[51]

That record of the identity in God's mind is symbolized in the Bible as a name written in a book in heaven, the book of life. Revelation 20:12 says, "And I saw the dead, small and great, standing before God, and books were opened. And another book was opened, which is the book of life. And the dead were judged according to their works, by the things which were written in the books."[52] These records provide an uninterrupted ideological presence in the sight of God despite death.

In that way it is possible to see how the works of the saints follow them after death,[53] they are written in the book. Moses also recognized the existence of a book that records the names or identities of the persons in heaven (Exod 32:32).[54] Therefore, the special covenantal relationship with

---

49. See the idea of God acting in Exod 1:17, 20; and the apparent absence inferred in Exod 2:23–25 which are the background of this text.

50. See also this expression of taking people as alive when they are dead in 4 Macc 16:24–25, and 4 Macc 7:19.

51. Andreasen, "Death," 318.

52. Daniel 7:10 also mention these books as the basis of judgment. See also *Adventists Believe*, 354, 356, 361 and 362 in relation to these books. See also Smith, *After Life*, 189, 190.

53. Rev 14:13 says, "And I heard a voice from heaven, saying, "Write, 'Blessed are the dead who die in the Lord from now on!'" 'Yes,' says the Spirit, 'that they may rest from their labors, for their deeds follow with them.'"

54. Compare with Ps 139:16.

Theological Implications

his people can be seen by the reference to a special place in God's records,[55] the book of life.[56]

Jesus already spoke about this special ideological presence in the sight of God on the occasion of the resurrection of Lazarus. Jesus said to Mary, "I am the resurrection and the life; he who believes in Me shall live even if he dies" (John 11:25). Although the passage is speaking about the death of Lazarus, and the comparison with sleep, there is another dimension in Jesus' explanation. The first and most obvious understanding of his words implies resurrection after death. He says that even if someone dies (κἂν ἀποθάνῃ (John 11:25), in the future he will live (ζήσεται) because of his faith in Jesus. He continues "and everyone who lives and believes in Me shall never die. Do you believe this?" (John 11:26). Because of the hope of resurrection, the life provided through faith in Jesus cannot be disrupted by death even if it occurs.

However, and in consonance with Jesus' statement, there is another understanding of the phrase, which is not contradictory but complementary. John records the word of Jesus: "He who believes in Me will live even *if* [κἂν] he dies,"[57] John uses only four times the conditional adverb-conjunction κἂν[58] that introduces a condition (protasis) for something to be fulfilled (apodosis).[59] In all of them it seems that the apodosis of the conditional sentence happens at the same time as the protasis.

John 8:14 says, "Even if [κἂν] I bear witness of Myself, My witness is true." In this expression, the witness of Jesus is true while he is bearing witness of himself. Both verbs, to bear witness in the protasis as well as *is* in the apodosis, are in present tense. The same happens in John 10:38 that renders, "though [κἂν] you do not believe [present tense] Me, believe [present tense] the works." Jesus tells his hearers that they should at least believe in his works even if at the same time they do not believe him.

In John 8:55 the verb in the protasis appears in aorist and the verb in the apodosis in future. It reads, "and if [κἂν] I say [aorist] that I do not know Him, I shall be [future] a liar." Jesus would be making himself a liar

---

55. See a special book recording names in Exod 32:32, 33. See also Ps 56:8 and Mal 3:16, 17; Ps 69:28 (29 on MT) mentions two different records, of the living, and of the righteous. Also the image of a book of covenant (Exod 24:7) implies the names of the covenantal parts on it, to erase one of the names break the covenant with this part.

56. Phil 4:3; Rev 3:5; 13:8; 17:8; 20:12, 15; 21:27; 22:19.

57. John 11:25. The emphasis is mine.

58. It is a contraction of the conjunction καί plus the conditional adverb ἐάν.

59. John 8:14, 55; 10:38; 11:25.

if he were to say that he did not know God. The future tense of the verb in the apodosis puts the whole sentence in a supposed future. He is not a liar in the moment he speaks, because he is not saying that he does not know God. But at the very moment (as is the punctual stress of aorist) he will say so (if such could ever be the case) that he will. On the other hand, if he says in that very present moment that he does not know God then he becomes a liar in that present time. This is the sense of the subjunctive construction. There is a correspondence in the tense of both verbs. They happen at the same time. The same combination of tenses, aorist/future, appears in 11:25, which could give the same sense to the construction.

There are other three instances in the NT in which a subjunctive construction begins with κἄν and is followed by a future active verb, as in John 11:25.[60] In these instances the same syntactical phenomenon can be seen. The actions referred to by both the subjunctive verb of the protasis and the indicative verb in the future tense in the apodosis, both occur at essentially the same time. Also the indicative verb in the apodosis stresses or even determines the time when the subjunctive verb in the protasis happens. In the case of John 11:25 the tense of the construction is some point in the future for both "to die" and "to live."

If this syntactical discussion provides a key to understand John 11:25, then the words of Jesus can be understood not only as pointing to the resurrection but also to a further meaning, namely, that "because someone believes in Jesus, even if he is dead he is alive"; or "even if he will die he will be alive." Life happens when death happens. The suggestion then is that the one who dies is considered as alive even if he is dead. The context makes clear that Jesus is speaking about physical death, and this understanding does not change the biblical concept of death, which is lack of life. The life here should refer to the same image Jesus recalls in Luke 20:38 where he refers to the dead as living ones. This life is the ideological presence of dead people in the sight of God.[61] The real existence before death and the real

---

60. Matt 21:21; 26:35; and Heb 12:20. See also 4 Macc 18:14.

61. This ideological presence does not demerit the eternal death as reward for unbelievers. In Luke 20:38 Jesus says that, for God, *all* live, but in John 11:25 he speaks of those who believe. John 11:26 helps explain the apparent difference. Jesus says "and everyone who lives and believes in Me shall never die." But the Greek stresses not the life that comes with faith, but the temporariness of the death. The Greek says, "He will not die forever" (οὐ μὴ ἀποθάνῃ εἰς τὸν αἰῶνα). The implicit truth is that those who do not believe will eventually die forever. The permanent character of death goes beyond the resurrection of the unbelievers. For them, the eschatological resurrection is a small temporal parenthesis of life in the eternal death they fell into when they died. This temporal

Theological Implications

existence after the resurrection are linked through this "ideological state of presence" during death.

Thus, even if someone is dead, which implies he is no longer in existence, there is identity related to him in the sense that people remember him, God keeps him in mind and his name is written in a book. Such is the case of the patriarchs Abraham, Isaac, and Jacob; and the case of all who have died. There is no difference. Paul calls this state a "naked state," since though dead, without life, and no real existence, the person has his identity kept in the mind of God waiting for the resurrection.

In Luke 20:38 Jesus clarifies that God is not God of the dead. This statement may also mean that while the dead are in that condition, even if ideologically alive in the sight of God, this ideological presence is not an existence at all. They have no God because they are not and they have nothing. This is a reaffirmation of the biblical concept of death. That is the reason why resurrection is needed.

Because the one who dies is not, and cannot perceive anything, the lapse of time called death is not perceived, they just jump from the sensorial existence before death to the sensorial existence after the resurrection in a sensorial continuity and there is no gap. The covenant is not broken.

If identity and existence are understood in this way, many of the Pauline allusions to this matter make sense. In 1 Cor 15:35 Paul asks about the body the dead will come with, not because they can switch from one body to another, or because they are in some place without one, but their ideological presence is awaiting to be alive again in a bodily form regardless of the nature of that body. The first person perspective sees itself as having a bodily nature before death and another after resurrection without changing the identity. In 1 Cor 15:49 Paul adds that the same first person plural (we) that have borne an earthly image will also bear the heavenly after resurrection.

Paul says in Phil 1:21 that "to die is gain." Yes, if there is no perception of time or anything in death, if the dead will perceptibly wait only for a twinkle of an eye to see Jesus in the morning of the resurrection, then indeed to die is gain. Death can be seen as "to depart and be with Christ" (1:23) which is much better[62] than "to remain on in the flesh" (Phil 1:24).

---

existence comes in order to give account for their deeds when they were alive. See on this the following section On Judgment in p. 144.

62. Compare this concept of departing and being at the resurrection with the same idea on 2 Tim 4:6–8. Paul recognizes that there is a lapse of time (ἐν ἐκείνῃ τῇ ἡμέρᾳ 4:8) but he will not be conscious (4:17, 18).

But still this "departing and being with the Lord" has to undergo the biblical process of resurrection (3:10, 11) through which Jesus "will transform the body of our humble state into conformity with the body of his glory, by the exertion of the power that He has even to subject all things to himself" (Phil 3:21).

Paul can also see the immortality as something already achieved through Jesus (2 Tim 1:10), although consummated or made physical at the Parousia through resurrection or transformation (1 Cor 15:35–55; 1 Thess 4:13–17). This reality is not only true because Jesus' resurrection warrants the immortality. It is true because at the very moment they receive the gospel and accept Jesus and his warranty of immortality—they indeed receive it. What makes it possible is the lack of lapse of time during death in the perception at death, and the total assurance of resurrection and immortality they will receive due to their faith in Jesus. Jesus himself says that whoever believes in him *has* already eternal life.[63]

In this perspective, eternal life starts indeed when the eternal life from Christ is accepted. This life is indeed eternal. Death is just a little parenthesis in the eternal life that permits everyone to be at the same time before the throne of God, regardless of the lapse of time during which they were unconscious at death. Living ones and resurrected ones from all ages appear at the same time to receive the fulfillment of their faith. This is the sense of the images of nakedness and sleep—the assurance of resurrection and the null length of time between death and resurrection.

This is also the reason why the Bible uses the image of the dead coming from the earth, graves, or sea at resurrection. Sleep or nakedness is compared also with the inert disintegrated body waiting in the grave for the resurrection time.

The image of the dead rising from their graves is a biblical description of how the phenomenon of resurrection will take place. It happened when Jesus rose; the stone of the tomb was rolled away by an angel to let him come out (Luke 24:2) from the same place he was put three days earlier. In the same way Lazarus came out from the tomb, so too did the resurrected ones who rose with Jesus (Matt 27:52, 53). At the eschatological resurrection also, "all who are in the tombs shall hear his voice" (John 5:28). This was anticipated to happen this way since the time of Daniel: "Those who

---

63. E.g. John 3:36; 5:24; 6:47.

Theological Implications

sleep in the dust of the ground will awake" (Dan 12:2).[64] Even the sea will deliver those who ended in it (Rev 20:13).

This description is in disagreement with the idea of souls coming from heaven to take a new body. It also strengthens the monist idea of the human being, since a body is linked to resurrection. It is a description of God recreating the dead at the same place they ceased to exist. Warren W. Wiersbe states that resurrection "is not reconstruction. It does not imply that God 'puts the pieces back together again.' The resurrection body is a new body, a glorified body, suited to the new heavenly environment";[65] however, God will do it in the same place people died.

This image of people coming out from the place they laid before could be seen as a synecdoche of physical death (since commonly the dead are buried) in contrast with the figurative spiritual death.[66] The Bible presents this image of the dead coming from graves as the description of an event. Such are the cases of Lazarus and the resurrected of Jesus, mentioned already. We can say that indeed the dead will come from the place they were buried in because God, having the power to recreate the dead in heaven itself, has decided to recreate them in the place where they closed their eyes the last time. So then, when they open the eyes again, the change through resurrection will seem to them like a "twinkle of an eye" and their identity may be reinforced in the eyes of those who waited for them.

This link to the earth (and also the sea or dust) is a kind of maneuver that gives the person an anchor for the first-person perspective in terms of the continuity of identity from the past death to the resurrection. God formed Adam from the dust because he wanted Adam to have his identity linked to the earth as a representative of those who would come after (1 Cor 15:47 cf. 45). In the same way Eve was made from a rib of Adam (Gen 2:22) so her identity would be linked to Adam and he could see her as "bone of my bones, and flesh of my flesh" and call her "woman, because she was taken out of man" (Gen 2:23). At resurrection the dead will be linked to their past in this earth before being translated into heaven, in order to strengthen their identity.

---

64. The OT places the dead in the dust or earth. See for instances Gen 3:19; Job 34:15; and Eccl 3:20. It is comprehensible that those who died are joined to those who died before in the same place (Deut 32:50), and all will come from there.

65. Wiersbe, *The Bible Exposition Commentary*, s.v. "John 5:19–47."

66. Calvin, *2 Corinthians*, s.v. "John 5:25."

Therefore, the description of the event of resurrection, speaking of the dead coming out from the graves, strengthens the idea of continuity of identity. It is also a maneuver to strengthen the monist conception of the human being. This physical event happens regardless of the changes on the geography of the place (many years have passed since the dead closed his eyes the last time) but attached to the need of the resurrected ones to perceive their own identity.

On Judgment

The pastoral and theological conclusion of Paul in 2 Cor 5:10 includes judgment and moral behavior. Paul's conclusion is derived from his exposition of change of natures, either by resurrection (4:13–5:1) or transformation (5:2–4), as was shown in the exegesis. The image of being present or absent at home in the body, or with the Lord in 5:6–9, as well as the possibility to please God either by being present or by being absent in 5:10, has another theological implication: the passage speaks about an ideological presence in the mind of God while people are materially and in reality inexistent. This implication has a strong relation with the concept of judgment. Paul presents judgment as appearing "before the judgment seat of Christ" (2 Cor 5:10). The previous verse (5:9) introduces the conclusion of the subject and the pericope.[67] It appeals to believers to be pleasing to God whether being present or being absent.

Since it was argued that being absent (naked) of any body, whether earthly or heavenly, means being dead, and hence, to be present means to be alive, then the question arises, how can someone being absent of all (dead) be pleasing to the Lord? The passage (2 Cor 5:10) adds that to appear before the judgment seat of God does not necessarily require a body. A look at the passage helps to see this inference. The text reads,

> Τοὺς γὰρ πάντας ἡμᾶς φανερωθῆναι δεῖ ἔμπροσθεν τοῦ βήματος τοῦ Χριστοῦ,
>
> For all of us must be made to appear before the judgment seat of Christ,
>
> ἵνα κομίσηται ἕκαστος τὰ διὰ τοῦ σώματος πρὸς ἃ ἔπραξεν,
>
> that each one may be recompensed for what he did through the body

---

67. See the use of διό on page 149.

Theological Implications

εἴτε ἀγαθὸν εἴτε φαῦλον.

whether good or evil.

In this passage the particle δεῖ, "it is necessary," makes clear that the inclusion of all (πάντας) in this process is not avoidable. Judgment is clear by the use of βήματος (judgment seat). This judgment could include the process of weighing evidences and gathering data, and the pronouncement of a verdict. Moreover, the text includes the idea of reward (κομίσηται). The aorist force of ἔπραξεν, "to perform," points to an act already done, which implies a past tense since it was done τὰ διὰ τοῦ σώματος, "through the body."

The word φανερόωis, from which φανερωθῆναι comes, is used forty-nine times in the NT, nine of them in 2 Cor. Its lexical meaning is "to cause to become visible, reveal, expose publicly (relatively more focus on the sensory aspect than on the cognitive)," and "to cause to become known, disclose, show, or make known."[68] It is applied mostly to things or knowledge, but when it is used to denote the visible appearance of persons, it refers almost exclusively to Jesus, referring to his incarnation,[69] resurrection,[70] or second coming.[71] The only possible physical allusions to other persons are Col 3:4, that reads, "When Christ, who is our life, is revealed [φανερωθῇ], then you also will be revealed [φανερωθήσεσθε] with him in glory," and possibly 2 Cor 5:10.

A point to notice is that the references to Jesus can also be understood as the revelation of what he is, beyond his physical aspect, but also including it. The question is if when it refers to the believers (twice) it necessarily infers physical appearance. There is not enough grammatical or lexical evidence to arrive at a verdict; however, the context can give a clue to determine this aspect. Col 3:3 says, "For you have died and your life is hidden with Christ in God." It is clearly a reference to a spiritual life in the Christian experience; the believers "have died" and also "have been raised up with Christ" (συνηγέρθητε τῷ Χριστῷ, 3:1). Col 2:12 says that this happened through the baptism.

Therefore, according to the context, the subject is a spiritual death and resurrection rather than an anthropological one. In that way, the

---

68. Bauer, BDAG, s.v. "φανερόω."
69. 1 Tim 3:16, 1 John 3:5; and 3:8.
70. Mark 16:12, 14; John 21:1, and 14.
71. Col 3:4; 1 Pet 5:4; 1 John 2:28.

manifestation of Jesus, the spiritual source of this new Christian life, implies the manifestation also of believers. The consequence is a change of the behavior of the believers. Paul says, "Put to death, then, your members that are upon the earth" (Col 3:5, Νεκρώσατε οὖν τὰ μέλη τὰ ἐπὶ τῆς γῆς).

In relation to 2 Cor 5:10 also the context helps to determine if the appearance is physical or not. The text can be translated as follows:

For all of us must to be manifested before the judgment seat of Christ

Τοὺς γὰρ πάντας ἡμᾶς φανερωθῆναι δεῖ ἔμπροσθεν τοῦ βήματος τοῦ Χριστοῦ,

that each one may receive for what was performed in the body,

ἵνα κομίσηται ἕκαστος τὰ διὰ τοῦ σώματος πρὸς ἃ ἔπραξεν,

whether good or evil.

εἴτε ἀγαθὸν εἴτε φαῦλον.

The context in 5:9 says that believers can please God, either being present or being absent. According to what was shown in this study the expression means to be alive or dead. The way to please him is through the life they lived. Paul uses the reference to his ambition to please God as an introduction to speak about the judgment. In 5:10 he adds that "all of us" (πάντας ἡμᾶς) must be manifest before Christ. This *all* includes the present ones and the absent ones. The implication according to the monist-mortalist point of view is that the presence cannot be physical since the dead have not yet resurrected, they are still absent.

Paul believes that judgment comes after death (Heb 9:27), and that the subjects of judgment are the deeds performed in life. It is not hard to see a non-physical appearance in this text. People may not appear physically before the judgment seat of Jesus, but they are made known through their deeds. Hence, if being without a body excludes the possibility of a physical real appearance, the records of the deeds and of the life of the dead are manifested before the throne of Jesus without the physical appearance of the person. It is important to note that, "Paul has no intention of outlining the events of the Parousia."[72] He is more interested in the implications of

---

72. The final judgment, for example, is omitted, though it is clearly assumed in other parts of the first letter to Corinthians (3:8, 13–15; 5:5; 6:2–3; 9:27). Garland, *1 Corinthians*, 743.

Theological Implications

these events, such as the hope of change, resurrection, and judgment in the life of believers.

What people will receive at resurrection, according to their deeds, is a heavenly immortal nature, or a body that can experience the final death.[73] Then the judgment to determine their fate has to be done while people are dead, since there are no more acts after that. Paul makes clear that the objects of judgment are the acts while people were alive. A physical presence before the throne of Christ implies having a body. It already implies a reward: resurrection in a transformed nature. But if a conscious appearance can be possible without a body then resurrection has lost its value.[74]

Therefore, Paul says that through our deeds and life we are manifested before God to be judged. All people are ideologically present before his throne. This presence, even though not a physical one, constitutes the base of judgment, and can please (5:9) or displease the Lord. In this sense someone could be found naked (*gymnos* as it has been defined in this book), which means at the same time "out of the body" and "not at home with the Lord," totally absent, and still be pleasing to the Lord.

---

73. Paul has no interest in the fate of unbelievers in 2 Cor 5, or in 1 Cor 15. He does not mention it specifically; however, the inclusion of them in resurrection and before the throne of God, and the subsequent final destruction infers that they resurrect with the same nature they had before death.

74. George R. Night points this out as a reason to believe in conditional immortality rather than immortality of the soul. He even links this theology with the ministry of Jesus in the heavenly sanctuary. See Night, *A Brief History of Seventh-Day Adventists*, 43.

Chapter 5
Conclusion

IN THE IDEOLOGICAL BATTLE to discover the nature of the human being, death appears as an inexpugnable boundary. The Bible speaks of death and resurrection in language that reflects the teachings from God for all times and nations, but that is limited to the environment of those who used it. In that context, the image of *gymnos* (naked) in 2 Cor 5:3 seems to give a glimpse of what death is. Its context and relation to other images used by the same author in the same background brings more evidence for a monist and mortalist view of the human self.

The way people understand life and death, and their relation to resurrection and immortality, respond to either a dualist or monist perspective of the human being. Under dualism, nakedness represents the soul without the body during the lapse of death, either in a conscious or unconscious state, in the presence of the Lord or in an obscure intermediate place. Nakedness also could mean homelessness, if the dwelling places in the text mean earthly and heavenly houses. In that view, during death, the so-called soul sleeps, waiting for its reunion with the body at resurrection. The body at resurrection could be different but the soul remains the same. This continuity of the soul, conscious or not, links the individual before death with the same individual after resurrection.

Monism, by contrast, sustains the unity of the composition of the human being and infers the total dissolution of the human being at death. The so-called soul sleepers, mortalists or conditionalists, while defending the non-immortality-of-the-soul and the non-eternal-punishment, have fallen on the side of dualism when it comes to the first death—the period before resurrection. They infer some kind of unconscious or imperfect

Conclusion

existence apart from the body, for believers that are waiting for resurrection. Some even see a kind of special proximity with Christ during that "state." Nonetheless, when they define human self and life, they do it with a monist terminology. They say that man is an indivisible unit. This possible misunderstanding of the conception of death and life has led theologians and philosophers to a variety of tags for the different views.

To avoid the misunderstanding these tags have had through history, I have suggested in this book the nomenclature of monist-mortalism to define the anthropological composition of the human being, especially when referring to the state of death and to resurrection. Under this perspective, and following an anthropological approach to 2 Cor 5:3, *gymnos* (gymnos) has been understood as standing for death itself, meaning cessation of life. This conception of death is similar to the Christian annihilation with the difference that Christian annihilation has mainly used it to speak of the "second death"—the death that the unbelievers will receive as a reward after resurrection. In a monist conception of the human being, sleep is a simple metaphor for unconsciousness that links the identity of the individual before death with the same identity after resurrection.

I recognize that the study presented in this book lies on a different understanding of 2 Cor 5:3 and its images. As it was argued, the mind-set of Paul and the issue being discussed in the passage, as well as the way the images and terms are used in their own context, bring evidence for a monist-mortalistic view of the passage.

A comparison with 1 Cor 15 as part of the background of the passage shows that the best reading of the passage is an anthropologic one. A comparison of the images used in 1 Cor 15:35–55 shows that the change on the nature of the body takes place through either resurrection or transformation; this last is a term used in this study to refer to the change of nature without death at the Parousia. The body, which is perishable, without glory, from the earth and natural, represents the whole person. It is changed into an imperishable, glorious, from-heaven, spiritual, and yet, physical-nature through resurrection or without death. In this sense, the body at resurrection is a new body. Thus, resurrection represents a re-creation of the person. Paul compares Adam with Christ to denote this change of nature with the difference that Christ is the "life-giving spirit" (*pneuma* ζῳοποιοῦν, 1 Cor 15:45) that man cannot be; however this characteristic of Jesus gives him the power to recreate the believers that died. His resurrection experience also gives some glimpses of the bodily nature of the resurrection.

The Naked State of Human Being

This issue of bodily-spiritual resurrection, which contrasts with the body before death, plus the issue of a monist view of the human being, combine to solve the problem of the earthly existence and tribulations that is an excuse for Paul's opponents against his ministry, and the concern of believers regarding physical sufferings. This is the knowledge the Corinthians already had and is marked by οἴδαμεν γὰρ in 2 Cor 5:1.

Paul uses in 2 Cor 5:1–10 the images of houses for the nature of human existence. The temporality of earthly life contrasts with the lastingness of its heavenly counterpart. The use of the variants of the verb ἐνδύω (to clothe) and the contrasting comparison of the images involved in the pericope, point to the issue of transformation (ἐπενδύσασθαι, to cloth-over in 5:2, 4) in addition to resurrection as inferred before (ἐγερεῖ, to raise up in 4:14). The verb ἐνδύω is not applied to robes since, what are to be clothed are houses. But it refers to a change of different existences, where death is swallowed by life (2 Cor 5:4 cf. 1 Cor 15:54). The earthly tent stands for the present earthly existence (that infers a body) and the heavenly building for the existence after the change. The process of change corresponds to the same process in 1 Cor 15:35–55, which forms a background pericope. A comparison of terms and expressions corroborates it.

Paul expresses his desire to avoid the state of nakedness. He prefers to be found clothed when the change comes. This is another argument against the Hellenistic reading of the image where nakedness of the soul is desirable. There are different cultural and historical meanings of *gymnos* in the Bible, such as exposedness, shame, death, and emptiness. They converge into the weight of the Pauline desire to avoid it. But according to the context, the primary meaning of *gymnos* is emptiness of life, a period of nonexistence, which death represents. In other words, it is the meaning of death, with the implications on nonexistence, that is stressed.

The literary context of *gymnos*, such as the conditional sentence in which it is placed, as well as a comparison with the same term in 1 Cor 15:37, gives support to that reading of *gymnos*. Another support is the use of the image of being present-absent with regards to the body and the Lord. To be absent is to be dead. By avoiding death Paul wanted to be alive at the Parousia in a moment when the possibility of the Parousia happening in his time was becoming blurred.

When *gymnos* is compared to *koimaomai*, and to the bare grain (1 Cor 15:37, 51), it is clear that even if nothing survives death, there is a link between the person before death and after the resurrection, so that the

Conclusion

resurrected ones can be accountable for their deeds, either good or evil. The nature of this death and the identity continuity is necessary for the righteous as well as for the unrighteous in light of the judgment. Then, the idea of identity is also present in the image of nakedness.

Another image that strengthens the idea of continuity of identity is the image of change in the phrase "in the twinkling of an eye." The expression embraces both the resurrection and transformation; therefore, the period of death in the sight of those who experience it happens in "an indivisible unit of time." For them, there is no lapse of time. Their identity is kept without alteration regardless of the time they were in the graves.

The monist-mortalistc view of death presented in this study agrees with the testimony of the OT regarding life and death. It gives a fresher scriptural monist meaning to the interpretation of 2 Cor 4:7–5:10 based in its connection with 2 Cor 15:35–55 and the anthropological reading of the passage, as the majority of scholars do. It also agrees with the testimony of Jesus about death using the euphemism of sleep (John 11:11–27). The same experiences—resurrection and transformation—can be traced in the OT. And it solves the apparent dualism of Paul's expression "absent from the body and present to the Lord."[1]

There is, however, another consideration of the images in the text that cannot be limited to the Corinthian correspondence due to its theological character. These images infer the continuity of identity. Philosophers and theologians use the brain process of memory as equivalent to identity. The process of memory links the things someone learns with his past and his present. It forms his character. On the other hand, the memory in others represents the concept others have of him. The Bible speaks of identity in terms of memory and name. Then, the name or memory of someone in the mind of God links the identity of the person until resurrection. A clear biblical example of this is presented by the question made to Jesus regarding the continuity of the covenant after the resurrection (Luke 20:38). Jesus explains that the mention of the patriarchs to Moses in Exod 3:6 speaks of resurrection and the continuity of the covenant with them. The assurance of resurrection gives continuity to the patriarchs so God can introduce himself as their God even if they are dead.

---

1. Chapter 3 ended with this consideration. The following theological considerations are presented in chapter 4.

The Naked State of Human Being

However, Jesus introduces as corollary the expression "for all live to him,"[2] (to God). Different suggestions have been given to interpret this sentence, even directly linked to resurrection. But a brief analysis helped to read it as, "All are alive in the sight of God." This presence in the sight of God is called in this study an ideological presence—a record of their life and identity in the mind of God. They were not lost in the mind of God, but his memory is kept for their re-creation through resurrection. God's relationship with the patriarchs is seen as continuing despite death. Jesus already spoke about this special ideological presence in the sight of God on the occasion of the resurrection of Lazarus when he said, "I am the resurrection and the life; he who believes in Me shall live even if he dies" (John 11:25), which can be proved by a syntactical analysis of the phrase.

The identity kept in the mind of God is not an entity, but just a record (memory) of their life (deeds). God sees them as if they were present before him (ideological presence) even to the point of judging them. Thus, dead people can be present before the judgment seat of Christ (2 Cor 5:10) without being really (physically) present there. Only the records of their lives are there and these are taken into account in the judgment. This understanding of "being in the presence of God" could solve many difficulties in the interpretation of some other passages with a monist-mortalistic point of view.

The last theological consideration regarding identity comes with the images of the dead coming from the graves, or from the sea, at resurrection. This issue represents the provision God gives to link the identity on the new body[3] with the previous existence or body. God leads the attention of the resurrected ones and their acquaintances to the realities of death, resurrection, and the continuity of their identity by making them open their eyes in the same place that they closed them at death.

Thus, the dead ones can receive their reward on the basis of what they did before they died; however, the very nature and moment of resurrection implies a reward. Resurrection with an immortal body implies their acceptance of the provisions of God and being found worthy by the blood

---

2. This is the common translation into English; although I prefer to take a dative of sphere applied to "him."

3. The new immortal body according to Paul is reserved for believers; however, the unbelievers will also have a "new" body at resurrection, since the previous one was dissolved and God brings them all to life (Dan 12:2, cf. John 5:28, 29). The difference is the nature of the body; believers will receive an immortal one and unbelievers a perishable one.

Conclusion

of Jesus. On the contrary, resurrection with a perishable body (the same nature with the previous one) implies their final fate, death. Therefore, the judgment of their *deeds* (2 Cor 5:10) was done after they died (Heb 9:27) and before the resurrection.[4]

In conclusion, an anthropological reading of the image of *gymnos* makes more sense in the context of 2 Cor 4:7–5:10. It agrees with the use of other images referring to death, and with the main stream of the interpretations of the passage made by the majority of scholars. The difference is not the anthropologic nature of the image, but the implications on the composition of the human being. A monist-mortalistic reading of *gymnos* (and the others) has more advantages when facing the weight of the evidence of the immediate context, the consideration of the background, the wide context of the Bible, and the other anthropological teachings of the Scriptures, including the OT and the NT.

Further Considerations

There are some observations derived from this study that can be useful for further studies. Further studies can be done in the area of biblical studies, theology, or even practical issues. This section considers some of them that recognize that there could be more.

Some exegetical studies can be made on passages that use the metaphor of sleep, beyond the Corinthian correspondence (1 Thess 4:13–18 among others), to enlighten the monist-mortalism view and its relation with identity. A further exegetical study on what I call here "ideological presence" (or ideological existence) would also be helpful, considering the biblical inferences that allude to it. It is my conviction that the concept can be developed and is helpful to explain some misunderstood passages. Also I see a need of a biblical examination of the incarnation of Jesus under a monist-mortalism perspective in passages such as Phil 2:5–11 or Heb 5:7 (the days of his flesh), as well as his death in the light of John 10:18, "No one has taken it away from Me, but I lay it down on My own initiative. I have authority to lay it down, and I have authority to take it up again. This commandment I received from My Father."

---

4. This consideration of judgment speaks exclusively of the judgment that determines the fate of people. Millennial and post-millennial judgments are not the issue of Pauline concern in 2 Cor 5:10 in my view.

For theological interest, there is a need to define and specify some terms and expressions to describe the monist state of death, such as biblical mortalism, thnetopsychism, psychopannychism, soul sleep, and biblical annihilation. They have to be separated from each other or explained in order to see the differences. Their definition should be either as complete monist or dualist views. Here the option of the term monist-mortalism is suggested as representative of the view of the human being sustained throughout this study. Perhaps some other views could have the same meaning in some circles, but the overlapping meanings of terms with divergent ideas makes them blurred.

There are some expressions in monist literature speaking about the state of death that should be reviewed or explained in their proper context to avoid the appearance of dualism. Some examples of these expressions are "death is not complete annihilation," "death is temporary unconsciousness," "the dead remain in the grave until resurrection," and "the person returns to dust."[5] Although the expressions are taken from biblical images, they have been presented as descriptions of facts. It seems that the Bible does not use them strictly in that sense.

There is also a need for a precise theological definition of person in a biblical basis and a term to refer to the person in monist literature. The word soul, that sometimes has been used to define it in monist circles, does not represent the variety of uses the Bible (OT and NT) does of it. The same is the case with terms translated as spirit or the uses of body.

Finally, the concept of identity, referred to as memory and name in the Bible, could bring more theological or systematic studies that fit with the monist-mortalist view of life and death. In the area of applied studies there could be further considerations regarding issues, such as a person that loses consciousness (or that never had it fully), the loss of memory, and mental disorders.

Applications

The message of the second Pauline letter to Corinthians is opportune and full of comfort for those who are crossing tribulations and for those who are under attack in their own ministry as Paul was. Here the meaning of tribulation goes against the common view that takes it as punishment from

---

5 *Adventists Believe*, 390–92.

Conclusion

God. The hope of an immortal body through resurrection[6] or transformation[7] renews the inner man, even though the outer man is decaying (2 Cor 4:16). It produces "for us an eternal weight of glory far beyond all comparison" (2 Cor 4:17).

But if death comes for us, there is no need for despair, since death works as a bridge on time from the moment of death to the second coming of Jesus. Death is just a parenthesis in life when the acceptance of Jesus gives the assurance of eternal life. In this sense the believer can say as Paul, "For to me, to live is Christ, and to die is gain" (Phil 1:21). This fearless way of living does not seek death, since as Paul says, "But if I am to live on in the flesh, this will mean fruitful labor for me; and I do not know which to choose" (Phil 1:22). Paul himself groans to avoid death (2 Cor 5:4) because of the things he could do until Jesus appears (5:10).

On the other hand, if a beloved one dies, the anxiety produced by not knowing where he or she is, and the ignorance of his or her well-being, disappears by seeing death as nakedness—a period of nonexistence. This could be perturbing if we do not know that the identities of our beloved ones are kept safe in the mind of a powerful God. But that assurance makes us live in accordance to our faith to meet the same people, with the same identity at the Second Coming. The monist-mortalism approach to death also encourages people to live this life wisely, since it is the only chance of life. After death the fate is sealed and the following moment of life is at the throne of Jesus at the Second Coming. There are no "souls" suffering in hell or experiencing bliss in heaven while they see the course of the life of their beloved ones. There are no "souls" hidden in an obscure place waiting to receive a body.

Understanding this concept of death also rejects the search of communication with dead people. All spirit communications will be seen as communications with real, live spirits, either from the kingdom of God or the kingdom of his enemy. These spirits are not dead people, but the agents that work for either our salvation or perdition. This truth becomes relevant in the sight of the belief that one of the "two great errors" at the end of time that the enemy of God will use to "bring the people under his deceptions" will be "the immortality of the soul," which "lays the foundation of spiritualism."[8] The reaction and response of believers in the face

---

6. See Ps 17:15; 49:15; Isa 26:19; Dan 12:2; 12:13; Hos 13:14.
7. 1 Thess 4:17 and 1 Cor 15:51–52.
8. White, *The Great Controversy*, 588.

of spiritual manifestations, meaning communication with people who are dead, will depend in good amount on their understanding of the state of the dead.

The other side of the monist-mortalistic view of death is its view of life. In this sense the person is an indivisible unity. It leads us to see the importance of the body as what we are now, our earthly tents. We are our bodies. The quality of life the individual has in this life contributes to the well-being of the total individual. What is introduced to the body through the mouth has as much influence as what is introduced through the eyes or ears. The mood or attitude also affects the person as much as the sickness affects it.

As the body dies, the person also dies and there is nothing that represents him but the memory on the mind of his acquaintances. Thus, organ donations (when decisions over the life of the donor are not involved) can be done with a free conscience. Cremation also is left for other considerations, but not for biblical considerations on life, death, or resurrection. What happens with the body after death does not affect the person (although it can affect the memory and respect on the acquaintances). In this sense the practice to visit cemeteries should be separated from the idea of visiting the dead, either to speak with them or any other intention, but could have just an intention to pay respect to the "memory" of them for the sake or testimony of the acquaintances.

Bibliography

Aland, Barbara, et al, eds. *Nestle-Aland Novum Testamentum Graece (Greek Edition).* 27th revised ed. Stuttgart, Germany: Deutsche Bibelgesellschaft, 2006.
Alger, William Rounseville. *The Destiny of the Soul: A Critical History of the Doctrine of a Future Life.* 10th ed. New York: W. J. Widdleton, 1878.
Allis, Oswald T. *The Five Books of Moses.* Phillipsburg, NJ: P&R, 1949.
Andreasen, Niels-Erik A. "Death: Origin, Nature, and Final Eradication." In *Handbook of Seventh-day Adventist Theology,* edited by Raoul Dederen, 314–46. Hagerstown, MD: Review and Herald, 2000.
Ankerberg, John. "Response to J. I. Packer." In *Evangelical Affirmations,* ed. K. S. Kantzer and Carl F. Henry, 137–48. Grand Rapids, MI: Zondervan, 1990.
Bacchiocchi, Samuele. *Immortality or Resurrection? A Biblical Study on Human Nature and Destiny.* Berrien Springs, MI: Biblical Perspective, 2001.
Baker, Lynne Rudder. "Death and the Afterlife." In *The Oxford Handbook of Philosophy of Religion,* edited by William J. Wainwright, 366–91. New York: Oxford University Press, 2005.
———. *Persons and Bodies: A Constitution View.* New York: Cambridge University Press, 2000.
Balz, Horst Robert. "Γυμνός." In *Exegetical Dictionary of the New Testament.* Edited by Horst Robert Balz and Gerhard Schneider, 1:265–66. Grand Rapids, MI: Eerdmans, 1993.
Barclay, William. *The Letters to the Corinthians.* 2nd ed., The Daily Study Bible. Louisville, KY: Westminster, 2000.
Barnett, Paul. *The Message of 2 Corinthians: Power in Weakness.* The Bible Speaks Today. Leicester, England: Inter-Varsity Press, 1988.
———. *The Second Epistle to the Corinthians.* The New International Commentary on the New Testament. Grand Rapids, MI: Eerdmans, 1997.
Barton, Bruce B., and Grant R. Osborne. *1 & 2 Corinthians.* Life Application Bible Commentary. Wheaton, IL: Tyndale House, 1999.
Bauckham, Richard. "Universalism: A Historical Survey." In *Themelios* 4, no. 2 (1978): 47–59. http://www.theologicalstudies.org.uk/article_universalism_bauckham.html#3.

Bibliography

Bauer, Walter. *A Greek-English Lexicon of the New Testament and Other Early Christian Literature*. Revised and edited by Frederick W. Danker. 3rd ed. Chicago, IL: University of Chicago Press, 2000.

Beck, James R., and Bruce Demarest. *The Human Person in Theology and Psychology: A Biblical Anthropology for the Twenty-First Century*. Grand Rapids, MI: Kregel, 2005.

Bedard, Stephen J. "Hellenistic Influence on the Idea of Resurrection in Jewish Apocalyptic Literature." In *Journal of Greco-Roman Christianity and Judaism* 5 (2008): 174–89.

Belleville, Linda L. *2 Corinthians*. The InterVarsity Press New Testament Commentary Series vol. 8. Downers Grove, IL: InterVarsity Press, 1996.

Berecz, John M. "Towards a Monistic Philosophy of Man." In *Andrews University Seminary Studies Journal* 14 (1976): 279–88.

Berkhof, Louis. *Systematic Theology*. Grand Rapids, MI: Eerdmans, 1953.

Bibelgesellschaft. *Biblia Hebraica Stuttgartensia*. 5th ed. Stuttgart, Germany: Deutsche Bibelgesellschaft, 1997.

Bonfante, Larissa. "Nudity as a Costume in Classical Art." In *American Journal of Archaeology* 93 (1989): 543–70.

Bracken Joseph A. "Bodily Resurrection and the Dialectic of Spirit and Matter." *Theological Studies* 66, no. 4 (2005): 770–82.

Bruce, Frederick F. *1 and 2 Corinthians*. London, England: HarperCollins, 1971.

———. *Paul: Apostle of the Free Spirit*. Exeter, NH: Pater-Noster, 1977.

———. "Paul on Immortality." In *Scottish Journal of Theology* 24 (1971): 469–72.

Brunner, Emil. *Eternal Hope*. Philadelphia, PA: Westminster Press, 1954.

Brunt, John C. "Resurrection and Glorification." In *Handbook of Seventh-day Adventist Theology*, ed. Raoul Dederen, 347–74. Hagerstown, MD: Review and Herald, 2000.

Bultmann, Rudolf. *Primitive Christianity in ItsContemporary Setting*. Translated by R. H. Fuller. Cleveland, OH: World, 1966.

Burns, Norman Thomas. "Tradition of Christian Mortalism in England, 1530–1660." In *Mennonite Quarterly Review* 43, no. 2 (1969): 170–71.

Buttrick, George Arthur, ed. *The Interpreter's Dictionary of the Bible*. Nashville, TN: Abingdon, 1962.

Cairus, Aecio E. "The Doctrine of Man." In *Handbook of Seventh-day Adventist Theology*, ed. Raoul Dederen, 205–32. Hagerstown, MD: Review and Herald, 2000.

Calvin, John. *Calvin's Commentaries: 2 Corinthians*. Electronic ed., Logos Library System. Albany, OR: Ages Software, 1998.

Carrez, Maurice. "With What Body Do the Dead Rise Again?" In *Immortality and Resurrection*, ed. Pierre Benoit and Roland Murphy, 92–102. New York: Herder and Herder, 1970.

Clarke, Adam. *Clarke's Commentary: First Corinthians*. Electronic ed., Logos Library System; Clarke's Commentaries. Albany, OR: Ages Software, 1999.

———. *Clarke's Commentary: Second Corinthians*. Electronic ed., Logos Library System; Clarke's Commentaries. Albany, OR: Ages Software, 1999.

Clarke, William Newton. *An Outline of Christian Theology*. New York: Scribner, 1900.

Clement of Alexandria. *The Stromata or Miscellanies*. Translated by Alexander Roberts, James Donaldson and A. Cleveland Coxe. The Ante-Nicene Fathers: Translations of The Writings of the Fathers Down to AD 325. Grand Rapids, MI: Eerdmans, 1997, 2:229–568.

BIBLIOGRAPHY

Conzelmann, Hans. *1 Corinthians: A Commentary on the First Epistle to the Corinthians.* Hermeneia, a Critical and Historical Commentary on the Bible. Philadelphia, PA: Fortress, 1975.

Cooper, John W. *Body Soul and Life Everlasting, Biblical Anthropology and the Monism-Dualism Debate.* Grand Rapids, MI: Eerdmans, 1989.

Criswell, W. A., ed. *The Believer's Study Bible:New King James Version.* Nashville, TN: Thomas Nelson, 1991.

Cullmann, Oscar. *Immortality of the Soul or Resurrection of the Dead?: The Witness of the New Testament.* London, England: Epworth, 1958.

Dahl, Murdoch E. "The Semitic Totality View." In *The Resurrection of the Body.* London, England: SCM, 1962.

Davis, Stephen T. *Risen Indeed: Making Sense of the Resurrection.* Grand Rapids, MI: Eerdmans, 1993.

Davis, Stephen T., et al, eds. *The Resurrection: An Interdisciplinary Symposium on the Resurrection of Jesus.*Oxford, England: Oxford University Press, 1997.

Delitzsch, Franz. *A System of Biblical Psychology.*Grand Rapids, MI: Baker, 1966.

Dewart, Joanne E. McWilliam. *Death and Resurrection: Message of the Fathers of the Church.* Wilmington, DE: Michael Glazier, 1986.

DeWolf, L. Harold. *A Theology of the Living Church.*New York, NY: Harper & Row, 1960.

Edwards, David L., and John Stott. *Essentials: A Liberal-Evangelical Dialogue.* London, England: Hodder & Stoughton, 1988.

Ellis, E.E. "The Structure of Pauline Eschatology (2 Cor 5.1–10)." In *Paul and His Recent Interpreters.* Grand Rapids, MI: Eerdmans, 1961.

Erickson, Millard J. *Christian Theology.* 2nd ed. 1988. Reprint. Grand Rapids, MI: Baker, 2007.

———. *The Concise Dictionary of Christian Theology.* Rev. ed., 1st Crossway ed. Wheaton, IL: Crossway, 2001.

Fee, Gordon D. *New Testament Exegesis: A Handbook for Students and Pastors.* 3rd ed. Louisville, KY: Westminster John Knox, 2002.

Freedman, David Noel, et al, eds. *Eerdmans Dictionary of the Bible.* Grand Rapids, MI: Eerdmans, 2000.

Friberg, Timothy, et al. *Analytical Lexicon of the Greek New Testament.* Grand Rapids, MI: Baker, 2000.

Froom, LeRoy Edwin. *The Conditionalist Faith of Our Fathers: The Conflict of the Ages Over the Nature and Destiny of Man*, vol. 1. Washington, DC: Review and Herald, 1966.

Fudge, Edward. *The Fire That Consumes: A Biblical and Historical Study of Final Punishment.* Houston, TX: Providential, 1982.

Garber, Daniel, and Michael Ayers, ed. *The Cambridge History of Seventeenth-Century Philosophy,* 2 Vols. New York: Cambridge University Press, 2003.

Garland, David E. *1 Corinthians.* Baker Exegetical Commentary on the New Testament. Grand Rapids, MI: Baker Academic, 2003.

Geisler, Norman L. *Baker Encyclopedia of Christian Apologetics.* Baker Reference Library. Grand Rapids, MI: Baker, 1999.

———. *The Battle for the Resurrection.* Nashville, TN: Thomas Nelson, 1989.

General Conference of Seventh-Day Adventists, Ministerial Association. *Seventh-Day Adventists Believe: A Biblical Exposition of Fundamental Doctrines.* Silver Spring, MD: General Conference of Seventh-Day Adventists, 2005.

Bibliography

Gijsbers, Alan J. "The Dialogue Between Neuroscience and Theology." In *College of Science Advising Center* 5 (2003). http://www.iscast.org/rough_diamonds/past_papers/Gijsbers_A_2003-07_Neuroscience_and_Theology.pdf.

Gillman, John. "A Thematic Comparison: 1 Cor 15:50–57 and 2 Cor 5:1–5." In *Journal of Biblical Literature* 107, no. 3 (1988): 439–54.

Gingrich, F. Wilbur. *Shorter Lexicon of the Greek New Testament*. 2nd ed. Revised by Frederick W. Danker. Chicago, IL: University of Chicago Press, 1983.

Grassmick, John D. *Principles and Practice of Greek Exegesis*. Dallas, TX: Dallas Theological Seminary, 1976.

Gundry, Robert H. "Human Being." In *Harper's Bible Dictionary*. Edited by Paul J. Achtemeier. San Francisco, CA: Harper & Row, 1985. 410–11.

———. *Soma in Biblical Theology, With Emphasis on Pauline Anthropology*. New York: Cambridge University Press, 1976.

Handy, Lowell K. "Serpent (Religious Symbol)." *The Anchor Bible Dictionary*. Edited by David Noel Freedman, 5:1113–1116. Garden, NY: Doubleday, 1996..

Harris, Murray J. "2 Corinthians 5:1–10: Watershed in Paul's Eschatology?" In *Tyndale Bulletin* 22 (1971): 32–57.

———. "Paul's View of Death in 2 Corinthians 5:1–10." In *New Dimensions in New Testament Study*, ed. R. N. Longenecker and M. C. Tenney, 317–28. Grand Rapids, MI: Eerdmans, 1974.

———. *Raised Immortal: Resurrection and Immortality in the New Testament*. Grand Rapids, MI: Eerdmans, 1983.

Hauck, Friedrich. "κοιμάομαι." In *Theological Dictionary of the New Testament*. Edited by Gerhard Kittel, Geoffrey William Bromiley and Gerhard Friedrich. Translated by Geoffrey W. Bromiley. Grand Rapids, MI: Eerdmans, 1976. 3:789–809.

Heidegger, Martin. *Pathmarks*. Edited by William McNeill. New York: Cambridge University Press, 1998.

Helm, Paul. "Intermediate State." In *Baker Encyclopedia of the Bible*. Edited by Walter A. Elwell and Barry J. Beitzel, 1:1043–1044.. Grand Rapids, MI: Baker Book House, 1988.

Hendrick, Charles W., and Robert Hodgson, eds., *Nag HammadiGnosticism, and Early Christianity*. Peabody, MA: Hendrickson, 1986.

Henry, Matthew. *Matthew Henry's Commentary on the Whole Bible: Complete and Unabridged in One Volume*. Peabody, MA: Hendrickson, 1996.

Herodotus. *The Histories*. Translated by A. D. Godley. Cambridge, MA: Harvard University Press, 1920.

Hick, John. *Death and Eternal Life*. Louisville, KY: Westminster John Knox, 1994.

Hill, Edmund. *Being Human: A Biblical Perspective*. 1984. Reprint. London, England: Geoffrey Chapman, 1988.

Hocking, David L. *Who Am I and What Difference Does It Make?* Portland, OR: Multnomah, 1985.

Hodge, Charles. *2 Corinthians*. The Crossway Classic Commentaries. Wheaton, IL: Crossway, 1995.

———. *An Exposition of the Second Epistle to the Corinthians*. 1859. Reprint. Grand Rapids, MI: Baker Book House, 1980.

Hoekema, Anthony. *The Four Major Cults*. 1986. Reprint. Grand Rapids, MI: Eerdmans, 1963.

Bibliography

Hughes, Philip E. *Paul's Second Epistle to the Corinthians*. The New International Commentary on the New Testament. Grand Rapids, MI: Eerdmans,1962.
Jaeger, Werner. "The Greek Ideas of Immortality." In *Immortality and Resurrection*, ed. Krister Stendahl, 97–114. New York: Macmillan, 1965.
Jamieson, Roberto, et al. *Comentario Exegetico y Explicativo de la BibliaTomo 2: El Nuevo Testamento*. El Paso, TX: Casa Bautista de Publicaciones, 2002.
Jeffrey, David L. *A Dictionary of Biblical Tradition in English Literature*. Grand Rapids, MI: Eerdmans, 1992.
Jewett, Robert. *Paul's Anthropological Terms: A Study of Their Use in Conflict Settings*. Leiden, Netherlands: Brill, 1971.
Johnson, Barton Warren. *The People's New Testament: With Explanatory Notes*. Oak Harbor, WA: Logos Research Systems, 1999.
Josephus, Flavius. *Antiquitates Judaicae*. Edited by B. Niese. Berlin, Germany: Weidmann, 1892, in the Perseus Digital Library, http://www.perseus.tufts.edu/hopper/text?doc=Perseus%3Atext%3A1999.01.0145%3Abook%3D5%3Awhiston+chapter%3D1%3Awhiston+section%3D12.
Kaiser, Otto, and Eduard Lohse. *Death and Life*. Nashville, TN: Abingdom, 1981.
Katz, Steven T. *Jewish Ideas and Concepts*. New York: Schocken, 1977.
Kennedy, Harry A. Alexander. *St Paul's Conceptions of the Last Things*. London, England: Hodder and Stoughton, 1904.
Kesley, David H. "Human Being." In *Christian Theology: An Introduction to Its Traditions and Tasks*, ed. Peter Crafts Hodgson and Robert Harlen King, 167–93. Minneapolis, MN: Fortress, 1994.
Kistemaker, Simon J., and William Hendriksen. *Exposition of the First Epistle to the Corinthians*. New Testament Commentary 18. Grand Rapids, MI: Baker Book House. 2001.
———. *Exposition of the Second Epistle to the Corinthians*. New Testament Commentary 19. Grand Rapids, MI: Baker Book House. 1997.
Kleine, Heribert. "'Οστράκινος." In *Exegetical Dictionary of the New Testament*. Translation of: Exegetisches Worterbuch Zum Neuen Testament. Edited by Horst Robert Balz and Gerhard Schneider, 2:537–539. Grand Rapids, MI: Eerdmans, 1993.
Ladd, George Eldon. "Eschatology." In *The International Standard Bible Encyclopedia*. Ed. Geoffrey W. Bromiley, 2:130–43. 1986, Reprint. Grand Rapids, MI: Eerdmans, 1992.
———. *A Theology of the New Testament*. Revised and edited by Donald A. Hagner. Grand Rapids, MI: Eerdmans, 1993.
Layton, Bentley. *The Gnostics Scriptures.* Garden, NY: Doubleday, 1987.
Leedy, Randy A. *BibleWorks New Testament Greek Sentence Diagrams* (2006). Bible Works Electronic Software v. 8.0.013Z1, 2009.
Liddell, Henry George, et al. *A Greek-English Lexicon, With a Revised Supplement*. New York, NY: Oxford University Press, 1996.
Logan, Alastair H. B., and J. M. Wedderburn, eds. *The New Testament and Gnosis: Essays in Honour of Robert Mcl. Wilson*. New York: T. & T. Clark, 2004.
Louw, Johannes P., and Eugene A. Nida. *Greek-English Lexicon of the New Testament Based on Semantic Domains*. 2nd ed. New York: United Bible Societies, 1989.
Lowery, David K. "2 Corinthians." In *The Bible Knowledge Commentary: An Exposition of the Scriptures*. Edited by John F. Walvoord, Roy B. Zuck and Dallas Theological Seminary, 2:551–85. Wheaton, IL: Victor, 1985.
MacArthur, John. *2 Corinthians*. Chicago, IL: Moody, 2003.

Bibliography

MacCant, Jerry W. "Competing Pauline Eschatologies: An Exegetical Comparison of 1 Corinthians 15 and 2 Corinthians 5." In *Wesleyan Theological Journal* 29 (1994): 23–49.

MacKay, Donald. *Brains, Machines and Persons.* Grand Rapids, MI: Eerdmans, 1980.

Martin, Dale B. *The Corinthian Body.* New Haven, CT: Yale University Press, 1995.

Martin, Ralph P. *2 Corinthians.* Word Biblical Commentary Series 40. Waco, TX: Word, 1986.

———. *The Spirit and the Congregation: Studies in 1 Corinthians 12-15.* Grand Rapids, MI: Eerdmans, 1984.

Martin-Achard, Robert. "Resurrection." In *The Anchor Bible Dictionary.* Edited by David Noel Freedman, 5:680–84. Garden, NY: Doubleday, 1996.

McCasland, Selby Vernon. "The Basis of the Resurrection Faith." In *Journal of Biblical Literature* 50, no. 3 (1931): 211–26.

McDonald, J.I.H. *The Resurrection: Narrative and Belief.* London, England: SPCK, 1989.

Methodius. *From the Discourse of Resurrection.* Translated by Alexander Roberts, James Donaldson and A. Cleveland Coxe. The Ante-Nicene Fathers:Translations of The Writings of the Fathers Down to AD 325, 6:364–378.. Grand Rapids, MI: Eerdmans, 1997.

Metts, Roy. "Death, Discipleship, and Discourse Strategies: 2 Cor 5:1–10 Once Again." In *Criswell Theological Review* 4 (1989): 57–76.

Metzger, Bruce M. *A Textual Commentary on the Greek New Testament.* 2nd ed. Stuttgart, Germany: Deutsche Bibelgesellschaft, 1994.

Milne, Bruce. *Know the Truth: A Handbook of Christian Belief.* Downers Grove, IL: InterVarsity Press, 1983.

Morris, Robert L. *Hellenika: A Beginning Greek Textbook Based on The Koine Greek of the New Testament.* Mishawaka, IN: Bethel College, 2005.

Motyer, Alec. "Significance of Names." In *Baker Encyclopedia of the Bible.* Edited by Walter A. Elwell and Barry J. Beitzel, 2:1522–1524. Grand Rapids, MI: Baker Bock House, 1988.

Mouratidis, John. "The Origin of Nudity in Greek Athletics." In *Journal of Sport History* 12, no. 3 (1985): 213–32.

Myers, Allen C., ed. *Eerdmans Bible Dictionary.* Grand Rapids, MI: Eerdmans, 1987.

Neufeld, Don F. ed. *Seventh-Day Adventist Encyclopedia,* 2nd ed. Commentary Reference Series 10. Hagerstown, MD: Review and Herald, 1995.

Niebuhr, Reinhold. *The Nature and Destiny of Man.* New York: Scribner's, 1941.

Night, George. *A Brief History of Seventh-Day Adventists.* 2nd ed. Hagerstown, MD: Review and Herald, 2004.

Niswonger, Richard L. *New Testament History.* Grand Rapids, MI: Zondervan, 1988.

Noonan, Harold W. *Personal Identity.* 2nd ed. New York: Routledge Taylor & Francis, 2003.

O'Collins, Gerald. *Interpreting the Resurrection: Examining the Major Problems in the Stories of Jesus' Resurrection.* New York: Paulist, 1988.

Oepke, Albrecht. "Γυμνός." In *Theological Dictionary of the New Testament.* Edited by Gerhard Kittel, Geoffrey William Bromiley and Gerhard Friedrich. Translated by Geoffrey W. Bromiley, 1:173–76. Grand Rapids, MI: Eerdmans, 1976.

Osei-Bonsu, Joseph. "Does 2 Cor 5:1–10 Teach the Reception of the Resurrection Body at the Moment of Death?" In *Journal for the Study of the New Testament* 23 (1986): 81–101.

Bibliography

Owen, Derwyn R. G. *Body and Soul: A Study of the Christian View of Man*. Philadelphia, PA: Westminster, 1956.

Pagels, Elaine H. "'The Mystery of the Resurrection': A Gnostic Reading of 1 Corinthians 15." In *Journal of Biblical Literature* 93, no. 2 (1974): 276-88.

Papademetriou, George C. "The Human Body According to Saint Gregory Palamas." In *Greek Orthodox Theological Review* 34, no. 1 (1989): 1-9.

Papaioannou, Kim. "The Geography of Hell in the Teaching of Jesus: A Study of Geographic Locations Associated With Hell in the Synoptic Gospels." PhD Dissertation. Durham University, England, 2004.

Parfit, Derek. "Personal Identity." In *Personal Identity*, ed. John Perry, 135-224. London, England: University of California Press, 1975.

Patterson, Dorothy Kelley, and Rhonda Kelley. *The Woman's Study Bible: The New King James Version*. Nashville, TN: Thomas Nelson, 1995.

Peel, Malcolm Lee. *The Epistle to Rheginos: A Valentinian Letter on the Resurrection: Introduction, Translation, Analysis and Exposition*. London, England: SCM, 1969.

Petavel, Emmanuel. *The Problem of Immortality*. London, England: Elliot Stock, 1892.

Peterson, Robert A. *Hell on Trial: The Case for Eternal Punishment*. Phillipsburgh, NJ: P&R, 1995.

Philo. *The Works of Philo: Complete and Unabridged*. Translated by Charles Duke Yonge. Peabody, MA: Hendrickson, 1996.

Pinnock, Clark. "The Destruction of the Finally Impenitent." In *Criswell Theological Review* 4 (1990): 243-59.

Plato. *Plato in Twelve Volumes*. Translated by Harold North Fowler; Introduction by W.R.M. Lamb. Cambridge, MA: Harvard University Press, 1966. http://www.perseus.tufts.edu/hopper/text?doc=Perseus%3Atext%3A1999.01.0170%3Atext%3DPhaedo%3Asection%3D67d.

Plummer, Alfred. *A Critical and Exegetical Commentary on the Second Epistle of St. Paul to the Corinthians*. New York: Scribner, 1915.

Price, Henry H. "Personal Survival and the Idea of Another World." In *Classical and Contemporary Readings in the Philosophy of Religion*, ed. John Hick, 364-86. Englewood Cliffs, NJ: Prentice-Hall, 1964.

Reichenbach, Bruce R. *Is Man the Phoenix? A Study of Immortality*. Grand Rapids, MI: Eerdmans, 1983.

———. "Resurrection of the Body, Re-Creation and Interim Existence." In *Journal of Theology for Southern Africa* 21 (1977): 33-42.

Reid, Thomas. "Of Identity." In *Personal Identity*, ed. John Perry, 107-12. London, England: University of California Press, 1975.

Richards, Kent Harold. "Death." In *The Anchor Bible Dictionary*. Edited by David Noel Freedman, 2:108-10. Garden, NY: Doubleday, 1996.

Richards, W. Larry. *1 Corinthians: The Essentials and Nonessentials of Christian Living*. Nampa, ID: Pacific, 1997.

Robinson, B. A. "Religious Beliefs of Americans, About Ghosts, Satan, Heaven, Hell, etc." In *Religious Tolerance: Ontario Consultants on Religious Tolerance*. http://www.religioustolerance.org/chr_poll3.htm.

Robinson, H. Wheeler. *The Christian Doctrine of Man*. Edinburg, TX: Clarck, 1911.

———. "Hebrew Psychology." In *The People and the Book*. Edited by Arthur S. Peake, 361-66. Oxford, England: Clarendond, 1925..

Bibliography

Robinson, John A.T. *The Body: A Study in Pauline Theology*. Philadelphia, PA: Westminster, 1952.

Rohde, Erwin. *Psyche: The Cult of Souls and Belief in Immortality Among the Greeks*. New York: Harper & Row, 1925.

Romanides, John S. "Man and His True Life According to the Greek Orthodox Service Book." In *The Greek Orthodox Theological Review* 1 (1954): 63–83.

Rorty, Richaard. *Contincengy, Irony, and Solidarity*. 1989. Reprint. New York: Cambridge University Press, 1999.

Roukema, Reimer. *Gnosis and Faith in Early Christianity: An Introduction to Gnosticism*. London, England: S.C.M., 1999.

Rust, Eric C. "Interpreting the Resurrection." In *Journal of Bible and Religion* 29, no. 1 (1961): 25–34.

Ryken, Leland, et al, eds. *Dictionary of Biblical Imagery*. Downers Grove, IL: InterVarsity, 1998.

Sand, Alexander. *Der Begriff "Fleisch" in den Paulinischen Hauptbriefen*. Regensburg, Germany: Pustet, 1967.

Satlow, Michael L. "Jewish Constructions of Nakedness in Late Antiquity." In *Journal of Biblical Literature* 116, no. 3 (1997): 429–54.

Schweizer, Eduard. "Σάρξ in the Greek World." *Theological Dictionary of the New Testament*. Edited by Gerhard Kittel, Geoffrey William Bromiley and Gerhard Friedrich. Translated by Geoffrey W. Bromiley, 7:97–105. Grand Rapids, MI: Eerdmans, 1976.

Schweizer, Eduard. "Ψυχή in the NT." In *Theological Dictionary of the New Testament*. Edited by Gerhard Kittel, Geoffrey William Bromiley, and Gerhard Friedrich. Translated by Geoffrey W. Bromiley, 9:637–56. Grand Rapids, MI: Eerdmans, 1976.

Setzer, Claudia. *Resurrection of the Body in Early Judaism and Early Christianity: Doctrine, Community, and Self-Definition*. Boston, MA: Brill, 2004.

Sevenster, J. N. "Some Remarks on the Γυμνός in II Cor. v. 3." In *Studia Paulinain Honorem Johannis de Zwann Septuagenarii*, ed. J. N. Sevenster and W. C. van Unnik, 202–14. Haarlem, Netherlands: De Erven F. Bohn N.V., 1953.

Shillington, V. George. *2 Corinthians*. Believers Church Bible Commentary. Scottdale, PA: Herald, 1998.

Shoemaker, Sydney. "Personal Identity." In *Encyclopedia Britannica Online*. http://www.britannica.com/EBchecked/topic/452945/personal-identity.

Simpson, Michael. *The Theology of Death and Eternal Life*. Hales Corner, WI: Clergy Book Service, 1971.

Smith, F. LaGard. *After Life: A Glimpse of Eternity Beyond Death's Door, Sheol, Heaven, Resurrection, Hades, Hell, Judgment, Purgatory, Limbo, Rapture*. Nashville, TN: Cotswold, 2003.

Smith, Jonathan Z. "The Garments of Shame." In *History of Religions* 5 (1966): 217–38.

Smith, Uriah. *Here and Hereafter or Man in Life and Death: The State of the Dead, the Reward of the Righteous, and the Punishment of the Wicked*. Washington, DC: Review and Herald, 1897.

Stacey, W. David. *The Pauline View of Manin Relation to Its Judaic and Helenistic Background*. New York: Macmillan, 1956.

Swinburne, Richard. *The Evolution of the Soul*. Oxford, England: Oxford University Press, 1997.

Bibliography

Tate, Marvin E. "The Comprehensive Nature of Salvation in Biblical Perspective." In *Review and Expositor*, 91 (1994): 469–85.

Thayer, Joseph Henry, trans and ed. *A Greek-English Lexicon of the New Testament: Being Grimm's Wilke's Clavis Novi Testamenti*. Grand Rapids, MI: Baker Academic, 1977.

Thomson, Ann. *Bodies of Thought: Science, Religion, and the Soul in the Early Enlightenment*. Oxford, England: Oxford University Press, 2008.

Tipler, Frank J. *The Physics of Immortality: Modern Cosmology, God, and the Resurrection of the Dead*. New York: Anchor, 1994.

Tischendorf, Constantin von, ed. *Bibliorum Codex Sinaiticus Petropolitanus*. Hildesheim, Germany: Gorgias, 1862.

———, ed. *Novum Testamentum Vaticanum*. Lipsiae, Germany: Giesecke et Devrient, 1857.

Travis, Stephen H. *I Believe in the Second Coming of Jesus*. Grand Rapids, MI: Eerdmans, 1982.

Trick, Bradley R. "Death, Covenants, and the Proof of Resurrection in Mark 12:18–27." In *Novum Testamentum* 49, no. 3 (2007): 232–56.

Van Biema, David. "Christians Wrong About Heaven, Says Bishop." *Time*, February 07, 2008. http://www.time com/time/world/article/0,8599,1710844,00.html.

Vidal, Fernando. "Brains, Bodies, Selves, and Science: Anthropologies of Identity and the Resurrection of the Body." *Critical Inquiry* 28, no. 4 (Summer, 2002): 930–974.

Vine, W.E., and F.F. Bruce. *Vine's Expository Dictionary of Old and New Testament Words*. Old Tappan, NJ: Revell, 1981.

Völkel, Martin. "Κοιμάομαι." In *Exegetical Dictionary of the New Testament*. Translation of: Exegetisches Worterbuch Zum Neuen Testament. Edited by Horst Robert Balz and Gerhard Schneider, 2:301–302. Grand Rapids, MI: Eerdmans, 1993.

Wall, Joe L. *Going for the Gold: Reward and Loss at the Judgement of Believers*. Chicago, IL: Moody, 1991.

Wallace, Daniel. *Greek Grammar, Beyond the Basics, Exegetical Syntax of the New Testament*. Grand Rapids, MI: Zondervan, 1996.

Walsh, Brian, and Richard Middleton. "The Development of Dualism." In *The Transforming Vision: Shaping a Christian World View*. Downers Grove, IL: InterVarsity, 1984.

Walter, Tony. *The Eclipse of Eternity: A Sociology of the Afterlife*. New York: Palgrave Macmillan, 1996. Quoted in Samuele Bacchiocchi, *Immortality or Resurrection? A Biblical Study on Human Nature and Destiny*, 10. Berrien Springs, MI: Biblical Perspective, 2001.

Weiss, Herold. *Paul of Tarsus: His Gospel and Life*. Berrien Springs, MI: Andrews University Press, 1986.

Westphal, Merold. "Continental Philosophy of Religion." In *The Oxford Handbook of Philosophy of Religion*, ed. William J. Wainwright, 472–93. Oxford, England: Oxford University Press, 2005.

Whidden, Woodrow, et al. *The Trinity: Understanding God's Love, His Plan of Salvation, and Christian Relationships*. Hagerstown, MD: Review and Herald, 2002.

White, Ellen G. *The Great Controversy Between Christ and Satan: the Conflict of the Ages in the Christian Dispensation*. Mountain View, CA: Pacific, 1950.

Wiersbe, Warren W. *The Bible Exposition Commentary: An Exposition of the New Testament Comprising the Entire*. Wheaton, IL: Victor, 1996.

Wilckens, Ulrich. *Resurrection: Biblical Testimony to the Resurrection: An Historical Examination and Explanation*. Atlanta, GA: John Knox, 1978.

Bibliography

Williamson, Gerald Irving. *The Westminster Confession of Faith for Study Classes*. 2nd ed. Phillipsburg, NJ: P&R, 2004.

Wilson, Michael P. "Nakedness, Bodiliness and the New Creation." In *Modern Believing* 47, no. 3 (2006): 42–50.

Wolfson, Harry A. "Immortality and Resurrection in the Philosophy of the Church Fathers." In *Harvard Divinity School Bulletin* 22 (1956): 5–40.

Wright, Nicholas Thomas. *The Resurrection of the Son of God*. Minneapolis, MN: Fortress, 2003.

Zodhiates, Spiros, ed. *The Complete Word Study Dictionary: New Testament*. Chattanooga, TN: AMG, 2000.

Zurchier, Jean R. "The Christian View of Man I." *Andrews University Seminary Studies* 2 (1964): 156–68.

———. "The Christian View of Man II." *Andrews University Seminary Studies* 3 (1965): 66–83.

———. "The Christian View of Man III." *Andrews University Seminary Studies* 4 (1966): 89–103.

www.ingramcontent.com/pod-product-compliance
Lightning Source LLC
Chambersburg PA
CBHW070922180426
43192CB00037B/1707